THE ARCHITECT KING

GEORGE III AND THE CULTURE OF THE ENLIGHTENMENT

THE ARCHITECT KING

GEORGE III AND THE CULTURE OF THE ENLIGHTENMENT

David Watkin

ROYAL COLLECTION PUBLICATIONS

TO
THE KING.

I HUMBLY beg leave to lay at Your MAJESTY's feet the following Differtation upon an Art of which You are the firft Judge, as well as the moft munificent Encourager.

A Sketch of the prefent little Performance was gracioufly received by Your MAJESTY many years ago, and found a kind reception in the world, under the Influence of Your Patronage. This is more ample, I wifh it may be more perfect than the original; that it may have a jufter title to Your Indulgence, and better pretenfions to the favor of the Publick.
I am,

May it pleafe Your MAJESTY,

Your MAJESTY's

dutiful fervant and faithful fubject,

WILLIAM CHAMBERS.

Dedicated

by Permission to

HIS ROYAL HIGHNESS

THE PRINCE OF WALES

This publication has been generously supported by

THE BASIL SAMUEL CHARITABLE TRUST

THE BAMFORD CHARITABLE FOUNDATION

Published by
Royal Collection Enterprises Limited
St James's Palace
London SW1A 1JR

For a complete catalogue of current publications, please write to
the above address or visit the website at www.royal.gov.uk

ISBN 1 902163 50 8

British Library Cataloguing in Publication Data
A catalogue record of this book is available from the British Library.

Designed by Judith Ash
Produced by Book Production Consultants plc, Cambridge
Printed and bound in Singapore by Kyodo Printing Co. (S'pore)
Pte Ltd

ILLUSTRATIONS
Frontispiece: Allan Ramsay, *George III*, 1761–2. Oil on canvas.
RCIN 405307
Opposite dedication: Giovanni Battista Cipriani, *Frontispiece to
William Chambers's Dissertation on Oriental Gardening*, 1772.
Engraving. RCIN 604541

CONTENTS

7 Architecture and Court Culture in England and on the Continent

Conclusion   206

ACKNOWLEDGEMENTS

One of the aims of this book is to relate the interests of King George III and his family in architecture, gardening, the applied arts, and the sciences, to the culture of the Enlightenment, and in particular to the court culture of the Holy Roman Empire. In this preliminary attempt at tackling a vast subject which historians are beginning to explore, I am particularly grateful for help with the sections covering Hanover and the Holy Roman Empire to the following scholars in England and Germany who have kindly read early drafts of the text and generously shared their knowledge with me: Professor T. C. W. Blanning, Professor Marcus Köhler, Dr Jarl Kremeier, Dr Robert Oresko, Dr Clarissa Campbell Orr, Dr Torsten Riotte, Dr Wilfried Rogasch, and Dr Brendan Simms. Mr Peter Barber, Map Librarian at the British Library, enabled me to see hundreds of relevant drawings in George III's Topographical Collection, notably the extensive record commissioned by the King of his Hanoverian Electorate.

Mr Francis Russell has kindly allowed me to consult the typescript of his monograph on the Earl of Bute before its publication in 2004. Miss Flora Fraser, author of a forthcoming, fully documented book, *The Daughters of George III*, has provided helpful information, as have the following in their comments on drafts of this book: Dr John Adamson, Mr Paul Doyle, Mr John Harris, Dr Richard John, Mr Jonathan Marsden, Sir Hugh Roberts, Dr Simon Thurley, and Dr Giles Worsley. My greatest debt is to the Hon. Lady Roberts, Librarian and Curator of the Print Room, Windsor Castle, who made available to me the vast collection of drawings in her care, and who also made invaluable contributions to virtually every page of this book.

David Watkin
Peterhouse, Cambridge
July 2003

INTRODUCTION

'Building, I am told, is the King's favourite study.' *Horace Walpole, 1761*

Kingship and architecture have been associated since the earliest times. Always seen as the most creative and artistic form of expression for a ruler, architecture is at once prestigious and useful, serving to represent the ruler and his state to the world and to provide lasting memorials of his fame. In the civilisations of the Middle East, the kings of Mesopotamia are thus remembered in their ziggurats, the pharaohs of Egypt in their pyramids, and King Solomon in the Temple of Jerusalem. The number of builder-kings is especially notable in France: the Frankish Emperor Charlemagne, St Louis (Louis IX), and François I, but especially Louis XIV, whose extraordinarily detailed attention to design and construction (he acted on at least one occasion as a designer[1]) anticipated in some respects the activities of George III. If great builders like Henry VIII in England, Charles V in Spain, and the Popes in Rome, were not obvious role models for George III, then Edward III, as the builder of much of Windsor Castle, was certainly close to his heart. Among his eighteenth-century contemporaries, George III shared the interest in architecture of Frederick the Great and Catherine the Great who, though they were more extensive builders than he, did not equal him as a collector of books, paintings, drawings, and scientific instruments.

John Brooke's authoritative biography, *King George III* (1972), with a Foreword by The Prince of Wales, inaugurated the rehabilitation of a monarch who had been criticised in the nineteenth century for interfering too much in the processes of government, and was known to many in the twentieth century principally for losing the American colonies and as a simple-minded farmer who went mad. By contrast, John Brooke, followed by Christopher Hibbert in *George III. A Personal History* (1998), established him as a man of broad cultural outlook and a patron of authors, artists, architects, gardeners, musicians, and scientists, with a serious professional interest in modern developments in agriculture. Exhibitions at The Queen's Gallery, Buckingham Palace, about the patronage of the King and Queen have been accompanied by full scholarly catalogues,[2] but the present book is the first to concentrate on George III's involvement with architecture, his first love in the arts.

The interpretation offered here also takes advantage of the recent shift in historical writing towards rehabilitating the importance of the courts of early modern Europe.[3] The leading trends of twentieth-century historical writing, whether liberal or Marxist in inspiration, had

---

1   Berger, *Royal Passion*, pp. 1–4.
2   *George III, Collector and Patron*, and, of special relevance to the present book, *George III and Queen Charlotte. Patronage, Collecting and Court Taste*, J. Roberts ed., London 2004.
3   The Society for Court Studies was founded in 1995, while the annual

Royal Collection Studies course, organised by the Attingham Trust since 1996 and attended by many scholars drawn from museums and royal collections, has played an important role in this reassessment of art in the context of the court.

tended to ignore the role of *ancien-régime* courts. One distinguished pioneer in adopting a broader approach was Ragnhild Hatton, 'a "truly" European historian',[4] who published what is still the finest biography of any of the Hanoverian monarchs, *George I. Elector and King* (1978). In this revisionist rehabilitation of George I and his court, she wrote 'That George was in tune with the Early Enlightenment ideas both in domestic and foreign affairs has been postulated in this study.'[5]

Hatton has been followed by scholars from the late twentieth century in Europe and the United States of America who, in opening up a rich treasury of neglected material, objects, and archives, have reassessed the court as the formative institution in the political and cultural life of Europe between the Renaissance and the French Revolution.[6] The same years have seen an interpretation of the Holy Roman Empire not as a doomed, reactionary survival but as an institution in which German *ancien-régime* states fostered rather than suppressed the Enlightenment.[7]

King of England, Elector of Hanover

The accession to the throne of the 22-year-old George, Prince of Wales, in October 1760 was greeted with rejoicing on the same scale as that at the Restoration of the Monarchy exactly a century before. He was hailed with particular delight by the world of the arts. Hogarth captured the mood of near-euphoria in the engraving which he produced as the frontispiece to the catalogue of the first exhibition of the Society of Artists of Great Britain in May 1761 (fig. 1).[8] In it, a bust of the young King surmounts a fountainhead or reservoir featuring a lion's mask from which water gushes forth. This fills a watering-can held by a figure of Britannia, who uses it to nourish the growth of three young trees, labelled Painting, Sculpture, and Architecture. The centrality of the King is underlined by a quotation from Juvenal, 'Et spes & ratio Studiorum in Caesare tantum' (The hope and purpose of learning depend on Caesar only). The charm and dignity of the young King, which were also widely appreciated, were given expression by James Boswell, who wrote after witnessing the State Opening of Parliament in November 1762 that, 'It was a very noble thing. I here beheld the King of Great Britain on his throne with the crown on his head addressing both the Lords and the Commons. His Majesty spoke better than any man I ever heard: with dignity, delicacy, and ease. I admired him. I wished much to be acquainted with him.'[9]

4 Oresko, *Sovereignty*, p. 23.
5 Hatton, *George I*, p. 290.
6 See Gagliardo, *Reich and Nation*, and Blanning, *Culture of Power*.
7 For an overview of this, see Umbach, *Enlightenment, passim*, and

P. Wilson, *Holy Roman Empire*.
8 See Paulson, *Hogarth's Graphic Work*, pp. 193–4, no. 243, and pl. 236.
9 Pottle, *Boswell's London Journal*, p. 49.

FIG. 1 C. Grignion after William Hogarth, *Frontispiece to the catalogue of the Society of Artists exhibition*, 1761. Engraving. RCIN 812005

GEORGIUS III REX MDCCLXI

PAINTING

SCULPTURE

ARCHITECTURE

W. Hogarth invᵗ. et del.

C. Grignion sculp.

Et spes & ratio Studiorum in Cæsare tantum.

Juv.

Published according to Act of Parliament May 7, 1761.

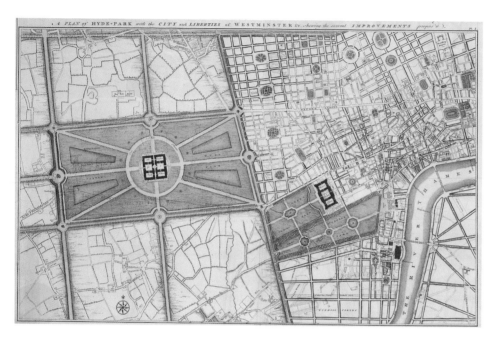

The mood of hope which evidently prevailed among the members of the Society of Artists at the start of the new reign was more than fulfilled in 1761–2 with the King's creation, or re-creation, of three royal offices of sculptor, architect, and painter. Such appointments were part of the growing contemporary belief in the importance to the nation of the promotion of the arts. This led to the foundation of the Royal Academy in 1768 in which both the King and many members of the Society of Artists played a leading role.

In 1766 John Gwynn (1713–86), an architect and architectural writer who became a foundation member of the Royal Academy, dedicated to George III his far-sighted book, *London and Westminster Improved, Illustrated by Plans. To which is prefixed, A Discourse on Publick Magnificence* (fig. 2). In it, Gwynn argued that 'public magnificence may be considered as a political and moral advantage to every nation.'[10] Acknowledging the architectural primacy of Paris, he went on to claim that 'publick works of real magnificence . . . [are] as necessary to the community as health and clothing to the human body', stressing that 'it is entirely owing to the encouragement of works of this sort that the kingdom of France has obtained a

---

10   Gwynn, *London and Westminster Improved*, p. xiv.

superiority over the rest of the world in the polite arts.' He proposed to help raise London to the level of Paris by building two new royal palaces, one in Hyde Park, the other in Green Park, which would have meant demolishing St James's Palace and Buckingham House. He also planned to demolish the Houses of Parliament and replace them with grandiose new buildings. The model for all this was contemporary France as in the creation of the vast Place Louis Quinze (now de la Concorde), built in 1755–74 from designs by Ange-Jacques Gabriel, the *premier architecte du roi*, and a role model for George III's architect, William Chambers.

Acceptance of the kind of programme outlined by John Gwynn in 1766 seemed confirmed by George III's appointment of Chambers and Adam as Royal Architects; by the creation of a state coach as a public display of great magnificence; and by the commissioning of festival architecture of the kind familiar in the *Service des Menus-Plaisirs* at the court of France. This mood was sustained by the King's involvement with the Royal Academy.

RELIGION, WAR, AND POLITICS

The firm religious faith of George III enabled him to occupy without affectation the traditional role of Christian monarch, the spiritual father of his people. It has been suggested that his court saw itself as 'a centre of Protestant Enlightenment, with contacts to like-minded writers and scholars in Germany, including the electoral university in Hanover, who were on guard against the tendency towards Deism or materialism.'[11] The theme of exemplary piety was stated in his lavish remodelling and furnishing of St George's Chapel, Windsor, as a setting for the sacred rituals of the Knights of the Garter, and even more ambitiously in his commissioning of Benjamin West (1738–1820) to provide no fewer than 35 paintings for a proposed new chapel at the Castle. These were on the theme of revealed religion, following a scheme devised by the King's close friend, Bishop Hurd, in consultation with the other bishops. It is remarkable that when John Pye calculated that the King had paid as much as £34,187 to West between 1769 and 1801, no less than £21,705 of this was for paintings of religious subjects.[12]

Fortified by his 'trust in divine Providence', a phrase he used repeatedly in his letters, the King was able to face with calmness and bravery the attempts on his life in 1786, 1795, and 1800. He commanded great public respect for his bearing on these occasions. He also gave notable public expression to the virtue of magnanimity by his proclamation of 17 April 1793 in support of the raising of funds to help French Roman Catholic priests. Referring to 'the

11   Campbell Orr, 'Queen Charlotte', p. 249.
12   Pye, *Patronage of British Art*, p. 230.

dreadful persecutions of the French Clergy which took place in France in August and September last', he described the priests as 'refugees in our British Dominions'. On the British annexation of Corsica in 1794, he insisted that the island should remain Catholic.

George III was involved with the Seven Years War (1756–63), the War of American Independence (1776–83), and the wars against Revolutionary and Napoleonic France between 1793 and 1815. These were events of global significance, while his reign also saw the beginning of the Industrial Revolution in England. In a period of such change and uncertainty, the great length of his reign, and his innate conservatism, ultimately led him to be seen as a figure of reassuring stability and continuity, the father of his people.[13] He had been from the start anxious to play a greater role in directing the country's government than George I and George II, who had been overshadowed by the dominance of the ruling Whig families. That aristocracy had largely taken to itself the distribution of the numerous offices and pensions which George III aimed to re-establish as the patronage and bounty of the Crown. A small but significant instance of his probity in such appointments is the letter of 1768 in which his Prime Minister, the Duke of Grafton, turned down the application of the Poet Laureate, Thomas Warton, for the post of Regius Professor of Modern History at Oxford, on the grounds that 'the king has signalled his intentions that this office should never any more be held as a sinecure.'[14] Following his stormy relationship with the elder Pitt, who helped establish Britain's second Empire,[15] George III was fortunate to have as First Minister the younger Pitt, another of the greatest statesmen in British parliamentary history, who confirmed British dominance by creating the circumstances in which Napoleon could be defeated.

In 1770, taking advantage of the dissensions which divided the Whigs, George III appointed his protégé, Lord North, as First Minister. However, it was widely felt that the war in America was mishandled by Lord North and by the King, who passionately believed that the rebellion of the revolting colonies was treason and should be subdued, by force if necessary. The loss of the thirteen British colonies thus led to the resignation of North, and in December 1783 the King chose as First Minister William Pitt the younger. This was an act of great courage and perception, for Pitt was only 24 and had been in opposition to the Tories. Pitt remained in office until 1801, treading a careful path between supporters of the King and the Whigs, who sought to check the royal power in parliament. With the King's backing, Pitt won the general election of 1784 but the King's grave illness in 1788[16] brought a return of political instability.

13 Colley, 'Apotheosis of George III'.

14 Nichols, *Literary Anecdotes*, vol. v, 1812, p. 655. Warton, like his father before him, was Professor of Poetry at Oxford.

15 The first Empire can be reckoned as that of the Stuarts in the seventeenth century.

16 The identification of the illness as porphyria was first made in two articles in the *British Medical Journal* in 1966 and 1968 by Ida Macalpine and Richard Hunter, who subsequently published *George III and the Mad Business*.

THE KING'S ILLNESS

The King's periods of what used to be called madness, now generally accepted to be porphyria, began in October 1788 when he was aged 50, with an attack that lasted until the following February. This tragic malady, an hereditary derangement of the metabolism with varied, and unpleasant, symptoms, including delirium and delusions, may have been aggravated by arsenic poisoning, for it has recently been suggested that he may have been given arsenic as a medicine or ingested it from cosmetic products used on the skin and hair.[17] If this were the case, it might help explain why his symptoms were so alarmingly worse than those of other supposed victims of the malady.

When, by the beginning of 1789, he showed no signs of recovery, it seemed that the Prince of Wales would become Regent and would enjoy the full prerogatives of the Crown. Pitt was alarmed at this because the Prince was seen as profligate and irresponsible, having formed an alliance in 1783 with his father's, and Pitt's, greatest enemy, the arch-Whig, Charles James Fox. The Prince of Wales had also made an illegal marriage in 1785 with a Roman Catholic, Mrs Fitzherbert. Pitt therefore drafted a Regency Bill to limit the Prince of Wales's power were he to become Regent. The Prince had designs on the Regency of Hanover, and in 1788 preparations were made for him to hold this office during George III's illness.[18]

The Regency Bill would have passed had the King's illness lasted only a few days longer, but he recovered in February 1789. During his four months of incapacity, the foreign policy of Britain and of Hanover was paralysed, the implications for Hanover being especially serious since Emperor Joseph II had the ability to intervene in the Electorate.[19] On the King's recovery, he became an object of popular sympathy and even respect. The public supported the monarch and also resented the blatant machinations of his sons and of Fox to secure power for themselves during his illness. He thus 'became the first Hanoverian sovereign to achieve popularity',[20] so that a great Thanksgiving Service to celebrate his recovery was held in St Paul's Cathedral on St George's Day, 23 April 1789. It is attractive that one of his first thoughts on his recovery was to establish an Order of Minerva to be bestowed upon men of letters and learning.[21] However, there is documentary evidence to show that his wife and daughters, who lived in close association, feared during the rest of his life that his recurrent ambitions for building threatened a return of his illness.

The King's illness recurred in milder form in 1801 and more seriously, though fairly briefly,

17 Tests on five strands of his hair in the possession of the Wellcome Society, and on loan to the Science Museum, were subjected to newly developed chemical tests in 2003 which revealed extraordinary levels of heavy-metal contamination. See *Medicine Man. The Forgotten Museum of Henry Wellcome*, British Museum 2003 (exh. cat.).

18 Burke, *Correspondence*, vol. v, p. 445, and Blanning and Haase, 'George III, Hanover and the Regency Crisis', in Black, *Knights Errant and True Englishmen*.

19 A point made in Oresko, *Sovereignty*, p. 13.

20 Plumb, *The First Four Georges*, p. 144.

21 Hibbert, *George III*, p. 291. The proposal was not adopted.

in 1804. The main celebrations of his Jubilee were held in 1809 with further celebrations on 25 October 1810, but that very day saw the final recurrence of the illness from which he was never to recover. Thus, the Prince of Wales eventually became Regent on 6 February 1811. The old King lived on for nearly nine years, virtually blind from 1805, deaf from 1817, and increasingly senile. When he died on 29 January 1820, in his eighty-second year, he was buried in St George's Chapel, Windsor, without a monument or inscription. George II had been buried in the vault of Henry VII's Chapel, Westminster Abbey, again without an inscription, while George I was buried at Herrenhausen. It is remarkable that no English monarch between Elizabeth I and Queen Victoria had a sculptured tomb.[22]

THE COURT OF HANOVER AND THE HOLY ROMAN EMPIRE

The house of Hanover belonged to the dynasty variously known as Welf, Guelph, Guelf, and Brunswick. The Brunswick lands, including Hanover, Göttingen, Calenberg, Celle, and Wolfenbüttel, were redivided several times between different branches of that family. From 1635 the surviving branches were those of Brunswick-Wolfenbüttel and Brunswick-Lüneburg; the latter, by then Electors of Hanover, inherited the throne of Great Britain in 1714. The senior branch, Dukes of Brunswick-Wolfenbüttel, remained in Germany at their residences of Wolfenbüttel and the nearby Schloss Salzdahlum. Their magnificent collection, finer than anything enjoyed by their Hanoverian cousins, included the celebrated library, amongst whose distinguished directors were the philosopher and polymath Gottfried Leibniz, from 1690 till 1717, and the playwright and author Gotthold Lessing, from 1770 to 1781.

In the absence of any surviving children of Queen Anne, the heir to the British throne was Sophia (1630–1714), a granddaughter of James I of England through her mother, Elizabeth, wife of the Elector Palatine. Sophia died in 1714, two months before Queen Anne. Thus it was that her son, Elector Georg Ludwig, became King George I of England. Since it is our aim to set the architectural interests of George III within a European, and especially German, context, we should briefly consider him in his capacity as *Georg, Kurfürst von Hannover*, and as Arch-Treasurer of the Holy Roman Empire, in which he was a member of the electoral college. Since 1356, the Empire had included seven electors but when these were increased to eight in 1648, the Dukes of Brunswick-Lüneburg had conceived the ambition of becoming a ninth. The office of elector was highly desirable since it completely separated the minor

---

22   N. Smith, *Royal Image*, p. 88.

German princelings from the chosen few who enjoyed the lucrative administrative offices of the Empire and elected the Emperor, the highest-ranking office in Europe. When a ninth electorate of the Empire was created in 1692 for Duke Ernest Augustus, Sophia's husband, it had been necessary to create an arch-office (*Erzamt*) for him, which happened to be Treasurer. Among the north German principalities, the largest ones were the three electoral courts at Berlin, Dresden, and Hanover. As Arch-Treasurer and Electoral Prince in the Holy Roman Empire, George III had a vote at the elections and was represented at the coronations of Joseph II in 1765, Leopold II in 1790, and Francis II in 1792, as Holy Roman Emperors. He was also represented at the coronations of German monarchs, whether Prussian or Austrian, and sent representatives to the accession of most, if not all, German princes. In addition, unlike George I or George II, he had more or less permanent diplomatic representation at the *Reichstag*, the imperial diet of the Holy Roman Empire which met continuously at Regensburg (Ratisbon) from 1663 till 1806.[23]

When he was still heir to the British throne, the Prince had complained at the age of 21 of the partiality of George II for 'that horrid Electorate which has always liv'd upon the very vitals of this poor Country'.[24] However, this opinion was doubtless coloured more by dislike of his grandfather than by any knowledge of Hanover. As monarch, his views changed so that, for example, in 1764 he inaugurated the systematic mapping of the Electorate, as we shall see shortly. He also learnt German, and spoke of *mein deutschen Vaterland* or *ma patrie Germanique*[25] by the 1780s. He sent three of his younger sons to be educated at the Hanoverian University of Göttingen, which had been founded by George II in 1737. It was known as the Georgia Augusta University after George II, whose style as Elector was George Augustus. The Hanoverian people had in general retained a warm affection for their Electors, despite their long absence in England. In turn, Georg Lichtenberg, who taught George III's sons at Göttingen, claimed of the King to a friend that 'he has always been convinced that the Germans could do everything as well as the English, and his only regret was that proof of this was so seldom forthcoming in England.'[26]

Imminent visits of George III to Hanover were reported in 1764,[27] and he even considered abdicating in 1782–3 and moving permanently to Hanover. Though in the end he never visited Hanover, it should be remembered that he never travelled to Ireland, Scotland, Wales or the north of England either. However, he occasionally expressed his intention of going to Hanover,

23 Horn, *British Diplomatic Representatives 1689–1789*, pp. 40–2. I am indebted to Dr Torsten Riotte and Dr Brendan Simms for this information and for their helpful comments on the whole of this section.

24 Prince of Wales to Lord Bute, 4 August 1759 (Sedgwick, *Letters from George III to Lord Bute*, p. 28).

25 Blanning and Haase, 'George III, Hanover and the Regency Crisis', in Black, *Knights Errant and True Englishmen*, p. 148, n. 10.

26 Mare and Quarrell, *Lichtenberg's Visits to England*, p. 82.

27 There were references to his imminent visits to Hanover in *Owen's Weekly Chronicle*, 17 and 21 March 1764 (cited in Black, 'The Crown, Hanover and the Shift in British Foreign Policy', in Black, *Knights Errant and True Englishmen*, p. 126).

notably in 1789 when, following his recovery from his first attack of porphyria, he proposed a visit in the summer with Queen Charlotte and his three eldest daughters.[28] The Queen referred to George III's 'paternalistic welfare for his Hanoverian subjects, suggesting that she saw him in his electoral capacity as traditional *Landesvater* or "father of his people."'[29] This was in the course of the correspondence of the Queen with her brother, Grand Duke Charles of Mecklenburg-Strelitz, civil and military governor of Hanover from 1776 to 1783, in which she discussed his career and his relation to other office holders. It seems clear that George III was himself imbued with German-style ideals of being a *Landesvater*, a benevolent paternal figure.

THE LEAGUE OF PRINCES

George III was a founder member and one of the leading promoters of the *Fürstenbund* (League of Princes), which was established in Berlin on 23 July 1785 by representatives of Prussia, Hanover, and Saxony.[30] A treaty relating to the domestic affairs of the Holy Roman Empire, it was intended to preserve the imperial *status quo* and to check Emperor Joseph II in his schemes for expansion. The *Fürstenbund* was soon joined by other German princes, including George III's cousin, Ernest II, Duke of Saxe-Gotha, William IX, Landgrave of Hesse-Kassel, Frederick William, Duke of Brunswick, Charles Augustus, Duke of Saxe-Weimar, and Prince Franz of Anhalt-Dessau who came to London in 1785 in order to discuss it with George III. Prince Franz sought to promote a league incorporating the English notion of the 'patriot king' as a protector of the smaller principalities. As we shall see, it has recently been suggested that some of the symbolism of the Picturesque English garden which he created at Wörlitz was related to such a concept.

In promoting the *Fürstenbund*, George III was not afraid to act independently and in opposition to the wishes of William Pitt and his Foreign Secretary, the Marquess of Carmarthen,[31] who both sought an alliance with Joseph II and the Habsburg monarchy. The *Fürstenbund*, which had been the object of much discussion and controversy on the continent, came to an end in 1790, following a reconciliation between Austria and Prussia. The King had been aided in his negotiations over the *Fürstenbund* by his second son, Prince Frederick,[32] who was on good terms with Frederick the Great, with the Prince of Prussia who became Frederick William II, and with the Duke of Brunswick. A frequent visitor to Prussia, Prince Frederick visited many of the less important princely courts in a major tour of 1783, which included Kassel and Gotha.

28 George III to Prince Adolphus, 24 March 1789 (Aspinall, *Correspondence*, vol. I, p. 403).

29 Campbell Orr, *Charlotte of Mecklenburg-Strelitz*.

30 For this episode, ignored or scarcely touched on in biographies of George III, see Blanning, '"That Horrid Electorate"'.

31 Secretary of State for Foreign Affairs 1783–91, he succeeded as 5th Duke of Leeds in 1789.

32 For Prince Frederick's letters to George III concerning the *Fürstenbund*, see Aspinall, *Correspondence*, vol. I, pp. 132–5, 184–5, and 194–5.

Sketch to a Curtain painted for His Majesty's Theatre at Hannover. 1789. represents Apollo attendet by the Dramatic Muses, disperses barbarism and inlightens the World

FIG. 3 Johann Heinrich Ramberg, '*Sketch to a Curtain painted for His Majesty's Theatre at Hannover. 1789. represents Apollo attendet by the Dramatic Muses, disperses barbarism and inlightens the world.*' Watercolour and pen and ink. London, British Library (K.Top.C.57-m)

MAPPING AND BUILDING IN THE ELECTORATE

Though it seems that there was little that George III could do to advance official mapping in England, he had the power in Hanover to commission a large-scale map of the Hanoverian lands, a vast project which was undertaken between 1764 and 1786 by J. G. du Plat and Johann Hogrewe.[33] It should be set in the context of his continuing interest in the forestry, agriculture, and manufactures of his province.[34] The material was assembled in eight volumes, containing maps as well as plans and views of his palaces and gardens in Germany, to form a Hanoverian collection, presumably for use in his official duties.[35] One charming image is a sketch for a curtain painted in 1789 for the royal theatre at Hanover by J. H. Ramberg (fig. 3), in which the King appears as Apollo with the dramatic Muses, dispersing barbarism and enlightening the world.

A major architectural undertaking in the electorate during his reign was Kloster Medingen, near Lüneburg, a former nunnery which had been converted at the Reformation

---

33   See Barber, 'Maps and Monarchs', in Oresko, *Sovereignty*, p. 106–7 and pl. 21.

34   On these interests, see Conrady, 'Die Wirksamkeit Königs Georgs III' and Achilles, 'George III. Als Königlicher Landwirt'.

35   British Library, Map Library, King George III's Topographical Collection. See the typescript by Peter Barber, 'Royal Geography'. For more on this collection, see below, ch. 3.

into a Protestant *Damenstift*, a charitable foundation for noble ladies, mostly daughters of the local minor aristocracy. After a fire destroyed most of the buildings in 1781, the Landbaumeister, Ziegler, designed a vast new building on an H-shaped plan with interiors in the Louis XVI style, which was built in 1781–8. The plans were shown to George III who contributed materials, including timber and nails.[36] In 1782 George III commissioned considerable work to be carried out at the Schloss at Osnabrück, built in 1668, to put it into habitable order for occupation by his son, Prince Frederick, in his capacity as Prince Bishop of Osnabrück and a Prince of the Holy Roman Empire. On the death in 1761 of Clement Augustus of Bavaria, Prince Bishop of Osnabrück, George III had the right to present a member of his family to the bishopric, for it alternated between a Catholic holder and a Protestant prince of the house of Brunswick-Lüneburg.[37] When held by a Protestant, it carried no ecclesiastical duties but, as head of state, the holder was the recipient of generous revenues. As there was no other candidate, Prince Frederick, the future Duke of York, though still a minor, was presented and elected by the chapter in 1764. It was in anticipation of his coming of age in 1784 that George III provided 20,000 Reichstaler to modernise the Schloss at Osnabrück. He had allowed the revenues of the bishopric to accumulate during his son's minority and presented them to him in 1784, in which year he created him Duke of York and Albany.

THE HANOVERIAN CRISIS OF 1806

In the course of the Napoleonic Wars, France compelled Prussia to exchange the Franconian province of Ansbach for the Hanoverian Electorate in December 1805. George III was keenly aware of the implications of this move and of the Peace of Paris of February 1806 by which Prussia was further forced to close the North Sea ports to ships under the British flag and to annex Hanover permanently. In fact, this accorded well with Prussia's ambitions for the Electorate, so that it became less valuable as an ally of Britain after 1805–6.[38] The active role which the King played during this crisis has led a recent historian to argue that the episode 'casts doubt on the idea of an "increasing emancipation of foreign policy from royal control" after 1782.'[39] In pursuit of his own career, Charles James Fox, normally seen as the King's great enemy, on this occasion most surprisingly supported the King's insistence on the restitution of his electoral land of Hanover rather than on the re-opening of the ports. George III's involvement was, of course, helped by the presence of the Hanoverian minister at the

---

36 I am indebted for information about this building, which still exists, to Dr Jarl Kremeier. See Mittig, *Kloster Medingen*.

37 This was because of the Alternatio Perpetua Osnabrugensis, a result of the Peace of Westphalia in 1648.

38 Simms, *Impact of Napoleon*.

39 Simms, 'An Odd Question Enough'. Simms also points out that in Brooke, *King George III*, no mention was made of the crisis, still less of George III's role in it.

German Chancery in London, who was able to articulate German views much more effectively than would have been the case without such an office.[40]

We should note in this context the moves from the 1790s to create a British Viceroy for the Electorate, an objective which was eventually achieved when it was elevated to a monarchy at the Treaty of Vienna in October 1814. The first Viceroy was the King's seventh son, Adolphus Frederick, Duke of Cambridge (1774–1850), who held the office from 1814 until 1837. Brutal coercion by Napoleon eventually led Emperor Francis II to renounce the historic Roman-German crown of the Holy Roman Empire in August 1806, but George III, along with other sovereigns such as Alexander I of Russia and the King of Sweden in his capacity as Duke of Western Pomerania, 'asserted that he would never recognise the abolition of the imperial constitution as valid, and would regard the Empire and its head as continuing.'[41]

QUEEN CHARLOTTE

We should not forget that Queen Charlotte (1744–1818), who became something of a German matriarch, was herself a Princess of the Holy Roman Empire, both by birth and by virtue of being Electress of Hanover.[42] When the Electorate became a kingdom, she was its first Queen and her birthday was celebrated in the ceremonial calendar of the new Guelphic Order. Queen Charlotte was aunt to two more German queens. These were sisters who were the daughters of her brother, Grand Duke Charles of Mecklenburg-Strelitz: Louise (1776–1810), wife of Frederick William III of Prussia; and Frederica (1778–1841), who married Queen Charlotte's son, Ernest Augustus, Duke of Cumberland, later King of Hanover. The second son of George III and Queen Charlotte, Frederick, Duke of York and Prince Bishop of Osnabrück, who was resident in Hanover from 1781 to 1787, married Frederica, niece of Frederick the Great. George III's sons Adolphus, Ernest, and Augustus, were all educated at Göttingen University, the first two holding rank in the Hanoverian army.

A Royal Topography

It will be helpful to summarise what we might call the topography of George III's life. We should note at the outset that he was the first Hanoverian King of England not to visit his Electorate and so he never saw, among its other sights, the famous formal gardens at Herrenhausen (fig. 8) which had largely been created by his great-grandmother, Electress

---

40 See Ellis, 'The Administrative Connection between Britain and Hanover'.

41 Gagliardo, *Reich and Nation*, p. 281.

42 See the ground-breaking study by Campbell Orr, *Charlotte of Mecklenburg-Strelitz*.

Sophia, of whom more in the next chapter. He was born in 1738 at Norfolk House, St James's Square, which his father, Prince Frederick, had rented from the Duke of Norfolk following his banishment from court. Prince George's first permanent London home, to which he moved with his parents when he was 4, was Leicester House, which filled much of the north side of Leicester Square.[43] The family occupied this large, old-fashioned mansion, built in the 1630s, in the winter, moving in the summer to Kew or to Cliveden House, Buckinghamshire. A beautiful house, with elaborate gardens sloping down to the River Thames, Cliveden had been built in the 1670s for George Villiers, 2nd Duke of Buckingham (1628–87), from designs by William Winde. Frederick, Prince of Wales, rented Cliveden and Hedsor Place from 1737 until his premature death in 1751.[44]

At the time of Prince Frederick's death, his son, Prince George, the future George III, was aged nearly 13. He was now created Prince of Wales (fig. 21), as heir apparent to the throne, and was set up in a separate establishment with his younger brother, Prince Edward, the future Duke of York, at Savile House.[45] This had been built in the 1680s, next door to Leicester House. The new Prince of Wales lived there when in London, until he succeeded to the throne on the death of his grandfather, George II, in October 1760, at Kensington Palace. The properties which he inherited on his accession included St James's Palace, built by Henry VIII and extended by Queen Anne, to which he reluctantly moved as it had been the official London residence of the monarch since the fire which had destroyed Whitehall Palace in 1698. George II had divided his time, when in London, between St James's Palace and Kensington Palace, bought by William III in 1689, with country residences at Hampton Court Palace, which had been taken over by Henry VIII, and at Richmond Lodge (fig. 5), which he reacquired himself.

George III chose not to live in any of the palaces associated with his grandfather, regarding them all as old-fashioned and uncomfortable. This was a pattern which had frequently occurred in British and continental monarchies. Following his marriage in 1761 to Princess Charlotte of Mecklenburg-Strelitz, he acquired Buckingham House (fig. 4) early in 1762 as a private residence. Here he lived 'in a retired manner, but easy of access',[46] though court ceremonies continued to take place at St James's Palace throughout the reign. Set amidst fields on the western edge of central London, Buckingham House was built in 1702–5 as his town house by John Sheffield, 1st Duke of Buckingham (1648–1721) of a new creation, probably from designs by William Talman or William Winde, the architect of Cliveden. George III

43 *Survey of London*, vol. xxxiv, *The Parish of St Anne Soho*, 1966, pp. 441–54 and pls. 46–9. Leicester House had been rented by the future George II in 1718 when, as Prince of Wales, he was banished from St James's Palace.

44 Crathorne, *Cliveden*, pp. 52–67.

45 *Survey of London, loc. cit.*, pp. 549–64 and pls. 46b and 48a.

46 Watkins, *Memoirs of … Her Most Excellent Majesty Sophie Charlotte*, p. 591.

FIG. 4 William Westall, *The entrance front, Buckingham House*, 1819. Watercolour and body-colour over pencil. RL 22137

FIG. 5 Thomas Sandby and Paul Sandby, *Richmond Lodge, c.*1770. Watercolour, pen and ink over pencil. RL 14711

employed Chambers to remodel Buckingham House,[47] though he always preferred living in the country, first at Kew and later at Windsor.

Since the two estates of Richmond and Kew occupied such a central place in his affections we should describe their history and layout. George III acquired them at two different times: Richmond Lodge (fig. 5) and Richmond Gardens on the death of his grandfather in 1760, and, adjacent to the east, the White House and Kew Gardens after his mother's death twelve years later. To the south is Richmond Park, where James I's deer park, greatly expanded by Charles I in the 1630s, remained popular for hunting well into the eighteenth century. Between the royal estate at Richmond and the curve of the river to the west were the remains of Richmond Palace, built by Henry VII. On the eastern edge of the Old Deer Park stood Richmond Lodge, remodelled for his own use by William III in the 1690s and again around 1702 by the Duke of Ormonde, Ranger of Richmond Park. Subsequently reacquired for George, Prince of Wales (later George II), in 1719, it was a rambling old building which George III, at his accession in 1760, asked William Chambers to modernise. However, this proposal was soon forgotten in the schemes for a grandiose new palace at Richmond which occupied the King and Chambers until the mid-1770s.

A great change came in George III's life when, on the death of his mother, the Dowager Princess of Wales, in 1772, he inherited the Kew estate, which was immediately adjoining the

47 J. Roberts, 'Chambers', pp. 46–8.

Richmond estate. It had been bought on a long lease in 1731 from the Capel family, Earls of Essex, by George III's father, Frederick, Prince of Wales. At the northern end of the gardens at Kew, landscaped for George III's parents by William Chambers (1723–96), was the White House which had been built in 1731–5 in a plain Palladian style, also for Frederick, Prince of Wales, by William Kent (1684–1748). On inheriting the Kew estate in February 1772, George III commissioned William Chambers to prepare plans for modernising and enlarging the White House,[48] but it seems that these were not executed. Nonetheless, the King and Queen moved to the White House on 14 May 1772 and demolished Richmond Lodge in July.

As the Richmond Palace project proved abortive, George III housed his two eldest sons with their tutors and servants in the Dutch House (Kew Palace; fig. 6), a redbrick gabled building of 1631 which was adjacent to the White House on the north. As his family grew, he lodged his other boys in houses round Kew Green. His daughters lived with him and the Queen at the White House which, before his decision to move to Windsor Castle, was his favourite home, though it must have acquired disagreeable associations as his place of confinement by Dr Willis during his illness in 1788. In 1801 he began building a vast new palace at Kew in the castellated Gothic style (figs. 103–4) from designs by James Wyatt (1746–1813). He accordingly arranged for Wyatt to demolish the White House in 1802 and moved temporarily into the Dutch House. However, construction of the Gothic palace at Kew was abandoned in 1811 following the onset of the King's final illness and the establishment of the Regency.

With his family scattered between the two houses in Kew Gardens and the cheerful residences round the Green, George III and Queen Charlotte had adopted, partly by chance, a highly unorthodox mode of living which combined the pastoral with the semi-public, but with virtually no recognisably royal elements. Even in London, they lived in comparative modesty, for Buckingham House was in origin the mansion of a nobleman, not the palace of a king. In the 1770s, however, George III began to feel the historical and romantic pull of Windsor, so that by the end of 1776 he had decided to make it, not Richmond or Kew, his principal residence. In the 1780s and '90s he employed first Chambers and then Yenn to refashion interiors in the Castle itself, a process which culminated in James Wyatt's remodelling in the castellated Gothic style of the royal apartments in Upper Ward in 1800–11 (fig. 99). Between his reign and that of Charles II, who died in 1685, Queen Anne had been the only monarch to show any affection for Windsor or to visit it frequently.[49] Thus, George III's decision to

48 For a plan by Chambers in the Royal Collection, see Cloake, *Richmond and Kew*, fig. 89.

49 H. Roberts, *King's Pleasure*, p. 3, citing Daniel and Samuel Lysons, *Magna Britannia, Berkshire*, p. 420.

FIG. 6 Thomas Sandby
and Paul Sandby,
The Dutch House, Kew,
*c.*1771/2. Watercolour,
pen and ink over pencil.
RL 14712

take up residence at the Castle was to have enormous significance for the image of the monarchy throughout the nineteenth and twentieth centuries and doubtless beyond.

From the complicated story of his numerous residences, two principal facts emerge: George III was following the precedent of many of his predecessors in his abortive projects for a palace, one notable example being the partially completed palace which Christopher Wren built for Charles II at Winchester in 1683–5. George III's acquisition of an ex-aristocratic mansion such as Buckingham House was even more characteristic of the British monarchy, for Whitehall, Hampton Court, and Kensington Palace, also fell into this category.

George III's Patronage of the Arts and Sciences

The extensive use by George III of his private funds, the Privy Purse, for the patronage of the arts can be interpreted not as a private indulgence but as one expression of the 'royal bounty' by which the enlightened monarch promotes the welfare of his subjects.[50] By the 1790s, he was giving away £14,000 annually, which amounted to roughly a quarter of the Privy Purse, while between 1769 and 1801 he paid over £34,000 to a single artist, Benjamin West.[51] George III was exceptional among British monarchs in the range of his architectural patronage,

50 Prochaska, *Royal Bounty*, ch. 1, 'Royalty and Philanthropy in the Reign of George III'.

51 Pye, *Patronage of British Art*, p. 230. Calculating that West had received about £1,500 annually from the King, Pye regretted the King's failure to commission work from Gainsborough, Reynolds, or Wilson (p. 140).

giving commissions to the four leading architects of the day: James 'Athenian' Stuart (1713–88), Sir William Chambers (1723–96), Robert Adam (1728–92), and James Wyatt (1746–1813), notably at Buckingham House, St James's Palace, the White House at Kew, Richmond Lodge, Windsor Castle, and in Windsor Great Park. Also employed by the King were William Robinson (?1720–75), Henry Emlyn (1729–1815), Thomas Sandby (1721–98), 'Capability' Brown (1715–83), and Chambers's pupil, John Yenn (1750–1821). Architects who made unexecuted plans for him included Thomas Wright (1711–86), James Adam (1732–94), and John Soane (1753–1837).

No fewer than four of these architects – Robert Adam, Chambers, Soane, and Stuart – successfully sought the permission of the King to dedicate their publications to him. The potential value of such marks of approval is demonstrated by James Adam who, referring to the ambition of his brother Robert to dedicate his *Ruins of the Palace of the Emperor Diocletian at Spalatro* (1764) to the King and Queen, confessed in 1761 that 'I have taken a sort of dread that the Athenian [Stuart] may have the same project & may be able to execute it through the M[arques]s of R[ockingha]me.'[52] In 1762 'Athenian' Stuart and his co-author Nicholas Revett (1720–1804) did indeed dedicate the first volume of their ground-breaking work, *The Antiquities of Athens*, to the King. Expressing the widely felt expectations of royal patronage at the start of the reign in the fulsome language of the day, Stuart and Revett claimed that

> Athens was particularly celebrated for those Arts, which amidst the cares of Government, and the glories of Conquest, Your Majesty deigns to patronize. The fame of Athens and of these remains of her ancient splendor, which we have described, would not sufficiently embolden us thus to approach Your Majesty, did we not behold, in the prospect which our own Country affords, the Arts of Elegance, and those of Empire equally flourishing, under the influence of a Sovereign in whose Mind they are united.

An important act of architectural patronage at the start of the King's reign was his commissioning in 1762 of a new edition and translation into English of *Les Édifices antiques de Rome* (Paris 1682) by Antoine Desgodetz (1653–1728). This was presumably at the suggestion of William Chambers, though Robert Adam had already considered publishing a new edition with the assistance of Charles-Louis Clérisseau (1721–1820), drawing master to both Chambers

---

52   James to William Adam, Florence, 16 February 1761, cited in Bristol, *James 'Athenian' Stuart*, p. 147.

and Adam in Rome. Originally published for the Académie Royale d'Architecture at the expense of Louis XIV, Desgodetz's authoritative work had as one of its principal aims to provide the young architects at the Académie with an accurate record of the best antique models to follow. It remained a standard source until well into the nineteenth century and was in some ways a parallel to Chambers's equally widely consulted *Treatise on Civil Architecture*.

The engraver and translator of the English edition, which appeared as *The Ancient Buildings of Rome* (2 vols., 1771, 1795),[53] was George Marshall, who took nine years to complete the task. In his folio volumes, which are exceptionally handsome products of the printer's and engraver's art, he reproduced Desgodetz's text in French as well as in translation. The first volume, though not the second, was published at the King's expense, while further evidence of the royal patronage which Marshall enjoyed is provided by his address in Kensington Palace.[54] In his Dedication, which has something of the grandiose flavour of Desgodetz's own dedication to Colbert, Marshall declared that 'Architecture may be termed with great propriety the Science of Kings' because, 'from the erection of the Egyptian pyramids to the present time, the world has owed to the magnificence of Monarchs the grandeur of its buildings.' Drawing attention to the King's training in architecture, Marshall observed of architecture that 'this splendid art may hope for your Majesty's protection by a more particular claim as it has long had the honour of your notice and attention. Other Princes could employ architects, your Majesty can direct them; other Princes have the pride of building, your Majesty has the science.'

Echoing the debates associated with the 'The Quarrel of the Ancients and the Moderns' in seventeenth- and eighteenth-century France, Marshall described his book as 'this representation of Roman art and Roman power, exerted in Edifices on which succeeding ages have gazed with wonder; and which are likely to stand unrivalled, unless your Majesty's influence should enable us to excel them.' He went on to stress in his Preface that a translation of Desgodetz's monograph on buildings which were 'models to all future generations' had been 'constantly in request as the standard of ancient and modern architecture'.

George III lived long enough to play a part in the Gothic Revival which undermined the classical world of Desgodetz and Marshall, a shift welcomed by the leading antiquarian, John Carter (1748–1817), who complained that admiration of 'the Roman and Grecian styles of architecture ... has necessarily turned the genius of Englishmen from their national architecture.'[55]

---

53 E. Harris and N. Savage, *Architectural Books*, p. 181.
54 According to the *Daily Advertiser*, 7 February 1772.
55 *Gentleman's Magazine*, vol. LXIX, 1799, i, p. 92.

The Gothic work which the King commissioned from Wyatt at Windsor while the country was threatened by a Napoleonic invasion could be identified with the promotion of Gothic on the grounds that it would reinforce the spirit of the nation in its opposition to both Napoleon and republicanism (see Chapter 5).

THE OFFICE OF WORKS AND THE ROYAL HOUSEHOLD

It should be explained that the King had direct access to the architects in the Office of His Majesty's Works, which was a department of the Royal Household until the mid-nineteenth century, when it became a ministry fully accountable to parliament. Within the Office of Works, the Surveyor of the King's Works from 1760 to 1778 was Thomas Worsley, MP, but Sir William Chambers contrived to exercise a stranglehold on royal patronage.[56] The King and his mentor from 1755, the Earl of Bute, sought to impose their will on the Office of Works by creating the new office of Architect of Works in November 1761, to be held jointly by Chambers and Robert Adam.

With his characteristic 'hands-on' approach, the King involved himself with many other appointments at the Office of Works.[57] Government business and architectural concerns appear side by side in his official correspondence, as in that of Frederick the Great, who was involved with commissioning and the choice of architect for virtually every building of significance erected during his reign.[58] For example, in a letter to the Prime Minister, William Pitt, of 15 March 1789, written very soon after his recovery from serious illness, the King began by giving him instructions about arranging the translation of the Bishop of Gloucester to the see of St Asaph, and went on to give detailed consideration to future appointments in the Office of Works. The letter is worth quoting at length since it gives such a vivid picture of his knowledge of the holders of comparatively minor offices.

> I find the Clerk of the Works at Hampton Court is expiring;[59] I have ordered Sir William Chambers to wait on Mr Rose[60] that Mr Pitt may be reminded when it shall happen of what I now mention that I would have Tinsley[61] [*sic*] the Clerk of the Works here [Windsor], removed to that place which will be on many accounts a desirable measure, and that Brown,[62] the labourer in trust at the Mewze, may be Clerk of the Works in his room at Windsor, who is an

56 Chambers was Comptroller of the King's Works from 1769 to 1782; from 1782 to 1796 he was Surveyor and Comptroller, as was his successor James Wyatt until 1813.

57 J. Roberts, 'Chambers', p. 45.

58 See Blanning, 'Frederick the Great and German Culture', in Oresko, *Sovereignty*, p. 530, and Giersberg, 'Friedrich II und die Architektur',

in Giersberg and Meckel, *Friedrich II und die Kunst*.

59 William Rice, who died on 6 May 1789.

60 George Rose, MP, Secretary to the Treasury and a close ally of Pitt.

61 Thomas Tildersly or Tildesley, Clerk of Works at Windsor Castle and the Queen's Lodge in 1787, and at Hampton Court and Bushey in 1791.

62 Robert Browne, junior, was Clerk of the Works at Richmond and Kew

active and discreet man, and by the Treasury placing a junior on the vacancy of the Resident Clerk, has had a mortification on a prior occasion.[63]

Many years earlier, while work at Buckingham House was under way in 1762, we find him writing to Lord Bute that 'I beg these things may be instantly put into hand there is one article I had forgot, that is grates in all the rooms that are furnish'd and also for E that is the place my page will wait in for the present. I have not touch'd on what is necessary for enabling meat to be warmed up in the kitchen.'[64] Such intimate acquaintance with details of the fabric and workings of the numerous royal residences was confirmed later in the reign when a contemporary recorded that

> So clear were his Majesty's perceptions of architectural construction, as I have been assured by Mr. Wyatt, that, during the alterations at Windsor Castle, made several years ago, and proceeding upon whilst the king was at Weymouth, his Majesty corresponded by letter with that great architect, and pointed out to him, by his acute recollections of every part of the site, capabilities for alteration and improvement, that had escaped the vigilance of those employed upon the spot . . . The localities of the late king's memory are said to have been such, as almost to exceed belief.[65]

In September 1804, he sent extremely detailed comments to Wyatt on designs for Windsor, including details of brackets and doorcases (see p. 154).[66] In the course of this book, it will be suggested that the King's concentration on detail may have proved problematic in another way by obstructing his creation of a larger picture. However, during his periods of illness he proposed strange and profligate architectural schemes; as Princess Augusta complained in July 1804, 'The ideas of building continue as extravagant as ever, altering every House, unroofing without end to add stories; in short, had He his own way at present, this, nor all the Countries in the World, could stand the expense.'[67]

We should not leave this subject without noting that the Hanoverian government also included an Office of Works. It is usually supposed that not much work was carried out beyond repairs and the building of country vicarages, but the archives have so far been little explored.[68]

Palaces from 1790 to 1820. He was responsible for arrangements for the coronation of George IV in 1820.

63 Aspinall, *Correspondence*, vol. I, p. 401.

64 Sedgwick, *Letters from George III to Lord Bute*, p. 101. 'E' refers to a ground-floor room on a sketch plan of Buckingham House.

65 Angelo, *Reminiscences*, vol. I, pp. 196–7.

66 Aspinall, *Correspondence*, vol. V, p. 228, 5 September 1804.

67 *Harcourt Papers*, vol. VI, pp. 188–90.

68 I am indebted to Dr Jarl Kremeier for information on this subject.

LANDSCAPE DESIGN, GARDENING, AND AGRICULTURE

In England in this period, interest in garden and landscape design went hand in hand with promotion of the latest improvements in agricultural techniques. It was these combined developments which attracted visitors to England from the continent of Europe, especially from the German courts. Rather as George III had a professional knowledge of architecture, so he acquired a detailed familiarity with agricultural techniques which went beyond anything normally expected of a country gentleman, still less of a monarch. He was also wise enough to take advice from the botanist and scientist, Sir Joseph Banks (1743–1820), President of the Royal Society from 1778 to 1820, whose career he promoted and whose interests in agriculture he shared. On the recommendation of Banks, the King imported sheep of French and Spanish descent to dispense with the need to import fine wool from Spain. The King's support of new developments in topics such as crop rotation was of a piece with the acquisition of agricultural books for his vast library, on some of which he made manuscript annotations. It is clear from an essay on agriculture which he wrote as a young man that a principal reason for his interest was that he saw it as 'that greatest of all manufactures'.[69]

As we shall see in Chapter 6, George III contributed to the developments in farming and gardening design in numerous ways, for example, in his most important commission in landscape design, which was at the Old Deer Park at Richmond, today the western portion of Kew Gardens. This was landscaped for the King by 'Capability' Brown from 1763, in which year Brown received the royal appointment of Master Gardener at Hampton Court. With Chambers and to a lesser extent with Brown, the King was on the kind of intimate terms that Louis XIV had enjoyed with Le Nôtre a hundred years earlier. After the death of his mother, the Dowager Princess of Wales, in 1772, the King replaced Lord Bute with Joseph Banks as horticultural and botanical adviser, thus stressing the garden's growing role as a centre for serious botanical study.[70]

At Windsor, the King employed Thomas Sandby to repair and re-create the great artificial lake, Virginia Water, and adorn it with a grotto and cascade. Jane Roberts has shown in *Royal Landscape* the King's unflagging concern with every feature of the extensive work of planting in the vicinity of Virginia Water, from lines of fencing to plantations. We shall also investigate the King's relations with Humphry Repton (1752–1818), 'Capability' Brown's successor as the principal landscape gardener in England.

---

69 RA GEO Add. 32/2020, cited in J. Roberts, *Royal Landscape*, p. 71.
70 See Desmond, *Kew*, pp. 85–103, and H. Carter, *Sir Joseph Banks*.

MACHINERY, MANUFACTURE, AND ASTRONOMY

By the mid-eighteenth century, the early stirrings of the Industrial Revolution had made London the leading centre in Europe for the design and manufacture of scientific instruments. The King played his part in this process by forming a remarkable collection of scientific instruments, models of engines and steam pumps, barometers and hygrometers, microscopes and orreries.[71] His characteristic attention to detail was demonstrated in his well-known familiarity with the assembly of watches, and, less known, in his ability as a turner in ivory, a royal skill exercised by Louis XV and XVI as well as by his friends Lord Bute and Thomas Worsley.

The King's interest in knowledge of the natural world and its practical implications was characteristic of much mid-eighteenth-century aristocratic culture. We have seen his belief in agriculture as 'that greatest of all manufactures', while he also discussed manufacturing industries at Buckingham House with Josiah Wedgwood (1730–95), the ceramics manufacturer and industrialist who became Potter to Her Majesty. With his watchword, 'All things yield to experiment', Wedgwood developed an export trade with Europe, America, and the Indies. As we shall see, John Adams, who became the first American Minister to Great Britain, visited Kew with Thomas Jefferson. Adams also made it his business to inspect Wedgwood's manufactory in 1783 where he admired the 'rich collection of utensils and furniture from the ruins of Herculaneum' as examples of the successful revival of 'the taste of the Greeks'.[72]

Wedgwood's partner from 1768, the Liverpool merchant Thomas Bentley (1731–80), was invited to an audience with the King in 1771, after which he noted that 'The King is well acquainted with business, and with the characters of the principal manufacturers, merchants and artists and seems to have the success of all our manufacturers much at heart, and to understand the importance of them.'[73] Though Wedgwood did not receive any significant orders from the King, in 1786 he gave him a pyrometer set in a mahogany case for his collection of scientific instruments.[74] This was a device of Wedgwood's own invention to measure the shrinkage of ceramic bodies at very high temperatures. His relationship with the King and Queen was remarkable since he was to be a radical in politics who supported the American War of Independence and even the French Revolution.

Described as 'undoubtedly the most scientifically and cartographically interested monarch that Britain has ever had',[75] George III gave key support to John Harrison (1693–1776) who

71 For his collection, now at the Science Museum, London, see Morton and Wess, *Public and Private Science*.

72 C.F. Adams, *Works of John Adams*, vol. 1, p. 407.

73 Hibbert, *George III*, p. 191.

74 See Reilly, *Wedgwood*, vol. 1, pp. 132–3.

75 Barber, 'Maps and Monarchs', in Oresko, *Sovereignty*, p. 105.

devised a marine chronometer capable of determining longitude at sea.[76] In mapping, by the later eighteenth century England had fallen behind other European countries, notably France, Austria, and Denmark, and even behind colonial possessions in India and eastern North America. Joseph Banks noted in 1791 that England, though 'the Queen of Scientific improvement', was not as well mapped as Bengal and Baher.[77] It was thus important that George III gave financial and moral assistance from 1784 to the Trigonometrical Survey, the fledgling Ordnance Survey which had long carried out enquiries into determining longitude. Indeed, it has been suggested that the King 'could have tipped the opinion of the government in its favour.'[78]

The most striking evidence of the King's involvement with the scientific revolution of the eighteenth century was his patronage of the German astronomer William Herschel (1738–1822), who was born in Hanover but came to England in 1757 to earn his living as a musician and to practise his hobby of astronomy. His discovery in 1781 of what turned out to be a new primary planet, Uranus, overthrew the entire conception of the solar system, which had been believed since the earliest times to consist of the sun and six planets, each capable of being seen by the naked eye. In 1782 the King invited Herschel to come with his telescope to an audience at Windsor Castle, where he subsequently became a regular visitor. In view of the observations made by Herschel, which led to the theory of the galaxies and the modern concept of the universe, it has been suggested that 'Perhaps the biggest thing King George ever did was to patronise Herschel.'[79]

Joseph Banks suggested to the King that Herschel might be given charge of the Observatory which had been built for the King at Richmond.[80] Instead, he gave Herschel a generous pension of £200 a year and paid 600 guineas each for four ten-foot telescopes made by him. The King gave one of these to the University of Göttingen in Hanover and sent Herschel and his brother to Göttingen to present it in person. The King also paid £4,000 for an immense telescope of 40 feet focal length and 49 inches aperture, the largest of its day, and provided Herschel with an annual sum of £200 for its maintenance.[81] Housed in a field near Herschel's house at Slough, it was supported within a towering pyramid of scaffolding which had some claim to be one of the most imposing constructions for which George III was responsible (fig. 7). It became an object of amazement, being compared in popular journals to the Seven Wonders of the World such as the Colossus at Rhodes, or to the Porcelain Tower of Nanking,

76 See Quill, *John Harrison*, ch. 20, 'King George and John Harrison'.

77 Royal Society Journal, Book 24, 1790–3, pp. 389–90, cited in Seymour, *History of the Ordnance Survey*, p. 1.

78 Seymour, *ibid.*, p. 22.

79 Brooke, *George III*, p. 303.

80 We shall investigate this building, initially erected to observe the Transit of Venus, in ch. 3.

81 See Hoskin, 'Herschel's 40 ft reflector'.

while the American author, Oliver Wendell Holmes (1809–94), claimed that 'it was a mighty bewilderment of slanted masts and spars and ladders and ropes, from the midst of which a vast tube, looking as if it might be a piece of ordnance such as the revolted angels battered the walls of Heaven with, according to Milton, lifted its muzzle defiantly towards the sky'.[82] It was thus appropriate that George III, helping an apprehensive Archbishop of Canterbury into the observation seat of the telescope, encouraged him by saying, 'Come, my Lord Bishop, I will show you the way to heaven.' Herschel, in turn, described George III to Banks, as 'the best of Kings, who is the liberal protector of every art and science'.[83] This was in a letter in which Herschel proposed naming the planet he had discovered 'Georgium Sidus' in honour of George III.

FIG. 7 *William Herschel's telescope*, 1786–7. Watercolour (artist unknown). 'Original sketch for engraving of 40 ft [telescope] presented to George III by His Majesty's devoted and loyal subject and most grateful servant, William Herschel'. Herschel family archive.

George III was more fortunately endowed with his youth and charm at the start of his reign than any of his immediate predecessors. The remainder of this book will be dedicated to considering how successfully he put into practice the lively interests in architecture, sciences, and the arts which his position allowed him to indulge, and to investigating the varied cultural concerns of George III in the context of his world, which was part *ancien régime*, part Enlightenment, and part Age of Improvement.

82 Holmes, *Poet at the Breakfast Table*, p. 199.
83 Letter printed in the *Philosophical Transactions*, vol. LXII, 1783, of the Royal Society. See Lubbock, *Herschel Chronicle*, p. 124.

THE ARCHITECTURAL PATRONAGE
OF THE ROYAL FAMILY

OPPOSITE Johann Georg
Ziesenis, *Queen Charlotte
when Princess of
Mecklenburg-Strelitz, in
front of Neustrelitz, c.*1761
(detail of fig. 15)

FIG. 8 *Maison de Plaisir
d'Herrenhausen.* Engraving.
RCIN 704535

The Early Hanoverians

Hanover, seat of the Dukes of Calenberg from 1636, became a cultural centre under George I's uncle, Duke John Frederick, who was reigning Duke at Hanover from 1665 to 1679. He rebuilt the Leineschloss, the residence at Hanover,[1] imported architects and musicians from Venice, and employed Leibniz as his librarian in 1676. His brother, George I's father, Ernest Augustus, Duke of Brunswick-Lüneburg (1629–98), Elector from 1692, and his celebrated wife, the Electress Sophia, followed his example on a slightly grander style. It was during their reign that, in 1692, the rulers of the small duchy of Calenberg became Dukes of Hanover and Electors in the Holy Roman Empire. Herrenhausen, the summer residence outside Hanover, was begun as a villa-cum-farm in 1650, but a new house was added by Duke John Frederick in 1665 and a new garden layout begun around 1673 (fig. 8). When Ernest Augustus and Sophia succeeded in 1679, they extended the garden in two stages: first, after 1689, by roughly doubling it in size with an envelope round three sides, and second, after 1696, by again doubling the size with an extension to the south which gave it its present rectangular shape. The creator of this vast Baroque garden, partly inspired by features of the work of Le Nôtre at Versailles, was the French landscape designer Martin Charbonnier (died 1720). He had been commissioned by Ernest Augustus and Sophia in 1683, having already designed gardens at the Prince Bishop's residence at Osnabrück, where the Schloss was built by Ernest Augustus from 1668 in a fairly advanced style for its date in Germany.[2] Though Hanover was a very rural state, the silver in the Harz mountains provided sufficient revenue for the electoral family to indulge in this grandeur.

KING GEORGE I

The Hanoverian monarchs, starting with King George I,[3] are sometimes seen as so lacking in interest in architecture and the arts that even the contributions of George III in this area have been under-appreciated.[4] The notion of creating an appropriate new royal palace, which obsessed

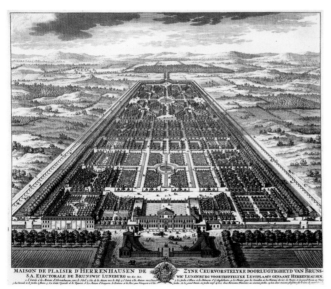

MAISON DE PLAISIR D'HERRENHAUSEN DE S.A. ELECTORALE DE BRUNSWIC LUNEBURG &c. &c. &c.   ZYNE CEURVORSTELYKE DOORLUGTIGHEYD VAN BRUNS- WIC LUNENBURG VOORTREFFELYKE LUSTPLAATS GENAAMT HERRENHAUSEN.

1   See Schnath, *Das Leineschloss.*
2   See Verspohl, *Das Osnabrücker Schloss.*
3   See Hatton, *George I* and Arciszewska, *The Hanoverian Court*

and the Triumph of Palladio.
4   For a rare study of a British royal household, see Beattie, *English Court in the Reign of George I.*

George III in the 1760s and '70s, went back to Charles I.
It recurred at the start of George I's reign in 1714 when
Sir John Vanbrugh (1664–1726) made several attempts
to interest the King in the creation of a magnificent
palace at St James's (fig. 9), at Kensington, or at
Hampton Court.[5] Vanbrugh gave some of his drawings captions in French, the language used in German
courts and also preferred to English in communica-
tions between George I and his court. On the scale of
the larger continental Baroque palaces, the plan for St
James's Palace incorporated nine interior courts, a
theatre, and two chapels.[6] One of these plans, despite
leaving much of the Tudor palace intact, included a
grandiose new south front (seen at the top of fig. 9)
which contained a square central hall with an internal
colonnade of free-standing columns.

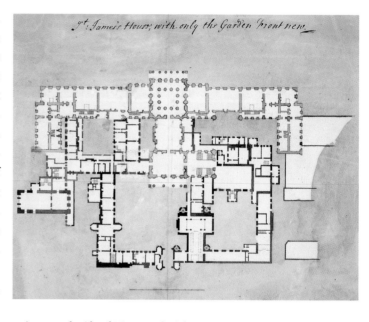

FIG. 9 Sir John
Vanbrugh, *Design for
St James's Palace: ground
plan, c.1715*. Pen and ink
and wash. RL 26300

George I's sister, Princess Sophia Charlotte (1668–1705), second wife of King Frederick I
in Prussia (formerly Elector Frederick III), was a highly cultivated woman and a friend of
Leibniz. From 1695, she built the beautiful garden residence outside Berlin which her
husband named Charlottenburg in her memory on her death in 1705.[7] On the advice of her
first cousin, Elisabeth Charlotte of the Palatinate, duchesse d'Orléans, she employed the
French gardener, Simon Godeau, to design its gardens. To prepare herself, she visited the
Hortus Palatinus at Heidelberg, laid out by her grandfather, Frederick of the Palatine, and
her mother's garden at Herrenhausen, travelling to France to see the gardens at Versailles, St
Cloud, and Fontainebleau. In raising Prussia to a monarchy in 1701 her husband was fired
by the example of his cousin, William of Orange, who had became King of England in 1689.
As part of his programme of achieving this status, King Frederick transformed on the grandest
scale the Schloss in Berlin, and founded the University of Halle, the Academy of Arts, and the
Academy of Sciences.[8]

George I was unique among the Hanoverian kings of Great Britain in commissioning work
at both Herrenhausen and London. He remodelled the Schloss at Herrenhausen in about

5   The drawings are in the Royal Library, Windsor Castle
    (RL 26299–26303, 29638), and All Souls College, Oxford, 1, 4.

6   For the plans for St James's and Kensington Palaces, see Downes,
    Vanbrugh, fig. 11.

7   See Kremeier, 'Iburg, Osnabrück, Hannover'.

8   For Frederick I and Sophia Charlotte as architectural patrons,
    see *Preussen 1701: Eine europäische Geschichte*, 2 vols., Berlin 2001,
    (exh. cat.), and MacDonagh, *Frederick the Great*, pp. 13–15.

1705, and commissioned a new hunting Schloss at Göhrde in the north of the Duchy of Lüneburg, paying for this with the income from that Duchy after he had inherited it in 1705. Göhrde was a minor palace with three wings round an open courtyard, vast stable buildings, and a theatre where plays and ballets were performed. George I was greatly attached to it because it was truly his own, Herrenhausen being occupied till her death in 1714 by his mother, the Electress Sophia, to whom his father had left it during her widowhood. After George I's own death in 1727, Göhrde fell into disuse; it was later demolished apart from two ranges of the outbuildings.[9]

Visiting Herrenhausen in 1716, George I was accompanied by William Benson (1682–1754), later Surveyor of the King's Works, who 'gave directions for that curious water-work in the gardens of Herenhausen [*sic*], which is known to excel the famous fountain of St. Cloud in France'.[10] This was the famous cascade at St Cloud by Antoine Le Pautre and Jules Hardouin-Mansart of 1667–*c*.1675. The later relationship between the gardens at Herrenhausen and at the Hanoverian court in England could be two-way. For example, Johann Jonas Christian Tatter, son of the court gardener at Herrenhausen, visited Kew in 1766 and made drawings of agricultural equipment and of the gardens. George I commissioned a number of utilitarian and government buildings in Hanover, including an archive-cum-library and stables, which were demolished after the Second World War.

During Benson's surveyorship, George I ordered the creation of a new state apartment of three imposing rooms at Kensington Palace.[11] These and the earlier state rooms were decorated for him by William Kent in the 1720s as some of the most striking interiors of their date in England. The Cupola Room and neo-antique ceiling of the Presence Chamber heralded the neo-classicism of the later eighteenth century, while Wren's staircase was transformed by Kent with rich illusionistic frescoes in the manner of Veronese. To George I we also owe the notion of extending Kensington Gardens eastwards towards Hyde Park and the creation of an ornamental lake, the 'Serpentine'.

In the winter of 1726–7 George I approved the designs of New Park Lodge (today White Lodge), in the New Park at Richmond (fig. 10).[12] Intended for the King's use when he was hunting in the Park, this elegant villa has been described as 'the most distinguished building put up by either George I or George II'.[13] The King was here in the forefront of taste for, as an early product of the Palladian Revival associated with the Earl of Burlington, it was

9   See Prüser, *Die Göhrde* and V. Köhler, 'Jagdschloss Göhrde'.

10 Nichols, *Literary Anecdotes*, vol. II, 1812, p. 138. See also Colvin, ed., *King's Works*, vol. V, *1660–1782*, p. 57, and the forthcoming study of the gardens at Herrenhausen by Dr Jarl Kremeier where it is suggested that Benson only put forward a few improvements to the water supply for the fountains when he visited Hanover.

11 Colvin, ed., *King's Works*, vol. V, *1660–1782*, pp. 194–202, where it is calculated that the very substantial sum of nearly £50,000 was spent on works at Kensington during George I's reign (1714–27).

12 *Vitruvius Britannicus*, vol. IV, pls. 1–4.

13 P. Willis, *Charles Bridgeman*, pp. 101–2. It is today the home of the Royal Ballet School.

designed by Roger Morris, the architectural protégé of George I's friend, Lord Herbert, after-wards 9th Earl of Pembroke. In the 1750s George III's aunt, Princess Amelia, who occupied the house as Ranger of Richmond Park, employed Stephen Wright, Clerk of Works, to add quadrant wings following a Palladian pattern. She employed a German gardener called Ludemann because, as she was recorded as saying in 1767, she liked to have a gardener 'who knows to how to handle American and other trees'.[14]

FIG. 10 T. Miller after J. Gandon, *Elevation of his Majesty's Lodge* [White Lodge] *in Richmond Park,* 1767 (from *Vitruvius Britannicus,* IV, pls. 1–2). Engraving. RCIN 703016

KING GEORGE II AND QUEEN CAROLINE

The future George II (reigned 1727–60) and Queen Caroline of Brandenburg-Ansbach (1683–1737) came to England from Hanover in 1714 as Prince and Princess of Wales. When he was banished from St James's Palace in 1718, the Prince of Wales rented Leicester House, Leicester Square, which had a Dutch garden, though this was modest in the extreme in comparison with Herrenhausen, his residence near Hanover.

In 1724 the King commissioned Charles Bridgeman, the distinguished landscape architect and a man of taste and distinction, to improve the gardens at Marble Hill House, the home

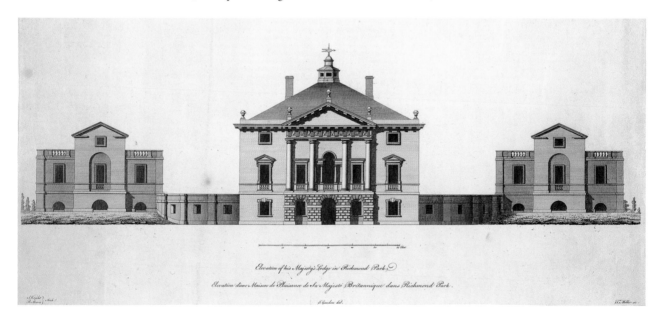

Elevation of his Majesty's Lodge in Richmond Park.

Elevation d'une Maison de Plaisance de Sa Majesté Britannique dans Richmond Park.

---

14   Johann Graefer to Baron Veltheim, 1767 (Landeshauptarchiv Sachsen-Anhalt, Aussenstelle Vernigerode, Rep. H. Harbke 1860, f. 164). I am indebted for this reference to Professor Marcus Köhler of the Fachhochschule Neubrandenburg.

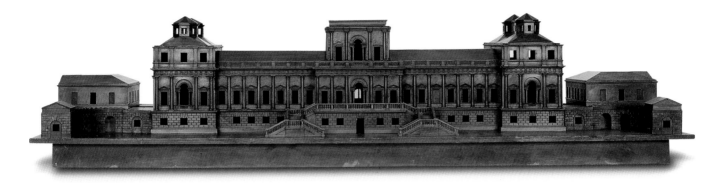

FIG. 11 William Kent, *Model of a design for a country palace for George II,* 1735. Pearwood. RCIN 79398

of his mistress, Henrietta Howard, Countess of Suffolk. Appointed Royal Gardener in 1728, Bridgeman remodelled Kensington Gardens for George II and Queen Caroline. Occupying an important transitional position between the old formal gardens of the seventeenth century and the new landscaped gardens of the later eighteenth century, he thus followed his formal Round Pond of 1728 at Kensington with the informal, or supposedly, natural lake, the 'Serpentine', of 1731. Queen Caroline also maintained the links between Herrenhausen and England by ensuring that Martin Charbonnier's son, Matthew, became a pupil of Bridgeman. In 1738 Bridgeman claimed of Matthew Charbonnier that this pupilage had been 'for his Improvement in the Art of Gardening, and that he has accordingly been Employed, & instructed by me therein, the whole time he has been in England, in drawing of Plans, & also in the practical parts of Gardening at his Majesty's Royal Gardens at Hampton Court.'[15]

William Kent designed a large palace at Richmond for George II and Queen Caroline in 1735, which was not executed, though an imposing pearwood model survives (fig. 11).[16] Its anti-Baroque style was due to the encouragement which seems to have been given to Kent in this project by his friend and patron, the Earl of Burlington. Though the palace was never built, George II's belief in the importance of architecture led him to appoint Burlington's protégé, Henry Flitcroft (1697–1769), as architectural tutor to his son, the Duke of Cumberland, in 1733. After a fire in 1741 at the Leineschloss, the King's residence at Hanover, George II added a new wing to it in 1742–6. Housing offices and archives, this was designed by Johann Paul Heumann, probably based on suggestions by J.-F. Blondel (1705–74), to whose studio Heumann sent his son to work in 1751.

15 Niedersächsisches Staatsarchiv Hannover, Dep. 103 XXIV Nr. 778.
16 Colvin, ed., *King's Works*, vol. v, *1660–1782*, pp. 220–1, and Millon, *The Triumph of the Baroque* (exh. cat.), no. 175, pp. 198 and 482.

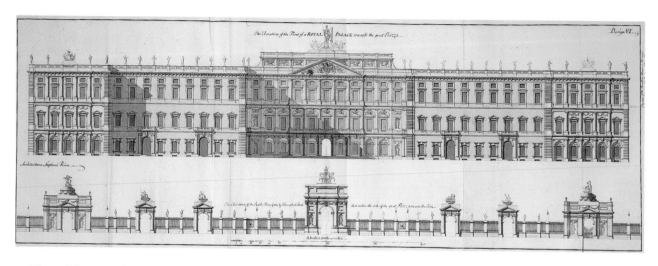

The architect Stephen Riou (1720–80) made presumably unsolicited designs for a palace for George II on a megalomaniac scale, which he described as 'begun in Rome in 1751, 1752, 1753, finished at London 1754' (fig. 12).[17] His façades of towering height, facing onto what he called 'the great Piazza', were in the grandiose language of papal Rome and would have been inconceivable in Georgian London. However, it was percipient of Riou to have proposed building the palace on the site of Buckingham House. Indeed, Sir Aston Webb's entrance front of Buckingham Palace of 1912–13 achieved something of the scale envisaged by Riou for the same site. Because of the parliamentary nature of the British constitution, money was not made available for a royal palace, but funds were readily granted for a major public building in George II's reign – the Horse Guards. Housing the Foot Guards and Horse Guards, which had been created for the King's personal protection, its plans were approved by George II. It was designed by William Kent, but its construction was supervised after his death in 1748 by John Vardy (d. 1756) and William Robinson in the Office of Works where they were joint Clerks of the Works at Whitehall, Westminster, and St James's Palace.

Queen Caroline, who was a passionate gardener at Richmond, was a woman of exceptional intellect and a friend of Leibniz, with whom she frequently corresponded.[18] She was well known for her weekly drawing rooms, court occasions at which she and her friends discussed topics such as theology and metaphysics. These interests found architectural

FIG. 12 Stephen Riou, *The Elevation of the Front of a Royal Palace towards the Great Piazza*, 1751–4. Pen and ink and wash. RL 18101

---

17   The MS volume, 'Designs for a Royal Palace', containing drawings
     and explanatory text, is in the Royal Library at Windsor Castle
     (RL 18098–18109).

18   See Marschner, 'Queen Caroline of Anspach', in Campbell Orr,
     Queenship in Britain 1660–1837.

FIG. 13 George III,
*William Kent's
Hermitage, Richmond,
c.1755. Pen and ink and
wash.* RL K 251

expression in the 1730s in the magnificent Library, 60 feet long and 30 feet wide, which William Kent built for her at St James's Palace, and in the Hermitage which she commissioned from Kent for the gardens at Richmond (fig. 13).[19] With busts by Guelfi and Rysbrack, the Hermitage celebrated natural philosophers and scientists, including Newton, Locke, William Wollaston, Boyle, Bacon, and her friend Samuel Clarke. This monument to national heroes in the form of a shrine to Newtonian science and to deist or Latitudinarian theology, was an early monument of the Enlightenment cult of reason and nature in a garden. With its octagonal plan and cupola, it may have been influenced by the grotto at Herrenhausen.[20]

FREDERICK, PRINCE OF WALES, PRINCESS AUGUSTA, AND KEW

The eldest son of George II and Queen Caroline was Prince Frederick (1707–51), the father of George III. Frederick was born and educated in Hanover. He was brought up at Schloss Herrenhausen and left for England with some reluctance in 1728, following his father's accession to the throne.[21] Created Prince of Wales in 1729, he was one of the most civilised to bear this title since the death in November 1612 of Prince Henry, elder brother of Charles I, at the age of 18. Indeed, Frederick, 'an emotional Jacobite'[22] with a strong affection for the Stuart dynasty and the paintings of Van Dyck, modelled himself as a collector on Charles I. He employed Joseph Goupy (d. 1763) as his drawing master in 1733, but his tastes were eclectic, for he was a patron of Rococo designers, a pioneer in the new gardening at Kew and Carlton House,[23] a collector of Old Master paintings,[24] a poet, and an accomplished cellist. A charming group portrait of 1733 by Philippe Mercier, showing the Prince playing the cello in the garden at Kew with his sisters,[25] conveys the civilised flavour of life at his court which could be paralleled in this respect at a number of German courts. Interested in astronomy, he was a friend of the natural philosopher John Theophilus Desaguliers (1683–1744), who may be said to have invented the planetarium. In 1736 he married Princess Augusta of Saxe-Gotha-Altenburg (1719–72), but the marriage, as well as his disagreements with his father over politics and money, led to his total estrangement from his parents. He and Princess Augusta were banished from court in 1737.

19 See Colton, 'Kent's Hermitage', and Giometti, 'Giovanni Battista Guelfi'.

20 For this analogy, see B. Adam, 'Die Grotten', in *Bericht über die 40*.

21 The importance of the Hanoverian upbringing of Frederick, Prince of Wales is stressed in the unpublished biography of him by the late Dr Frances Vivian.

22 Mowl and Earnshaw, *An Insular Rococo*, p. 177.

23 Coombs, 'The Garden at Carlton House'.

24 Rorschach, 'Frederick, Prince of Wales (1707–51), as Collector and Patron'.

25 National Portrait Gallery (no. 1556). In the background is the Dutch House at Kew, home of the Prince's sister, Anne, Princess Royal. The version in the Royal Collection (RCIN 402414) has a different setting.

Prince Frederick was a generous and loving father to his children and there can be little doubt that many of George III's interests, from architecture to astronomy, were inspired by his example. His sudden death in March 1751, when Prince George was little more than two months short of his thirteenth birthday, must have been traumatic for the boy. Ragnhild Hatton made the interesting suggestion that because he 'was adversely affected' by this loss, 'like many another prince in his position he became obsessed with his duties and with the need to set a good example.'[26]

In 1749, two years before his death, Prince Frederick built a chinoiserie garden building at Kew, the House of Confucius, which was designed by Joseph Goupy or William Chambers.[27] Chinese garden buildings were associated with the new appreciation of nature and the 'natural' style in gardening which also symbolised individual liberty and the politics of the country Whigs in opposition to Robert Walpole. For members of this 'Patriot Opposition' or country party, landscape design and the politics of 'retirement' into the countryside became a medium for the expression of patriotism. A contrast was drawn between 'corruption' and the figure of the 'patriot king', a role to which Frederick, Prince of Wales, aspired and which George III in some sense achieved. King Alfred was seen as the inventor of the English mixed constitution which Walpole had violated. A masque, *Alfred*, by David Mallett and James Thomson, was staged at Cliveden in 1740 for Prince Frederick, who erected a bust of Alfred at Carlton House and one of the Black Prince, who was seen as a model Prince of Wales. We shall see George III adopting a similar theme at Windsor Castle, while the Tory MP Henry Hoare built the gigantic Alfred's Tower at Stourhead, Wiltshire (1762–72), from designs by Henry Flitcroft. The Tower similarly identified George III, 'our truly British King', with King Alfred, 'the Bulwark of English Liberty',[28] so that it was appropriate that George III should give the name Alfred to a son, his ninth, born in 1780.[29]

By 1757 Princess Augusta had appointed William Chambers as her architect and as architectural tutor to her eldest son, Prince George.[30] With the encouragement of Lord Bute, she followed her late husband's example by developing the Picturesque gardens at Kew from 1757 to 1763 with a series of classical and exotic garden buildings by Chambers (fig. 14).[31] In 1772 George III inherited a garden unique in Europe, where it was all but universally admired. Chambers had long been his favourite architect, so that, once again, it is to his parents that the future George III was indebted in his role as a student, patron, and designer of architecture.

FIG. 14 E. Rooker after W. Marlow, *A View of the Wilderness with the Alhambra, the Pagoda, and the Mosque*, 1763 (from W. Chambers, *Kew*). Engraving. RCIN 702947.S

---

26 Hatton, *George I*, p. 286, citing the similar concerns of the Swedish king, Charles XII (1682–1718), who was 14 at the time of his father's death (see Ragnhild Hatton, *Charles XII of Sweden*, London 1968, p. 522).

27 For a discussion of this attribution, see Harris and Snodin, *Chambers*, pp. 56–7.

28 From the inscription on the tower, as proposed in a letter of 1762 from

Hoare to his son-in-law, Lord Bruce, a Gentleman of the Bedchamber to George III (cited in Woodbridge, *Landscape and Antiquity*, p. 55).

29 Prince Alfred died aged 2 in 1782.

30 For officers in her household from 1736 to 1772, see http://www.ihrinfo.ac.uk/office/augusta.html.

31 For an excellent account of these, see Desmond, *Kew*, pp. 44–63.

A View of the Wilderneſs, with the Alhambra, the Pagoda and the Mosque

WILLIAM AUGUSTUS, DUKE OF CUMBERLAND

Another influence on the young King was probably the architectural and landscaping activities of his uncle, William Augustus, Duke of Cumberland (1721–65), in his capacity as Ranger
of Windsor Great Park from 1746 to 1765.[32] Like his brother, the Prince of Wales, William
Augustus was provided, as we have seen, with an architectural tutor, Henry Flitcroft. A
leading architect in the Office of Works from 1726, thanks to the patronage of Lord Burlington,
he was tutor to the Duke of Cumberland from 1733 to 1737 at a salary of £50 a year. In tribute
to this association, Flitcroft prepared a bound volume of his drawings of the five orders, designs
for a large Palladian palace, a Doric pavilion, and other buildings, dedicated to the Duke.[33]

---

32 For a full account, see J. Roberts, *Royal Landscape, passim.*
33 British Library, King's MS 283. The perspective view of the palace is
    reproduced in J. Roberts, *Royal Landscape*, pl. 46, where it is dated to
    *c.*1747.

The most interesting activities of the Duke as Ranger were his works of the later 1740s and 1750s, including the creation of Virginia Water and the associated introduction of the taste for 'natural' garden design which his elder brother, Frederick, Prince of Wales, was pioneering at Carlton House and Kew in the same period. He also paralleled his brother's tastes by commissioning chinoiserie features at Virginia Water – the Mandarin Yacht and the Chinese Building – both to the design of unknown architects. The Yacht of 1753 was an astonishing creation, containing a central reception room with swept-up roofs ornamented with dolphins. Its sides were painted with large-scale, winged dragons below fretwork balustrades. Approached by Chinese bridges, the Chinese Building on China Island in Virginia Water was no less imaginative.

A design of around 1754 for a large colonnaded villa for the Duke of Cumberland by Richard Bentley (1708–82), a close associate of Horace Walpole, suggests a possible link between Cumberland's park buildings at Windsor and those in both Chinese and Gothic style built at Old Windsor for Walpole's friend, Richard Bateman.[34] Cumberland also built the Belvedere, a triangular crenellated tower with corner turrets overlooking Virginia Water. Designed by Thomas Sandby in about 1750 and enlarged by Wyatville for George IV, it forms the core of the present Fort Belvedere. Its Gothic flavour provided a precedent for George III's creation in the same style of Cranbourne Lodge and Cumberland Lodge at Windsor. The Duke of Cumberland had already employed Thomas Sandby to enlarge the Great (now Cumberland) Lodge in the Great Park at Windsor in about 1760.

EDWARD AUGUSTUS, DUKE OF YORK, AND WILLIAM HENRY, DUKE OF GLOUCESTER

George III's brother, the Duke of York (1739–67), second son of Frederick, Prince of Wales, commissioned designs from William Chambers in 1759 for a superb town house in Pall Mall in the most up-to-date Franco-Italian neo-classical manner.[35] This was before George III had bought Buckingham House. George I, his father, and uncles, were frequently in Italy, particularly in Venice where they rented the Ca' Foscari and boxes in opera houses. Italy seems not to have been visited by the royal family since George I, but in 1763–4 Prince Edward made a Grand Tour there.[36]

George III's favourite brother, the Duke of Gloucester (1743–1805), third son of Frederick, Prince of Wales, took a keen interest in the antiquities of Rome, where he had the leading dealer, Thomas Jenkins, as his guide in 1772, and undertook excavations with Prince Barberini

---

34   The Lewis Walpole Collection, Farmington, Connecticut. See
       J. Roberts, *Royal Landscape*, p. 48.
35   Harris and Snodin, *Chambers*, pp. 127–8.
36   Ingamells, *Dictionary*, pp. 402–4.

FIG. 15 Johann Georg
Ziesenis, *Queen Charlotte
when Princess of
Mecklenburg-Strelitz, in
front of Neustrelitz, c.*1761.
Oil on canvas.
RCIN 403562

in 1776. During visits to Italy in 1771–2, 1775–7, and 1786–7, he commissioned numerous paintings and portraits, and bought marble and alabaster chimneypieces and a painted mosaic table.[37] Though these activities in Italy were not followed by George III, they were by his son, Prince Augustus, the future Duke of Sussex, as we shall see in Chapter 7.

The Mecklenburg-Strelitz Family and Queen Charlotte

The family of Queen Charlotte, from the small state of Mecklenburg-Strelitz in north Germany, had modest architectural ambitions. George III's wife was born in 1744 as Princess (Sophie) Charlotte, daughter of the younger son of Duke Adolphus Frederick II of Mecklenburg-Strelitz (1658–1708). Her uncle, Adolphus Frederick III (1686–1752), was reigning Duke at the time of her birth. An early biographer mentioned that her birthplace, the summer residence at Mirow, resembled 'the castellated mansions of our old English nobility'.[38] This description was an early attempt to make the ducal family look English, for the residences of the Mecklenburg-Strelitz family were in the customary German Baroque style, though in the simpler form known as *Landbaukunst* (country building). Charlotte was born in the old manor house at Mirow, built in 1707–12 and remodelled in half-timbered form between 1735 and 1737 as a modest, H-shaped, stuccoed building with high mansard roofs and little decoration beyond rusticated angle pilasters. However, its interiors were remodelled in about 1760 with Baroque plasterwork by stuccoists from Potsdam, who were available as most work there had been halted by the Seven Years War.[39] This work was carried out for Adolphus Frederick IV (1738–94), Queen Charlotte's brother, who, though not wealthy, spent considerable sums at the palaces of Mirow and Neustrelitz. He had succeeded their uncle, Adolphus Frederick III, following the death of their father, Charles, earlier in 1752.

At Neustrelitz, which became a *Residenz* in 1701, there was already a Schloss, burned in 1712 in which year it was remodelled. Adolphus Frederick III built a new palace at Neustrelitz with formal gardens in 1726–31 to designs by Christoph Julius Löwe, a former gardener from Brunswick who now became the leading architect in Mecklenburg. Its half-timbered construction was replaced in 1755 by Löwe for Duke Adolphus Frederick IV.[40] Princess Charlotte was brought up in some state in the 1750s at her brother's residence at Neustrelitz, which appears in her portrait (fig. 15) by Johann Georg Ziesenis (1716–76), court painter and decorator in Hanover to George II and later to George III.[41]

37 *ibid.*, pp. 1033–5.

38 J. Watkins, *Memoirs of … Her Most Excellent Majesty Sophie Charlotte*, p. 30.

39 See Adamiak, *Schlösser und Gärten in Mecklenburg*, p. 262 and pls. 96–102.

40 Remodelled in 1862 and 1905, Neustrelitz was demolished in 1945 (*ibid.*, pp. 265–9 and pls. 265–8).

41 On Neustrelitz, see British Library, Map Library, K.Top. 101.22d and 22e.

To the north-east of the Schloss and garden at Neustrelitz, Princess Charlotte's uncle, Adolphus Frederick III, employed Löwe to lay out the new town of Neustrelitz in 1733 on a star plan, though this was not related to the Schloss as were the palace and town at Karlsruhe.[42] The departure of Princess Charlotte to marry George III in 1761 was marked by an illumination at Mirow. As we shall see, she commissioned such transparencies, a German and French custom, at the English court. As Queen of Great Britain she entertained her relatives at Richmond, especially her brothers, Prince Ernest of Mecklenburg-Strelitz, and Prince, later Grand Duke, Charles of Mecklenburg-Strelitz. We shall see the architectural fruits of these visits in Chapter 7.

We have noted the architectural commissions of Queen Charlotte's family in Mecklenburg and elsewhere, while recent research has established more clearly the extent to which she acted independently of the King in shared areas of interest such as music, architecture, gardening, and collecting, notably books, furniture, and pottery.[43] She drew and painted, especially flowers and landscapes, as well as patronising Gainsborough, Beechey, and particularly her fellow German, the raffish Johann Zoffany, born in 1733 near Frankfurt-am-Main. In 1761 she is said to have played English music on the harpsichord on the sea-crossing to England to meet her future husband for the first time, and appointed Johann Christian Bach, son of Johann Sebastian, her Music Master soon after he settled in London in 1762.

The ducal court in Hanover suffered musically in comparison with other German courts during the eighteenth century because of the absence of the Elector after 1714.[44] However, in England the passion of the King and Queen for Handel led them to attend the first of the Handel festivals in 1784 at Wyatt's Pantheon in Oxford Street and at Westminster Abbey. In both places substantial canopied royal boxes were erected from designs by James Wyatt (figs. 16, 17), who appropriately chose the classical style for the Pantheon and Gothic for Westminster Abbey.[45] A key figure in the Handel festival was the distinguished musician and historian, Dr Charles Burney (1726–1814), father of the Queen's Second Keeper of the Robes, Fanny Burney (1752–1840), Madame D'Arblay.[46] The author of *The Present State of Music in Germany, the Netherlands, and United Provinces* (2 vols., 1773), he was appointed Musician in Ordinary to George III in 1774. The King became a regular subscriber to the Concert of Ancient Music in 1785, granting it royal patronage and attending its performances with Queen Charlotte.[47] The Queen also supported music at the court through her household budget, while Burney chose to dedicate to her his *General History of Music* (4 vols., 1776–89), a monument of Enlightenment

FIG. 16 J. and W. Walker after J. Dixon, *View of the Magnificent box erected for their Majesties in Westminster Abbey*, 1784. Engraving. RCIN 702360

FIG. 17 W. Angus after J. Dixon, *Inside view of the Pantheon showing the Royal Box designed by James Wyatt for the Handel Commemoration*, 1784. Engraving. RCIN 702468

42　See M. Köhler, *Historische Gärten um Neubrandenburg*, pp. 97–106 and 114–19, and Nugent, *Travels through Germany*, vol. II, p. 344.

43　See Campbell Orr, 'Queen Charlotte', pp. 236–66, and 'Queen Charlotte as Patron'.

44　See Bauman, 'Courts and Municipalities in North Germany', p. 247.

45　Their appearance is known from engravings by William Angus and

James Walker respectively after drawings by J. Dixon (RCIN 702468 and 702360).

46　For officers in Queen Charlotte's household, see http://www.ihrinfo.ac.uk/office/queencharlotte.html.

47　For references to the musical life of the court, see Papendiek, *Court and Private Life, passim*.

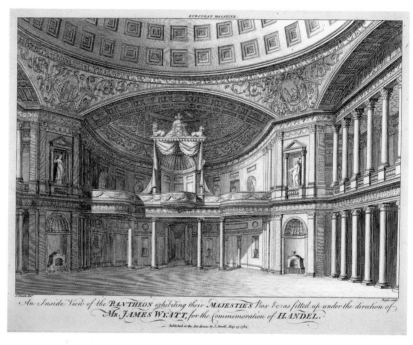

thought in which he had been inspired by the *Encyclopédie* and by Johnson's *Dictionary*.[48]

Queen Charlotte's interest in porcelain and pottery led her to commission a tea service from Josiah Wedgwood in 1765, after which he was appointed Potter to Her Majesty.[49] She become patroness of his factory at Burslem, where he named his cream-coloured earthenware Queen's Ware in her honour.[50] Her most remarkable act of architectural patronage was to commission the delectable neo-classical villa which James Wyatt built for her at Frogmore in 1793–5 (fig. 18), incorporating a seven-bay house of around 1680, probably designed by Hugh May (1621–84). Wyatt made further additions in 1801 and 1804, including a long, glazed loggia, full of plants and flowers. The Queen's love of gardening was supported by a serious interest in botanical literature which encouraged her to acquire two estates at Frogmore in 1790 and 1792, where she created an important Picturesque garden. This was inspired by the Rousseauesque flower garden at Nuneham Courtenay, Oxfordshire, created by her friends, the 2nd Earl Harcourt (1736–1809) and his wife. The Queen's circle included several

48 See Lonsdale, *Dr Charles Burney.*
49 See Reilly, *Wedgwood,* vol. i, pp. 200–2.
50 Uglow, *Lunar Men,* p. 88.

acquaintances or followers of Rousseau, notably one of her salaried Readers, Jean-André DeLuc (1727–1817), a native of Geneva and friend of Matthew Boulton; her botanical lecturer, the Unitarian dissenter James Edward Smith (1759–1828), a botanist and co-founder of the Linnean Society; and her close friends, the Harcourts, whom she appointed respectively her Master of the Horse and Lady of the Bedchamber; and the Duchess of Portland (1715–85), who has been described as 'the leading female collector, connoisseur and scientific amateur of her day'.[51]

The famous garden of sensibility at Nuneham Courtenay, inspired by Julie's garden in Rousseau's *Julie, ou la nouvelle Héloïse* (1761), was designed for George Simon Harcourt in 1772 before he succeeded to the property as 2nd Earl Harcourt on the death of his father in 1777. He and his wife continued to develop it during the next two decades.[52] Designed by the

51 Campbell Orr, 'Lost Royal Libraries and Hanoverian Court Culture',
    in Raven, *Lost Libraries*, where the household of the Duchess of Portland
    is described as 'the matrix in which Elizabeth Montagu,
    the queen of the bluestockings, developed her own literary
    leanings and learnt how a household could become a
    centre for female intellectuality'. (p. 133). See also Myers,
    Bluestocking Circle.

52 See Laird, 'Our equally favorite hobby horse'.

FIG. 18 Charles Wild, *The garden front, Frogmore House*, 1819. Watercolour and bodycolour over pencil. RL 22118

FIG. 19 W. Watts after Paul Sandby, *View of the Flower Garden at Nuneham from the Statue of Hebe to the Temple of Flora*, 1777 (J. Boydell, *A Collection of One Hundred and Eighty Select Views in England … drawn by P. Sandby*, vol. I, 1783, pl. 46). Engraving. RCIN 817092

View of the Flower Garden at Nuneham, from the Statue of Hebe, to the Temple of Flora.

Published according to the Act, by G. Kearsly, at No. 46, in Fleet Street. Aug.t 1. 1777

poet-gardener, William Mason (1724–97), author of *The English Garden. A Poem in Four Books* (1771–81), this novel flower garden featured a bust of Rousseau and an inscription from *La nouvelle Héloïse* at the entrance. Indeed the Harcourts established a spinning festival along Rousseauesque lines, at which prizes for craftsmanship were awarded annually along with awards for merit to virtuous tenants.[53]

Nuneham Courtenay was visited by George III and Queen Charlotte in 1784, 1786, and 1788, husband and wife appreciating its charms equally (fig. 19). The King wrote to Harcourt *en route* for Cheltenham in 1788 that he looked forward to being able to 'just cast an eye on the more beautiful flower Garden'.[54] Though the reactions of the King and Queen to the tributes to Rousseau in the garden and the mementoes of him in the house are not recorded, the Queen acquired his key writings for her library, while DeLuc 'explicitly praised George III

53 Campbell Orr, 'Queen Charlotte', p. 256.
54 Cited in J. Roberts, *Royal Landscape*, p. 68.

A Jubilee at Frogmore

and Queen Charlotte for appreciating the delights of domesticity and linked this to Rousseau's advocacy of the simple life.'[55] DeLuc was, however, worried about the questionable religious orthodoxy of Rousseau.

Envying what she described to Lady Harcourt as 'your little Paradise, Nuneham',[56] the Queen asked William Mason to design her a similar garden at Frogmore in 1791. Mason sent the Queen his assistant, Christopher Alderson, though a more important role was played by William Price, Equerry to the King from 1783 to 1787, the Queen's Vice-Chamberlain from 1792, and brother of the celebrated Picturesque theorist Sir Uvedale Price (1747–1829). Queen

FIG. 20 J. Merigot after Matthew Cotes Wyatt, *A Jubilee at Frogmore*, 1809. Etching and aquatint. RCIN 700895

---

55 Campbell Orr, 'Queen Charlotte', p. 240.

56 *ibid.*, p. 257 (Queen Charlotte to Elizabeth, Lady Harcourt,
     13 September 1786).

Charlotte and William Price planted thousands of trees and shrubs at Frogmore, transformed the rectangular canal into a lake, and built Gothic ruins from designs drawn by James Wyatt and Princess Elizabeth. The whole place became a Petit Trianon where, like Queen Marie-Antoinette at Versailles, she could escape from court life at Windsor. It was thus ironic that a party which Queen Charlotte planned to hold at Frogmore in 1793 to celebrate the anniversary of her husband's accession on 25 October 1760, had to be postponed until 8 November because of the execution of Marie-Antoinette on 16 October 1793. It was at Frogmore on 25 October 1809 that Queen Charlotte gave one of her most spectacular parties, to celebrate the jubilee of the King's accession (fig. 20). At this water pageant, for which she had issued a thousand tickets, there appeared 'as it were by magic, on the beautiful piece of water opposite the garden front of the house, two triumphal cars, drawn by two sea-horses each, one occupied by Neptune, and preceded by the other with a band of music'; an island rising from the water featured a transparency of 'a Grecian temple' designed by Wyatt which represented 'the Eye of Providence, fixed as it were, upon a beautiful image of his Majesty, surmounted by stars of lamps'.[57]

Reading extensively in modern literature, English, French, and German, and having her own private press and bindery at Frogmore, Queen Charlotte built up a large collection of books.[58] In her mellow and rather masculine-looking library, the rich colour of the golden-brown walls matched that of the bookcases, doors, and shutters, all grained in imitation of satinwood. The shelves were surmounted by black plaster busts of men of letters. As earlier at Buckingham House, her interest in interior design is shown in the interiors at Frogmore House, which proved so attractive that the Queen eventually granted permission for Frogmore to be opened by ticket to 'respectable parties'.[59]

---

57 *Reading Mercury*, 30 October 1809. See Hedley, *Queen Charlotte*, p. 234.
58 On her library, see Campbell Orr, 'Lost Royal Libraries and Hanoverian Court Culture', in Raven, *Lost Libraries*.
59 Watkin, *Royal Interiors*, pp. 90–7.

George III was unique amongst English monarchs in receiving a near professional training in architecture. In aristocratic families such training was, by contrast, probably more customary than is now appreciated, partly because its principal tangible records, ephemeral drawings, have rarely survived. The presence in the Royal Library at Windsor of hundreds of drawings connected with the architectural education of George III is a tribute to the seriousness with which successive monarchs and those who serve them have taken the keeping of records. In a great house such as Badminton, Gloucestershire, which has long been in the ownership of a single noble family, the archives also happen to contain extensive tuition drawings in architecture,[1] including schemes for a large palace, made in the 1720s by the young Henry Somerset, 3rd Duke of Beaufort (1707–45), a future collector and patron.[2]

A more famous nobleman architect, the 3rd Earl of Burlington (1694–1753), did not supervise the execution of his own designs, but employed a large number of clerks and executant architects, notably Samuel Savill, Daniel Garrett, Henry Flitcroft, William Kent, and Stephen Wright.[3] It is probable that many such amateur architects have long been forgotten. For example, George III's architectural tutor, William Chambers, a man of exacting standards, described the Marquis de Voyer d'Argenson as an 'Excellent Architect',[4] though we know of no work built from his designs. He was the patron from 1762 to 1778 of Chambers's friend, the architect, Charles de Wailly (1730–98).[5]

The Mentors

LORD BUTE

Prince George (fig. 21) was given an elaborate training in kingship in which architecture took its place. His tutor from 1749 was George Lewis Scott (1708–80), a Fellow of the Royal Society, a mathematician and a barrister, who counted Dr Johnson and Edward Gibbon among his friends. Scott gave the young Prince a sound mathematical and scientific training as well as instruction in history, classics, religion, agriculture, geography, and the English political and legal systems. Nor was the Prince's artistic education neglected, for he seems to have received some lessons from the painter Joseph Goupy, who had worked for his father since 1733. His education was not only determined by the example of his parents, who were sophisticated patrons of art and architecture, but also by the fact that, after his father's premature death in 1751, his chief mentor and adviser was John Stuart, 3rd Earl of Bute (1713–92), a serious and

1   Information from Mr John Harris.
2   Ingamells, *Dictionary*, pp. 67–9.
3   Hewlings, 'Chiswick House and Gardens', in Barnard and Clark,

Lord Burlington, p. 132.
4   British Library, Add. MS 41135, 37, cited in Harris, *Chambers*, p. 14.
5   *Charles de Wailly*, pp. 43–6.

cultured intellectual.[6] He was a second father to the Prince, who clearly adored him, and a friend of the Prince's father, Frederick, Prince of Wales, who had appointed him Lord of the Bedchamber in 1750. In that year Bute was also assisting in the design of the gardens at Kew. It was at the request of the young Prince George that Bute was appointed his Groom of the Stole in 1756. Already there were expectations that he would become First Minister in the next reign.

Bute kept a close watch over every aspect of the Prince's education, even to the extent of correcting his written exercises.[7] From the summer of 1755 he was in constant attendance on the Prince, who addressed him as 'My Dearest Friend' in letters from June 1757. It is impossible to over-emphasise the importance of Bute in shaping the tastes of the future George III in everything from art and architecture to the collection of scientific instruments. The King and his friends such as Bute, Harcourt, and Worsley all saw an interest in architecture as one of the attributes of a gentleman. During the first twenty years of the reign of George III, it became increasingly fashionable for people of leisure to practise the arts of paintings, modelling, and design. A talented practitioner was the King's friend and member of the Queen's Household, the 2nd Earl Harcourt. In 1787 we find him sending the Queen one of his drawings to copy. In her letter of thanks, she tells him that 'I will try to copy it in my humble way,' adding, 'though the King says it is the shabbiest way of drawing in the world,'[8] a comment which sheds interesting light on his own activities as a practitioner. He may have been aware that Reynolds had warned his pupils at the Royal Academy of the dangers of servile copying.[9]

On 27 October 1760, two days after the death of George II, Bute was sworn a member of the Privy Council and was appointed Groom of the Stole and First Gentleman of the Bedchamber to George III.[10] From May 1762 to April 1763 he was also First Lord of the Treasury and Keeper of the Privy Purse, the equivalent of the modern office of Prime Minister. In January 1761, near the start of the new reign, that great gossip Horace Walpole wrote to Henry Zouch[11] that 'The King and Lord Bute have certainly both of them great propensity to the arts . . . Building, I am told, is the King's favourite study.'[12] Chambers and the sculptor Joseph Wilton (1728–1803) – who had both worked for the Dowager Princess of Wales and Lord Bute, as well as Prince George – were rewarded with promotion soon after the start of the new reign. In August 1761 Wilton was appointed 'Sculptor in Ordinary to His Majesty', and in the following November Chambers and Robert Adam became joint holders

---

6   See the forthcoming monograph on him by Francis Russell, to whom I am grateful for allowing me to read the typescript.

7   For examples, see Brooke, *George III*, p. 55.

8   Whitley, *Artists and Their Friends*, vol. II, p. 73.

9   Reynolds, *Discourses*, Discourse VI, 1774, p. 100.

10   Bucholz and Sainty, *Officials of the Royal Household, 1660–1837*.

11   Henry Zouch (1726–95), political adviser to Lord Rockingham in Yorkshire in 1780 was the author of *Catalogue of the Royal and Noble Authors of England, with Lists of Their Works Printed at Strawberry Hill*, 1758.

12   Walpole, *Correspondence*, vol. XVI, p. 21.

FIG. 21 Jean-Étienne Liotard, *George, Prince of Wales (later George III)*, 1754. RCIN 400897

of the new post of Architect to the Board of Works, while in December Allan Ramsay (1713–84) was given the title of 'Principal Painter in Ordinary'.

Since all of these posts were newly created or re-created, they were evidently intended to be part of what has been described as Bute's and the King's 'larger political strategy to illustrate the young King's interest in Britain and all things British'.[13] The appointments of these three men, all of whom had up-to-date classical tastes, clearly established the belief of the King and his advisers in the importance of the patronage of architects and artists as part of the salvation or modernisation of British art. As we have seen, even Hogarth produced an engraving in which he hailed the young King as the fountainhead of British architecture, painting, and sculpture (fig. 1).[14] Walpole echoed this euphoria when he exclaimed 'If there are any talents among us, this seems the crisis for their appearance: The Throne itself is now the altar of the Graces, and whoever sacrifices to them becomingly, is sure that his offerings will be smiled upon by a Prince, who is at once the example and patron of accomplishments.'[15]

It was at this moment that Bute began giving ambitious commissions to Robert Adam, including his town mansion, Bute (later Lansdowne) House (from *c.* 1762), Berkeley Square, and Luton Hoo, his vast palace in Bedfordshire (1767–74). In the same decade he continued the process which he had begun in the 1730s of remodelling his Scottish seat, Mount Stuart, on the Isle of Bute. His choice of Adam rather than of Chambers was doubtless to allow Chambers to concentrate on the commissions which he might expect to receive following his royal appointment. Bute's choice did not dim the rivalry between Chambers and Adam, who had visited Chambers as early as 1758 and taken private pleasure in finding him 'drawing in a poor mean lodging up a long dark stair'. Chambers spoke of his royal pupil, which Adam felt too boastful, and showed him one of the Prince's drawings. Adam found the drawing 'simple enough, however it shows his love for the art'.[16]

LORD HARCOURT AND THOMAS WORSLEY

The young King was not only powerfully influenced by his association with Bute, but also by his friendship with Simon Harcourt, 1st Earl Harcourt (1714–77), and with Thomas Worsley (1710–78), the last of whom he had known all his life. A talented and active amateur architect, Worsley had been appointed an equerry to George II in 1743, while Harcourt, a member of George II's household from 1735 and the Prince's Governor in 1750–1, was a gifted amateur

13 Coutou, 'William Chambers and Joseph Wilton', in Harris and Snodin, *Chambers*, p. 179.
14 On this, see above in Introduction, p. 12.
15 Walpole, *Anecdotes of Painting*, vol. I, p. xx.
16 Fleming, *Robert Adam and His Circle*, p. 249.

artist and a close friend of Worsley. Bute's own intimate friendship with Worsley had begun when they were at Eton, Worsley writing to him in 1760 that they had 'respected, honoured, loved nearly 40 years together'.[17] Correspondence between them shows their great familiarity with the details of the orders and how to use them in design.[18] They were, for example, in close discussion over the building of Worsley's seat, Hovingham Hall, Yorkshire (1751–76). Arranged round two courtyards approached through an atrium, this was inspired by Palladio's reconstructions of the ancient Roman house in his illustrations to Daniele Barbaro's edition of Vitruvius of 1556 and in his *Quattro Libri dell'Architettura* (1570).[19]

Horace Walpole told Horace Mann in December 1760 that Thomas Worsley 'is made Master of the Board of Works; he was this King's equerry, and passes for having a taste for architecture of which I told you this king was fond.'[20] It was as part of Bute's plan for replacing the Whig officials whom the new King had inherited from his grandfather that he persuaded the King to appoint Worsley Surveyor General of the King's Works in December 1760.[21] Holding the Surveyorship till his death in 1778, Worsley thus oversaw works at Buckingham House. It was through association with such connoisseurs as Harcourt, Bute, and Worsley, that George III came in his youth to think it natural and appropriate for an educated man to be able to discuss the niceties of the classical orders with an architect, skills shared by his future friends and acquaintances such as Bishop Hurd and the 1st Duke of Northumberland.

The intimate relations between Worsley, Bute, and the King, is shown in the following extract from a letter from Worsley to Bute, evidently from the early 1760s, from which it is also clear that a bout of ill health did not deter the King from inspecting work in progress.

> I have been at St James's this afternoon: & to my great surprise & concern found the King walking about the new painted and white washed rooms, the

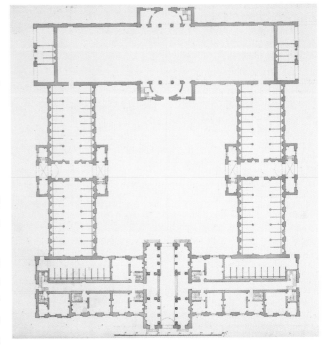

FIG. 22 Sir William Chambers, *Design for a Riding House and Stables*, c.1765. Pen and ink. RL 30484

17 Mount Stuart, Bute MSS, 13 November 1760. I am indebted to Dr Giles Worsley for information about Thomas Worsley.

18 For example, in a letter of 1756 from Worsley to Bute, cited in Francis Russell's forthcoming monograph on Bute.

19 Worsley, *Classical Architecture*, p. 141.

20 Walpole, *Correspondence*, vol. XXI, p. 460.

21 On a 'sudden and positive order' from the King (cited in J. Roberts, 'Chambers', p. 42).

windows all open, & he having taken a dose of physick this morning . . . I could not help saying afterwards to Mr Hawking I wish he had prevented the King's going about in new rooms at that time, but he said he could not prevent him.[22]

George III, Worsley, Harcourt, and Bute, all shared a passion for horses as well as for architecture. Bute sought Worsley's advice when building a riding house at Mount Stuart in 1761, signing himself in a letter to Worsley as 'your humble Ecuyer and Architect'.[23] As we shall see in Chapter 4, Worsley and Bute were doubtless involved in the design of the King's riding house at Buckingham House in 1762.[24] There are two sets of designs at Windsor for an ambitious riding house and stables, one of them being a quadrangle with a riding house of 203 feet by 50 feet in one range, two ranges of stables, and a fourth range with substantial houses, presumably for equerries (fig. 22).[25]

WILLIAM CHAMBERS

Apparently introduced into the household of Frederick, Prince of Wales by Bute, William Chambers was appointed in the summer of 1757 to be both architectural tutor to Frederick's eldest son and architect to his widowed mother, the Dowager Princess.[26] Chambers had begun his own professional training under Jacques-François Blondel in 1749–50 at his École des Arts in Paris, the most important architectural training ground in Europe. With memories of this education still fresh in his mind, Chambers gave the Prince architectural instruction on three days each week, frequently in the White House at Kew, commenting that 'my hands are full of work, but my pockets are not full of money. The prince employs me three mornings a week to teach him Architecture; the buildings and other decorations at Kew fill up the remaining time.'[27] The manuscript with illustrations of Chambers's general account of the orders made for the Prince and later reproduced in the published *Treatise*, remains in the Royal Collection (RL 30311, 30311A, etc). Chambers remodelled the grounds at Kew for the Dowager Princess of Wales, from 1757, providing a series of cross-axes terminated by 25 temples and other ornamental buildings. Construction of these continued into the reign of George III, notably the Mosque and Temple of the Sun, both of 1761, the Pagoda of 1761–2, and the never-completed Temple of Peace to celebrate the Treaty of Paris of 1763.

Chambers published his remarkable achievement at Kew in his book *Plans, Elevations,*

22 Mount Stuart, undated letter, no. 515; if pre-1762, it probably refers to St James's Palace; if later, to Buckingham House.

23 *ibid.*, undated letter, no. 165.

24 Dr Worsley informs me that there are drawings at Hovingham which are probably related to the riding house at Buckingham House.

25 Windsor Castle, RL 30467, 30480–4, 30486–90. See Giles Worsley,

'Catalogue of British Riding Houses', *Ancient Monuments Society Transactions*, forthcoming.

26 See Bucholz and Sainty, 'Office-Holders in Modern Britain. Household of Princess Augusta 1736-72' (http://www.ihrinfo.ac.uk/office/augusta.html).

27 Undated letter, *c.*1760 (Royal Academy Archives, CHA/3/17).

Sections, and Perspective Views of the Gardens and Buildings at Kew in Surrey (1763), while he also paid tribute to Bute by saying that the buildings at Kew had been planned by him and executed under his direction. He bound up the original drawings for the book for presentation to Bute.[28] Most unusually for their date, his buildings at Kew were in classical, oriental, and Gothic styles, perhaps because, as Francis Russell has suggested, Bute considered that such exotic modes complemented the botanical collections being built up by him and his agents. In another modern interpretation of Kew, it 'represented a spectrum of all world cultures and religions that were deemed important at the time' in which the British Empire 'provided a model of how these different cultures might relate to Britain.'[29] This was an expression of the support for the Empire by the anti-Walpole Patriot party, of which Frederick, Prince of Wales, had been an enthusiastic member.

Chambers's buildings also served an educational role associated with the history of architecture which was being taught to the Prince. Indeed, while he was receiving his tuition, Kew was a building site which cannot have been anything other than fascinating to the young man who could watch the process of construction in brick, stone, timber, and plaster, under the direction of Joshua Kirby (1716–74) as Clerk of the Works. Chambers was familiar with such methods of instruction from Blondel, who had taken his students on frequent tours of buildings as they were rising in Paris. Buildings such as the now demolished Mosque at Kew (fig. 14) were indebted to plates in the first comparative history of world architecture by Johann Bernhard Fischer von Erlach, the richly illustrated *Entwurff einer historischen Architektur* (Vienna 1721), of which a translation under the title, *A Plan of Civil and Historical Architecture*, was published in 1730 and 1737. Fischer von Erlach had visited London in 1704 when he had almost certainly met Christopher Wren and Nicholas Hawksmoor.[30]

It was to Bute that Chambers chose to dedicate the first two editions of his *Treatise on Civil Architecture* in 1759 and 1768. The relation between Chambers's *Treatise* and his role as architectural tutor to the Prince is strikingly demonstrated in a draft letter which Chambers wrote to him, as George III, seeking his permission to dedicate the third edition of 1791 to him. He described it as 'a work originally written for your Majesties information', thanking him for his 'encouragement [which] first prompted me to render publick what at first was certainly not designed for publication'.[31]

28   Now in the Metropolitan Museum, New York.

29   Umbach, *Enlightenment*, p. 64.

30   Hart, *Nicholas Hawksmoor*, p. 33.

31   J. Harris, *Chambers*, p. 129.

THE ROLE OF JOSHUA KIRBY

One of Bute's first acts, following his appointment to the Prince of Wales's Household in 1756, was to appoint the landscape artist from Ipswich, Joshua Kirby, to the unusual post of 'Designer in Perspective to his Royal Highness'. Kirby and his son, William, were later appointed Joint Clerks of the Works at Kew and Richmond, working directly under Chambers. A master of architectural perspective, Joshua Kirby had published *Dr Brook Taylor's Method of Perspective Made Easy* (1754).[32] Bute, possibly guided by Chambers, had seen that Kirby's simplification of Taylor's somewhat abstruse presentation of the principles of vanishing points made Kirby an appropriate tutor for the Prince. The instruction went so well that Kirby published *The Perspective of Architecture. A Work Entirely New; Deduced from the Principles of Dr Brook Taylor* (1761), which, he explained, had been 'begun by Command of His Present Majesty when Prince of Wales'. The extravagant production of what was simply a textbook bore testimony to the financial support of George III to whom it was dedicated as a work 'carried on under your eye'.

Indeed, some of the drawings of the orders seem to have been prepared with the use of a new instrument which was described by Kirby in his publication of 1761. The explanatory text was also separately issued (in the same year) as *The Description and Use of a New Instrument Called, an Architectonic Sector. By Which Any Part of Architecture may be Drawn With Facility and Exactness*. Kirby claimed that, with this instrument, 'persons wholly unacquainted with architecture may be enabled to delineate any part of it with elegance and exactness.' Twenty-three of the 25 plates show how the orders can be drawn with the help of the sector. It was thus intended to play a role in the growth of the ability to design, which was to contribute so much to the appearance of the towns and buildings of Georgian England. The first two plates in the book illustrate an architectonic sector made by George Adams the elder (d. 1773), Mathematical Instrument Maker to the King. Lord Bute was involved in the creation of this instrument about the use of which George III made many pages of notes.[33]

The Perspective of Architecture is memorable for its striking frontispiece (fig. 23), engraved in July 1760 after a drawing by Hogarth.[34] A rocky landscape includes a circular temple with a dome on a tall attic, obviously inspired by Chambers's Temple of Victory at Kew of 1759 (fig. 36). In the centre a seated cherub holds a copy of Palladio's *I Quattro Libri*, while a ray of light shoots diagonally across the scene to illuminate a perspectival diagram. Above this is a

32 See E. Harris and N. Savage, *Architectural Books*, pp. 254–8.

33 RA GEO Add. 32/1742–1760.

34 In the British Museum (Oppé, *Drawings of Hogarth*, no. 94, pl. 85).
    For the engraving, see Paulson, *Hogarth's Graphic Work*, p. 193 and pl. 235.

FRONTISPIECE.

column with a capital in a novel order which is a tribute to the Prince of Wales, for it incorporates his coronet, plumes of feathers, and the Garter star. Chambers would have known of the particularly French endeavour to create a new order worthy of the French nation, but this attempt is a remarkable foretaste of the Britannic order devised for George III in 1781. This was the work of one of his favourite architects, Henry Emlyn, who published it in *A Proposition for a New Order in Architecture, With Rules For Drawing the Several Parts* (1781, with later editions in 1784 and 1787; fig. 24). Dedicated to the Royal Academicians, it was described as featuring 'ornaments suited to the glory of the country, and its boasted order of Knighthood, to which it is designed to allude'.[35] Its coupled columns were a reference to 'the twin trees in Windsor Park', while the triglyphs took the form of the ostrich feathers of the

35   *Gentleman's Magazine*, vol. LII, 1782, p. 77.

FIG. 23 William Woollett
after William Hogarth,
*Frontispiece to Kirby's
Perspective of Architecture,*
1761. Engraving.
RCIN 1150778

FIG. 24 Henry Emlyn,
The Britannic Order
(H. Emlyn, *A Proposition
for a New Order in
Architecture,* pl. XXV,
third edn, 1797).
Engraving. RCIN 1150770

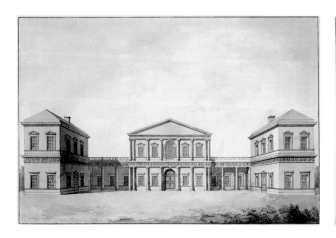

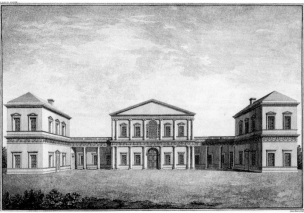

Prince of Wales's emblem. It has not previously been noted that Hogarth's attempt to create the Britannic order was made as early as 1760, the year before Emlyn began work as a carpenter at Windsor Castle.[36]

Plate LXIV in Kirby's *The Perspective of Architecture* is engraved from a drawing in the Prince's hand (figs. 25, 26). This is for a house, or public building, in the form of a U-shaped composition with a central, five-bay, pedimented range which has engaged Doric columns on the ground floor, and Ionic on the first. It is flanked by one-storeyed wings fronted with a Doric colonnade which lead on each side to three-bay wings which project forwards. The front of these is only two bays wide, an unclassical disposition which suggests that Chambers was not involved in the design. The original drawing, which survives in the Royal Library, is inscribed and dated 'G.P.W. 1760', and – evidently by Kirby – 'This Drawing was Designed & Executed for my Book on Perspective by His Majesty King George III'.[37] Plate LXXIII in Kirby's book is an engraving of a far more sophisticated design for a curving peristyle terminating in a shallow-domed pavilion. This was doubtless provided by Chambers for it is in the style which he had learnt from French students at the Académie Royale d'Architecture in Rome and was illustrated by his friend, Marie-Joseph Peyre, in *Oeuvres d'Architecture* (Paris 1765). It is also close to Chambers's own drawing of the Duc de Chartres's Casino in Paris, designed by Alexandre-Théodore Brongniart in 1773.[38]

Joshua Kirby supplied the drawings for three of the engraved plates in Chambers's *Plans . . . of the Gardens and Buildings at Kew*. Kirby's own approach was an empirical one in which he

FIG. 25 George III, *Building with wings, in perspective*, 1760. Pencil, pen and ink, and grey wash. RL K 93

FIG. 26 James Basire after George III, *Building with wings, in perspective*, 1761 (Joshua Kirby, *The Perspective of Architecture*, 1761, pl. LXIV). Engraving. RCIN 1150779

36 Even before this, Batty Langley had illustrated an English order with
    oak leaves, palms, star, and garter, in his *Ancient Masonry* (1733–6),
    p. 321. See E. Harris and N. Savage, *Architectural Books*, p. 268 and p. 270 n. 45.

37 J. Roberts, *Royal Artists*, pp. 58–61, and Oppé, *English Drawings*, no. 4.

38 J. Harris, 'Sir William Chambers and his Parisian Album', fig. 21.

argued that 'we form our common Judgement and Estimation of the Appearance of Objects from Custom and experience and not from mathematical Reason.' Though this subjective and associational approach is dependent on Locke and Addison, its architectural basis was in the French architect and theorist Claude Perrault (1613–88), who demolished the Renaissance belief that the rules of proportion in classical architecture were rooted in divine harmony. Perrault, by contrast, argued that these rules depended on nothing more than custom and 'fantaisie'.[39] The significance of this from the point of view of the education of the Prince of Wales was that it was William Chambers who was principally responsible for introducing Perrault's architectural philosophy to England in his *Treatise on Civil Architecture* of 1759. In 1768 Kirby became President of the Society of Artists of Great Britain, a body which he hoped would become the Royal Academy, but, as we shall see in Chapter 4, he was outwitted by Chambers.

The Prince's Drawings

The hundreds of drawings connected with the Prince's architectural instruction which are preserved in the Royal Library at Windsor must surely constitute the most complete surviving record of the organised architectural education of any future leader.[40] Though, with hardly any exceptions, they are not signed or dated, they are proof of the exceptional assiduity of the royal pupil.

EARLY LANDSCAPE DRAWINGS

Fifty-six drawings of landscapes, mostly incorporating buildings, survive in the Prince's hand.[41] Such topics formed part of a general education in painting and drawing, but were something of an innovation in architectural education, for they were related to the new emphasis on nature in early eighteenth-century England. Subsequently flowering into the Picturesque movement, this had been especially associated with William Kent, who saw architecture as linked to landscape both physically and in artistic representation. A series of eleven drawings in pencil, some with grey wash, signed *PW*,[42] include several which seem to have been made on the spot, including the building of a bridge, a house by a road, and the Hermitage in the gardens at Richmond (fig. 13), containing busts of natural philosophers and scientists. As we noted in Chapter 1, the Hermitage had been built in 1730 for his grand-mother, Queen Caroline, from designs by William Kent.[43] The composition of the Prince's

---

39 Perrault, *Les dix livres d'architecture*, Preface.
40 There is no published list or catalogue of these, for architectural drawings were excluded in Oppé, *English Drawings*. They are, however, included in summary form in the inventory of George III's collection of drawings (Inventory A, pp. 164/273 and 166/277).

41 For a checklist of the Prince's landscape drawings – excluding architectural drawings, with the exception of no. 4 above (see footnote 37) – see Oppé, *English Drawings*, pp. 19–20.
42 Oppé, *English Drawings*, no. 2.
43 See Sloan, 'A Noble Art', pl. 67.

OPPOSITE

FIG. 27 George III, *Syon House from Richmond Gardens*, c.1760. Black and white chalk on blue paper. RL K 237

FIG. 28 George III, *A ruined Corinthian temple in a landscape*, c.1760. Pencil, pen and ink, black and white chalk on blue paper. RL K 206

FIG. 29 J.J. Müller, *The Temple of Baal Shamin, Palmyra*, 1753 (R. Wood, *The Ruins of Palmyra*, 1753, pl. XXXI). Engraving. RCIN 1071056

THIS PAGE

FIG. 30 George III, *Landscape with the Tower of the Winds*, c.1760. Black and white chalk. RL K 214

FIG. 31 Le Bas after Julien-David Leroy, *Vue de la Tour des Vents à Athene*, 1758 (J.-D. Leroy, *Les Ruines des plus beaux monuments de la Grèce*, part II, pl. XIV, 1758). Engraving. RCIN 1071091

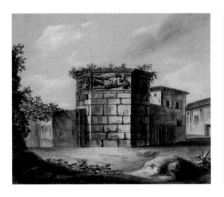 

drawing of it could be criticised for the large area of largely blank grass in the foreground. The Hermitage was to be swept away in about 1775 as part of the post-Kentian landscaping which, as we shall see in Chapter 6, the King carried out at Richmond Gardens.

A volume containing 45 drawings,[44] evidently later than the previous group, includes a highly finished view in black and white chalk on blue paper of Syon House, taken across the Thames from Richmond Gardens, with the tower of Isleworth parish church on the left (fig. 27).[45] A seat of the 1st Duke of Northumberland, a key figure in the Royal Household, Syon was, like the Hermitage, familiar to the Prince from boyhood. The composition of his drawing is close to that of a painting by Richard Wilson (1714–82) from the same spot.[46] 'Capability' Brown's landscaping of the setting of Syon around 1760 may have influenced George III, as we shall see later, while Robert Adam remodelled the interiors of the house in 1762–9.

These sketches by the King, though also probably the result of Kirby's teaching, have a personal flavour. Many of them show classical buildings and ruins in conjunction with English vernacular buildings and rural landscapes, recalling the technique of Kirby's friend Gainsborough, and also Robert Adam's views of ruins in landscapes.[47] They include *capricci* in which real buildings are transferred to imaginary settings, notably the sumptuous Corinthian temple of Baal Shamin of c.130 AD at Palmyra, which the Prince shows in a watery English landscape with a boat. His drawing of the temple (fig. 28) is based on plate XXXI in Robert Wood's book, *The Ruins of Palmyra* (1753; fig. 29). Here the Prince entered into the kind of process which was being adopted by Chambers at Kew, where he based his Temple of the Sun on Wood's plates of the Temple of Bacchus at Baalbek in his *Ruins of Balbec* (1757).

44 Oppé, *English Drawings*, no. 1, labelled *Landscapes drawn by H.M.*
45 Sloan, 'A Noble Art', pl. 68, and J. Roberts, *Royal Artists*, p. 64.
46 Neue Pinakothek, Munich.

47 Oppé, *English Drawings*, notes that no. 42 in cat. no. 1 is indebted to Richard Wilson's painting, *The Baths of Caracalla*.

FIG. 32 George III, *Capriccio with Roman ruins and Tudor buildings*, c.1760. Black and white chalk on blue paper. RL K 224

FIG. 33 Sir William Chambers and George III, *Elevation of a house with notes and observations*, c.1758. Pen and ink. RL K 1517

Another of these chalk drawings by the Prince shows the Tower of the Winds in Athens (fig. 30), a building of the mid-first century BC, half-buried and surrounded by vegetation. This unusual octagonal monument, echoed in pioneering buildings of the 1760s and '70s by 'Athenian' Stuart and James Wyatt, was to be influential on late eighteenth- and early nineteenth-century British architecture. The Prince's drawing is based on the view of the building included in Julien-David Leroy's *Les Ruines des plus beaux monuments de la Grèce* (fig. 31). Leroy, Professor at the Académie Royale d'Architecture in Paris from 1762, was a friend of Chambers who, however, always ridiculed Greek architecture, complaining that the Tower of the Winds 'resembles exactly one of the Dove houses usually erected on Gentlemen's Estates in the Country of England, excepting that . . . there is no Turret for the Pigeons to creep in & fly out at.'[48] Nonetheless, Chambers was concerned that the Prince should be aware of the latest archaeological discoveries described in books such as those by Wood and Leroy.

48   British Architectural Library MSS, CHA.1/1–1/13.

These 56 drawings by the young King include some inspired by artists such as Poussin and Claude, recalling English Picturesque gardens such as Stourhead. Others show English towns or scenery, including views of boats on the river Thames. Eleven of the drawings incorporate buildings, some of them ancient Roman and in English settings such as a Tudor courtyard, suggesting the Prince's sympathy for the traditional English scene (fig. 32).[49]

This trait is further indicated in a separate set of 38 slight drawings in the Prince's hand,[50] possibly from the early 1750s, which are related to Sébastien le Clerc's popular textbook, *Pratique de la géometrie* (Paris 1669). As many as six editions of an English translation of this book as *Practical Geometry* were published between 1671 and 1783. In Le Clerc's plates the upper half contains simple geometrical diagrams enlivened with unrelated scenes of classical buildings below. However, though Prince George copied the diagrams, he replaced the lower scenes with views of English landscapes and church towers.[51] Le Clerc's *Pratique* and his more widely read *Traité d'Architecture* (Paris 1714), the latter published in an English translation in 1714 and 1724, were known to Kirby and to Chambers. Chambers cited Le Clerc's *Traité* in his own *Treatise*, for his reading of Perrault had made him sympathetic to Le Clerc's aesthetic relativism.

EARLY ARCHITECTURAL DRAWINGS

It is probably right to suggest that a number of the architectural drawings were both designed and drawn by the Prince, while some were drawn by other hands to develop designs either

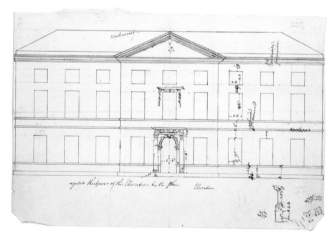

invented or approved by him as Prince of Wales or as King. The Prince's own laborious productions are punctuated with numerous compass points and sometimes feature amateurish touches such as blotched or patchy wash, and pencil lines of horizontal mouldings projecting beyond the edges of the façade. The precise role of Chambers in the process of production is unclear, for the assistance provided by him, Kirby, and William Robinson, Clerk of the Works at St James's from 1754 to 1766, seems to have been interlocking and is therefore difficult to disentangle. An unrelated drawing (fig. 33) for a façade bearing the inscription 'regulate the Spaces of this Elevation by the plan', and 'His

49 Reproduced for the first time by The Prince of Wales in *Vision of Britain*, p. 109.

50 Oppé, *English Drawings*, no. 3.

51 J. Roberts, *Royal Artists*, pp. 8–9 and 58.

majestys plan' on the verso,[52] seems to be an exercise in which the Prince was instructed to correct in ink the deliberately incorrect placing in pencil of the windows in the three central bays. The drawing shows that he did indeed perform this simple task by adjusting the position of the windows in conformity with the plan so as to produce symmetry.

It is likely that Chambers began by setting the Prince to study the details of the orders (fig. 34), then to produce variants of buildings in works such as *Vitruvius Britannicus*, and finally to echo his own garden buildings then rising at Kew and his designs for villas. Many of the drawings which illustrate the details of the orders, Tuscan, Doric, Ionic, Corinthian, and Composite, probably made in the late 1750s, are close to, though not copies of, those in Chambers's *Treatise on Civil Architecture* (1759), while others draw on the standard earlier sources such as Palladio's *I Quattro Libri dell'Architettura*, first published in 1570, and Roland Fréart de Chambray's *Parallel of the Antient Architecture with the Modern*, translated in 1664 by John Evelyn from the original French of 1650.

Characteristic of many is the drawing of the Doric order (RL K 448) showing the plinth, base moulding, capital, and entablature with triglyph in the frieze. This is a variant of the model of the Doric order both in plate VII of Kirby's *The Perspective of Architecture* and in Chambers's *Treatise*, inspired by the Theatre of Marcellus in Rome. The Prince adopted the shading à la Chambers but omitted the ornamental rosettes and husks in the neck of his capital. One of his drawings of the Composite order is also based on Kirby's example.[53]

One unusual drawing (RL K 1287) is for a high and narrow tower or belvedere of no fewer than five storeys piled on top of one another, surmounted by an open, circular rotunda of Corinthian columns. An exuberant youthful essay, this is a kind of exaggerated tower of the orders in which a heavy Doric order on the first floor rests somewhat incongruously on a lighter ground storey with a large Venetian archway.[54] The drawing bears all the numerous marks of the compass and divider points used in its construction, while the pencil lines of the entablature project beyond the elevation on either side. A related drawing shows a tower in which the four upper storeys rest on a more appropriately solid rusticated base.[55] These drawings can be linked to a design, possibly for a church, also with a domed Corinthian rotunda, which unexpectedly anticipates aspects of Chambers's designs of 1770 for St Marylebone church.[56] The Prince's drawings of temples serving as garden buildings often reflect designs published by Chambers in his *Treatise* and his *Plans . . . of the Gardens and*

FIG. 34 George III, *Details of the Composite order*, c.1759. Pencil, pen and ink, and wash. RL K 447

FIG. 35 George III, *Design for a temple based on Chambers's Temple of Victory, Kew*, c.1759. Pen and ink and wash. RL K 479

FIG. 36 E. Rooker after Sir William Chambers, *Temple of Victory, Kew*, 1763 (from W. Chambers, *Kew*). Engraving. RCIN 1150769

52　This may be a unique instance of an informative inscription on one of the King's drawings. The purpose of the majority of the drawings is far from clear.

53　As noted in J. Roberts, 'Chambers', p. 43 and pl. 60.

54　Reproduced for the first time by The Prince of Wales in *Vision of Britain*, p. 108.

55　Reproduced in J. Roberts, 'Chambers', pl. 62.

56　*ibid.*, pl. 63.

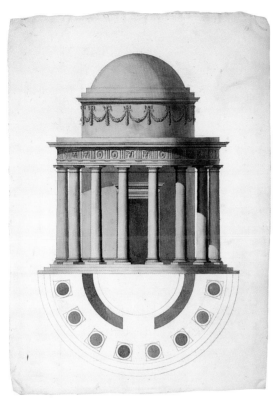

The Temple of Victory —

Buildings at Kew (1763). One drawing attributed to the Prince's hand (fig. 35) is for a circular peripteral temple closely based on Chambers's Temple of Victory at Kew (fig. 36), though with the order changed from Ionic to Doric. Based on a design in Perrault's edition of Vitruvius,[57] the Temple of Victory (now demolished) was built by Chambers in 1759 to commemorate the allied victory over the French at the Battle of Minden that August. Where the Prince's drawings differ from the published designs they may have been based on drawings given him by Chambers himself. One of the more attractive of these (RL K 1444) is the variant of the Theatre of Augusta at Kew, a long, one-storeyed structure with a Corinthian colonnade on a semicircular plan below a balustrade and central pediment. Built in 1760 for the Princess's theatricals, it was described by Chambers as 'an excellent piece of scenery for a theatre' in his book on Kew of 1763.

57   Perrault, *Les dix livres d'architecture*, pl. xxxvi.

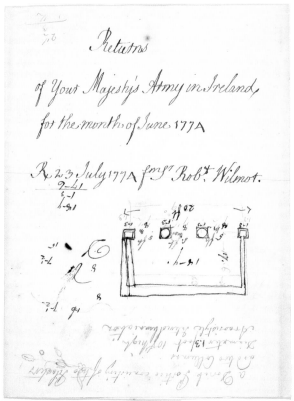

Another finely finished drawing is of a pedimented Corinthian temple with a rusticated windowless wall and an entablature in which the frieze is, unusually, a continuous Greek key scroll (fig. 37).[58] The frieze is interrupted by a central tablet filled with elegant swags, paterae, and urns. This Chambersian design appears to be the basis for an engraving which, dedicated to Bute's friend and the King's future Surveyor General, Thomas Worsley, was the ninth in a set of plates at the end of Chambers's *Treatise on Civil Architecture,* where it was entitled 'Design for a Corinthian Temple for Erection at Kew'. An early impression of this plate, formerly in the collection of Thomas Worsley, bears an inscription, possibly in his hand, stating that the design was by the Prince of Wales.[59]

58   J. Roberts, 'Chambers', pl. 64.
59   *ibid.,* p. 45.

FIG. 37 George III, *Design for a Corinthian temple for Kew*, c.1759. Pencil, pen and ink, and wash. RL K 1419

FIG. 38 George III, *Page of notes with design for a garden loggia*, 1774. Pen and ink with pencil. RL K 480

LATER ARCHITECTURAL DRAWINGS

A small sketch plan by the King in the Royal Library for what seems to be a garden loggia (fig. 38) reuses a wrapper of official papers received by the King in July 1774; it is inscribed 'Returns of Your Majesty's Army in Ireland for the month of June 1774'. The building may have been intended for the gardens of the palace at Richmond or for the adjacent gardens at Kew. The plan for a substantial construction, 20 feet long, is of special interest as it is a serious design with numerous measurements. Technically, the portico is distyle in antis, that is, it consists of two columns flanked by antae. It bears the inscription: 'a Dorick Portico consisting of two Pillasters and two Collumns. Diameter 1.3 foot 10ft. high. Aerosistyle Intercollumniation'.[60] It thus not only shows that the King had been taught the proportional system of Vitruvius, but that he had absorbed it. Intercolumniation, the distance between columns, is measured in multiples of the diameter of the column at its foot. Vitruvius cites five types from pycnostyle to his favourite, eustyle, where the intercolumniation is $2^1/_4$ times the diameter.[61] The King notes correctly that aerostyle intercolumniation is at least three times the diameter of the column, though he makes the forgivable error of writing 'aerosistyle' instead of 'aerostyle'.[62]

Aerostyle provided a wider gap between columns than Vitruvius liked, for it meant that the beams spanning them had to be of timber, not of stone or marble. However, this made its use appropriate for the construction of rustic temples in English landscaped gardens of the eighteenth century. The date of the wrapper is also significant for showing that the King's interest in architectural design survived long after his initial instruction. Indeed, the presence in the Royal Library of many designs by Chambers, especially for villas, including Hedsor Lodge, Buckinghamshire, which dates from as late as 1778, shows the continuing informal relation between the architect and his sovereign. It is also a reminder that the Office of Works was still effectively the King's Works.

Further late drawings made by the King seem to be for remodelling and extending the White House at Kew which had been built for Frederick, Prince of Wales, by William Kent in 1731–5. Chambers had made extensive alterations to the house in 1772–3 but the King spent much time in drawing plans, somewhat manically, for rebuilding the house during his enforced stay at Kew in 1788–9 while recovering from his first serious illness.[63] One of these plans (fig. 39) shows no fewer than four main staircases completely filling two of the four ranges surrounding the central space. Though these could be alternative proposals, they

60 J. Roberts, *Royal Artists*, p. 62.

61 Vitruvius, *De architectura*, book III, ch. iii, on the 'Elevations of Temples'.

62 Also, what are identified as 'Pillasters' at the angles of the façade are more properly described as antae or piers.

63 The plans are attached to a manuscript Service Sheet of 19 July 1785 discovered by Mr Peter Barber, Map Librarian at the British Library, in a volume of plans of palaces at Hanover of 1763 from George III's Topographical Collection (Maps 7 Tab. 17).

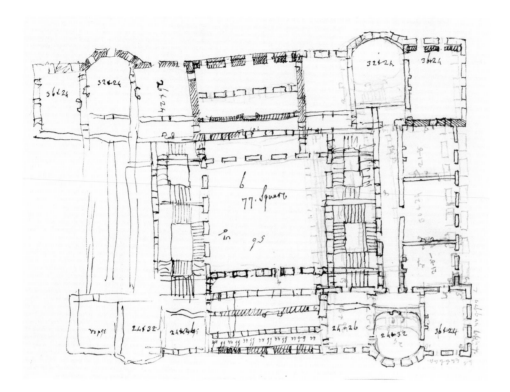

FIG. 39 George III, *Ground plan of courtyard building, c.*1788/9. Pen and ink. London, British Library (K.Top.C.57-a)

could equally well be the product of a disturbed mind which his family later associated with his interest in building schemes.

To sum up, George III's drawings and designs are competent rather than inventive, but his architectural training and the vast number of architectural drawings in his hand make him exceptional, not only among monarchs but among the gentleman patrons of eighteenth-century England. To practise the art of architectural design but not to supervise building construction was recommended by the 4th Earl of Chesterfield (1694–1773), Lord of the Bedchamber to George II, and an architectural patron of distinction at Chesterfield House, Mayfair, and at the Ranger's House, Blackheath. In one of the shrewd and sophisticated letters which Lord Chesterfield wrote to his illegitimate son, Philip Stanhope, he pointed out to him the value of architectural education to anyone entering polite society. In October

1749, when Philip, aged 17, was in Venice on his Grand Tour with his tutor, Walter Harte, Lord Chesterfield remarked, 'Mr Harte tells me, that he intends to give you, by means of Signor Vicentini, a general notion of Civil and Military Architecture; with which I am very well pleased. They are frequent subjects of conversation.' The boy's architectural instructor was the painter, etcher, and architect Antonio Visentini (1688–1782),[64] who worked extensively for Consul Joseph Smith (whose library and collection George III bought in 1762). At that time Visentini was giving instruction in architectural draughtsmanship in Venice to George III's future architect, James Wyatt; later in the decade he was also employed by Lord Bute. Lord Chesterfield went on to recommend his son to study Palladio's *Quattro Libri* in order to gain knowledge of the details of the orders and their use, adding that 'You may soon be acquainted with the considerable parts of Civil Architecture; and for the minute and mechanical parts of it, leave them to masons, bricklayers and Lord Burlington; who has, to a certain degree, lessened himself, by knowing them too well.'[65] This *hauteur* towards Burlington's practice may not have been an untypical reaction, but it would scarcely have troubled George III, the 'Farmer King' who was content to write letters about crop rotation for publication in the *Annals of Agriculture*.

---

64 See Vivian, 'Joseph Smith, Antonio Visentini, el il movimento neoclassico', pp. 340–58.

65 Chesterfield, *Letters*, vol. II, pp. 276–7.

A TASTE OF FRANCE:
WORKS AT THE START OF THE REIGN

The mood of cultural and political optimism in the opening years of the new King's reign was given glittering expression by the new Gold State Coach and by the sumptuous coronation portraits of the King and Queen by Allan Ramsay, completed in 1762.[1] Aware of contemporary French painting, Ramsay seems to have given his grandiose portrait of George III (frontispiece) something of the character of the state portrait of Louis XV by Louis-Michel van Loo (1707–71). He may also have deliberately echoed the portrait of 1742 by Louis-Michel's father, Jean-Baptiste van Loo (1684–1745), of the King's father, Frederick, Prince of Wales, in robes of state.[2]

The Gold State Coach

Soon after the accession of George III on 25 October 1760, the decision was made to commission a new state coach (figs. 40, 41) to replace the old-fashioned Baroque one made for Queen Anne. The King and Queen Charlotte travelled from St James's Palace to their coronation on 22 September 1761 in sedan chairs,[3] a mode of transport with a domestic flavour which was very different from that recommended by Dr Johnson and John Gwynn in the pamphlet of 1761, *Thoughts on the Coronation of his Present Majesty King George the Third*. Gwynn, as mentioned in the Introduction, was the author of *London and Westminster Improved* (1766), and had been considered for the post of architectural tutor to the King when he was still Prince of Wales; his recommendation was that the coronation should take a new and longer route, with a greater display of ceremonial magnificence and before a larger public than before. Because of delays to the process of design and manufacture, the King was only seen in public for the first time in the coach at the State Opening of Parliament on 25 November 1762. Innovations in carriage design aroused widespread public interest, notably on the birthdays of the King and Queen when spectacular carriage processions took place to St James's Palace with the nobility and gentry travelling in strict order of precedence.[4]

Described correctly at the time as 'the most superb and expensive of any ever built in this kingdom',[5] and widely discussed in contemporary newspapers, the King's new coach of 1762 was designed by his architectural mentor, William Chambers, built by Samuel Butler, and featured carvings and paintings by Chambers's friends, Joseph Wilton and Giovanni Battista Cipriani (1727–85) respectively. Chambers recommended his pupils in architecture, and probably his royal pupil, to 'Study painting and sculpture thoroughly [as] you cannot be a

1   Millar, *Later Georgian Pictures*, nos. 996 and 997.
2   *ibid.*, no. 536, and see Allen, 'Royal Portraits'.
3   *Gentleman's Magazine*, vol. XXXI, 1761, p. 428.

4   Wackernagel, 'Carlton House Mews'.
5   See Marsden and Hardy, 'O Fair Britannia Hail', p. 3.

FIG. 40 Sir William Chambers and Giovanni Battista Cipriani, *Design for the King's State Coach*, 1760. Pen and ink and watercolour over pencil. RL 17942

FIG. 41 The State Coach in the State Coach House at the Royal Mews, Buckingham Palace

master in Your own art without great judgement in these, which are so intimately connected with it.'[6] A study of George III and architecture must thus include the Gold State Coach which triumphantly unites those three arts.

It was commissioned by Francis Hastings, 10th Earl of Huntingdon (1729–89), Master of the Horse to the new King, whom he had served in the same capacity as Prince of Wales from 1756. He undertook extensive Grand Tours in Italy in 1754–6 and again in 1771–4, meeting Joseph Wilton and Sir Horace Mann in Florence, Robert Adam in Rome, and Sir James Gray in Naples. He studied the antique sculpture in the Medici collection with Wilton, formed a medal collection, and commissioned modern paintings. Described by the 4th Earl of Chesterfield as 'a bright exemplar of the union of a scholar with a man of the world',[7] the bachelor Lord Huntingdon was one of the most civilised members of the court of George III, whom he also served as Groom of the Stole from 1761 to 1770.[8]

Since the King had appointed Chambers and Adam as Joint Architects to the Office of Works in 1761, Adam was also asked for designs for the new state coach in that year but, if made, they do not survive. As Marsden and Hardy have observed in their definitive study of the coach as designed by Chambers, it served as 'a rolling manifesto' or 'triumphal peace

6   William Chambers to Edward Stevens, 5 August 1774 (Sir John Soane's Museum, Private Correspondence i.c. 7.1).

7   Ingamells, *Dictionary*, p. 537.

8   Chambers, Wilton, and Cipriani, who had met in Florence and Rome in the 1750s when Huntington was also in Italy, were all commissioned on their return by Augusta, Dowager Princess of Wales, to create her Gallery of Antiques at Kew in 1757.

chariot' for 'the first Hanoverian monarch to have been born in England, and one who declared that he "gloried in the name of Briton".'[9] Its iconography was devised by Thomas Hollis (1720–74), the antiquarian, collector, patron of Chambers, and friend of 'Athenian' Stuart and of Robert Adam. A key figure in the Society for the Promotion of Arts, Manufactures, and Commerce, he was described as a 'strenuous Whig' and even as a 'Republican'.[10] Nonetheless, he advised Cipriani on the subject-matter of the decorative painting of the royal coach and was probably the author of the account of it published in 1762.[11] This iconography should be seen against the background of the defence of England during the Seven Years War. The War concluded with the peace treaty with France arranged at the end of 1762 and proclaimed in March 1763, establishing England as the world's leading colonial power. First used at the time when the Treaty of Paris was being drawn up, the state coach was appropriately emblematic of the themes of victory and peace.

The victories during the War, and also in the 1780s, were particularly the achievement of the navy, the popularity of which greatly increased as a result. George III and his advisers were thus quick to associate him with national pride in the navy. He was, for example, represented in the iconography of the coach as commander of the empire of the sea, suggesting his imperial role among European monarchs. His coach is guarded by four figures of tritons, two at each end, the sea-gods who are the sons of Neptune and traditionally represented as men with fishes' tails. The tritons at the front of the coach blow conches to announce the arrival of the monarch of the sea, while those at the back carry tridents. They can here be related to Chambers's chapter on 'Persians and Caryatides' in his *Treatise on Civil Architecture* where he includes 'galleries of armour' among the situations in which 'Male figures may be introduced with propriety'.[12]

Twenty-four feet long, the coach is like a travelling temple, its roof in the form of a shallow dome surmounted by a group of three winged genii symbolising the kingdoms of England, Ireland, and Scotland. Standing on the shield of Britannia, these boys bear the regalia used at George III's coronation, the Sceptre, the Sword of State, and St Edward's Crown, the covered imperial crown introducing the imperial theme which features in the symbolic decoration of the coach and, as we shall see, of Somerset House. As well as personifying Neptune, the King was also represented as Apollo, leader of the Muses and inspirer of the arts. Thus, in his depiction of Air as one of the four elements, Cipriani showed Mars and Minerva defending and

9   Marsden and Hardy, 'O Fair Britannia Hail', quoting House of Lords, *Journal*, vol. xxx, 1760–1, 18 November 1760, p. 9.

10 I am indebted to Mr Jonathan Marsden for drawing my attention to the significance of this interesting figure, on whom see W.H. Bond,

Thomas Hollis of Lincoln's Inn, and Ingamells, *Dictionary*, pp. 512–13.

11 *London Chronicle*, 25–27 November 1762.

12 Chambers, *Treatise* (1759), London 1791, p. 73.

supporting the imperial crown, flanked by symbols of Painting, Sculpture, and Architecture as well as of Navigation and Study.

All the sides of the coach originally contained large panels of glass, a transparency which caused some surprise but was intended to enable the King, crown, and regalia to be seen as clearly as possible. The exposure of the King was as unprecedented as the televising of the Coronation of Queen Elizabeth II in 1953, but was in conformity with the calls for greater public display by John Gwynn and Dr Johnson in *Thoughts on the Coronation of His Present Majesty George the Third* (1761).[13] In Chapter 4 we shall see Somerset House as another symbolic celebration of the imperial power of Britain under the benevolent rule of George III; again, it was a work designed by William Chambers and adorned by Joseph Wilton and Giovanni Battista Cipriani.

Buckingham House

Following his marriage to Princess Charlotte of Mecklenburg-Strelitz in September 1761, there was news as early as the following month that the King was to build a new palace at Richmond from designs by William Chambers, who exhibited a design for it in 1762. However, at the start of 1762 the King bought the Crown lease of Buckingham House, though this, as he explained to Lord Bute, was 'not meant for a Palace, but a retreat'.[14] St James's Palace remained the official seat of the court and its ceremonies, while Buckingham House, renamed the Queen's House, was a private house for the King and Queen and their growing family. George III has sometimes been claimed as the first British monarch to attempt to make so clear a division between his public and private roles, but in fact the tradition of the privy palace had a long royal history.

Buckingham House was built in 1702–5 by William Winde, probably from designs by William Talman, and it is likely that Adam and Chambers, appointed to their joint offices in 1761, were expected to adapt it for the use of the King and Queen. It is intriguing to wonder whether George III and his architects knew the designs by Stephen Riou of the 1750s for a vast palace for George II on the site of Buckingham House (fig. 12).[15] Adam submitted designs to Thomas Worsley for altering Buckingham House and also elaborate proposals (Sir John Soane's Museum, Adam Drawings, vol. 54, nos. 135, 136) for adding three new ranges round a colonnaded courtyard to be entered through a series of triumphal arches, of which the

13   Johnson, *Works*, vol. x, *Political Writings*, pp. 292–300.

14   Quoted in Hedley, *Queen Charlotte*, p. 71. Nonetheless, the full and flattering account of it in *Gentleman's Magazine*, vol. XXXII, 1762, pp. 222–3, claims that it was 'purchased by the King for a Palace to the Queen's Majesty'.

15   See above, p. 42.

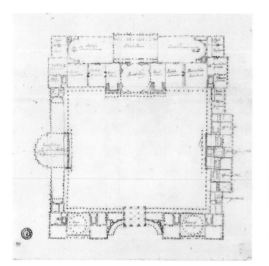

central one was inscribed 'Geor[…] Te[…]o Rex' (figs. 42, 43). As the King found Adam's work too fussy for his tastes, it was probably Chambers who, from September 1762, was responsible for most of the remodelling carried out from 1762 to 1774.[16] The large sum of £72,000 was spent on this work, which included simplifying the façade by removing swags, statues, and angle pilasters (fig. 4), and adding four great libraries which opened into each other at the south end of the house (fig. 44).

All this work has long since disappeared, mostly in the creation of Buckingham Palace by John Nash in the 1820s, but one survival of this early period is the Riding House, though it was refaced and embellished with pedimental sculpture in 1860. This long rectangular building in a severely Palladian style was constructed in 1762–6 on a site south-west of Buckingham House. It was a unique feature in a city palace, because riding houses are associated with country not town houses. An unusual attempt at creating *rus in urbe*, it must have been the outcome of discussions between the King, Chambers, and Worsley, who was the King's Equerry and unofficial riding-master. A passionate enthusiast for horses, he had designed his own riding house at Hovingham, Yorkshire. As we have seen, he was an intimate friend of Lord Bute, who had himself commissioned designs from Robert Adam for an ambitious riding house at Luton Hoo.

FIG. 42 Robert Adam, *Sketch plan for the Queen's House, c.*1762. London, Sir John Soane's Museum (Adam Drawings, vol. 54, no. 135)

FIG. 43 Robert Adam, *Triumphal arch for the Queen's House, c.*1762. London, Sir John Soane's Museum (Adam Drawings, vol. 54, no. 136)

16 Adam's designs are discussed in Rowan, '*Bob the Roman*', nos. 59–60. For the work carried out in Buckingham House in the 1760s and '70s, see Colvin, ed., *King's Works*, vol. v, *1660–1782*, pp. 134–8; Jackson-Stops, 'A noble simplicity'; and J. Roberts, 'Chambers', pp. 46–8.

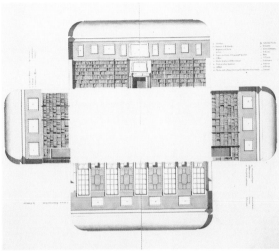

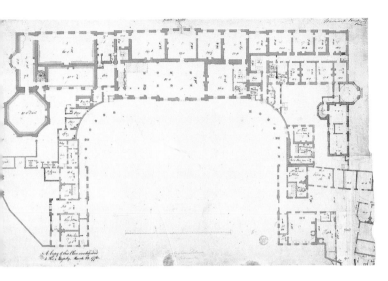

FIG. 44 Office of Sir William Chambers, *Plan of the Hall Floor of Buckingham House,* *c.*1770. Pen and ink. London, Westminster Public Library, Archives and Local Studies Section (Box 39/16)

FIG. 45 Anonymous English artist, *Hanging plan for the West Library, Buckingham House,* *c.*1774. Pencil, pen and ink, and wash. RL 26321

THE LIBRARIES

Immediately on his accession to the throne in 1760, George III had created a library in a range of rooms on the garden side of St James's Palace, ordering ten bookcases from William Vile.[17] These were to house the books which he was buying to replace those which had been given by George II in 1757 to the nation, about 9,000 in number.[18] The urgent need for even more library space at Buckingham House came about with George III's purchase on Bute's recommendation of the collection of Consul Joseph Smith (*c.*1674–1770) in 1762. The purchase was made with the assistance both of Bute's brother, James Stuart Mackenzie, and of Richard Dalton. A merchant banker, publisher, and bookseller, who served British interests in the Venetian Republic as consul from 1744 to 1760 and again in 1766, Smith was one of the most remarkable of all English collectors. His magnificent collection of paintings, drawings, prints, books, manuscripts, gems, coins, and medals was acquired by George III for £20,000 in December 1762.[19]

William Chambers built four libraries at Buckingham House, partly to house Smith's collection of books. The first was the Great or West Library, built in 1762–4, which was 60 feet long and 30 feet wide with a high coved ceiling, paintings hung above the bookcases, and, between the windows, mirrors with octagonal panes (fig. 45). Next came the South

---

17 See H. Roberts, 'Metamorphoses in Wood'.

18 See Brooke, 'The Library of George III'.

19 See Vivian, *Consul Smith Collection*; and *A King's Purchase*.

Library built in 1766–7 at right angles to this, with a canted bay to the garden and an entrance at the south end into the Octagon Library which was built at the same time.[20] Finally came the East Library (fig. 46), built against the back of the Great Library and raised by one storey in 1774 to create a Marine Gallery to display the King's models by John Chamberlaine of ships, sea ports, and fortifications.

The centrally planned, two-storeyed Octagon Library (fig. 47), 42 feet in diameter, was the most remarkable. With its vaulted ceiling lit by seven large Diocletian windows, and its

20 For illustrations of the Octagon Library and East Library, see Pyne's
    Royal Residences, vol. 1, with which figs. 46 and 47 are associated.

walls lined entirely with books uninterrupted by pictures or ornaments of any kind, it demonstrated the King's seriousness as a bibliophile. It had no palatial character and was a serious working library, almost its sole furniture being a giant octagonal desk, probably made by John Bradburn, Vile's successor as cabinet-maker to the Great Wardrobe from 1764.[21]

The King's passion for books and their arrangement was fired by Lord Bute, a serious bibliophile who acquired numerous architectural books and drawings. The King will have discussed the designs for the libraries with both Chambers and Bute, for whom Adam was

---

21   It was remodelled in 1836 and 1863 for the Royal Library at Windsor,
     where it remains (see H. Roberts, 'Metamorphoses in Wood').

designing a house in Berkeley Square from 1761 containing octagonal libraries. Further evidence of the King's close association with the libraries is that they opened out of his bedroom. In making acquisitions he wisely took advice from men like William Chambers, Samuel Johnson, Stephen Demainbray, Richard Dalton, his Librarian from 1760 to 1773 and Keeper of Medals and Drawings from 1773 to 1791, and Frederick Barnard, Librarian from 1774. With their advice on the purchase of drawings as well as books, George III 'conscientiously built up. . . one of the finest libraries ever created by one man', for, to him, 'a fine library was part of the royal prerogative'.[22] By the time of his death in 1820 it numbered over 65,000 volumes. It was divided into three parts which he called his 'Gentleman's' Library, his 'Nobleman's' Library, which he kept at Windsor, and his 'Royal' Library, kept at Buckingham House; these were described in a letter of about 1825 as 'all admirably selected with a view to their respective objects'.[23]

Though the King was well read, especially in contemporary literature and history, and could read and discuss the works of authors like Gibbon, Burke, Johnson, and Boswell, he was in no sense a scholar. This library was not primarily for his personal use. Books in that category he kept at Windsor. Open on a limited basis to scholars and distinguished visitors who had access to it, not from the King's bedroom but from the floor below, the Royal Library at Buckingham House was assembled as the kind of national library which England did not at that time possess. This may help to explain the institutional character which Chambers gave to the architecture of the rooms which housed it. Furthermore, the King saw it as 'a necessary appendage of monarchy. . . an important part of his *gloire* but also an essential reference source in the conduct of his *métier* as ruler'.[24] John Adams, who became first American Minister to Great Britain, visited Buckingham House in October 1783. He wrote:

> The King's library struck me with admiration. I wished for a week's time, but had but a few hours. The books were in perfect order, elegant in their editions, paper, binding, &c., but gaudy and extravagant in nothing. They were chosen with perfect taste and judgment; every book that a king ought to have always at hand . . . In every apartment of the whole house, the same taste, the same judgment. The same elegance, the same simplicity, without the smallest affectation, ostentation, profusion, or meanness. I could not but compare it, in my own mind, with Versailles, and not at all to the advantage of the latter.[25]

22   Miller, *That Noble Cabinet*, p. 125.
23   *ibid.*
24   Barber, 'Royal Geography', p. 9.
25   C.F. Adams, *Works of John Adams*, vol. 1, p. 405.

The favourable comparison to Versailles seems to have been a familiar topos, for an enthusiastic visitor from Germany in 1786, impressed by the fact that the libraries formed the largest apartment in Buckingham House, declared that 'Two are much larger and finer than the Versailles ones.'[26]

THE TOPOGRAPHICAL AND GEOGRAPHICAL COLLECTIONS

The King also housed in his library at Buckingham House his vast collection of topographical prints and drawings which he assembled so as to provide himself with visual records of buildings and towns of note throughout the world.[27] The universalist scope of this project was akin to that of Enlightenment undertakings such as the production of the *Encyclopédie*. Indeed, one of the key promoters of the scheme was that great lexicographer, Dr Johnson, who recommended it in a letter of 1768 to the King's future librarian, Frederick Barnard. Given to the British Museum in the 1820s by George IV as part of George III's library, the King's topographical collections contain roughly 40,000 graphic images. These are notably printed and manuscript atlases; architectural and garden plans; maps and records of military campaigns, fortifications, barracks, and canals; records of towns and of country houses; and thousands of the watercolour, engraved, etched, or aquatinted views that were produced in the later eighteenth and early nineteenth centuries as part of the English Picturesque movement. Some of these are the product of the new Romantic appreciation of the natural scenery of the Lake District and the mountains of Scotland, Ireland, and Wales, while there are also valuable records of medieval antiquities, including stained glass and brasses, as well as the ruins of monasteries and castles.

This important yet little known collection has recently been described as

> An expression of *British* and not simply English patriotism, assembled in a period when the industrial and agricultural revolutions, the fame of its political and economic theorists, its balanced political constitution, its evident and growing prosperity, its (relative) political liberty; and its growing military, commercial and imperial might were making Britain a world leader and a source of emulation and envy abroad.[28]

---

26 Williams, *Sophie in London*, p. 145.

27 These are now in the British Library, Map Library, K.Top.
    See Barber, 'Royal Geography'.

28 Barber, 'Royal Geography', p. 2.

About 40 per cent of the material is devoted to Great Britain, 10 per cent to the Colonies (including the United States of America), and 30 per cent to western Europe. Paris and Rome are represented in five and four volumes respectively, while New York is the only other city which is made the subject of a whole volume. We have already noted the surveys which the King commissioned of the states of Hanover and Osnabrück.

PAINTINGS AND DRAWINGS

As we have seen, the collection of Consul Joseph Smith – acquired by George III in 1762 – included quantities of paintings and drawings in addition to books and manuscripts. In the same year the King purchased, at the suggestion of Robert and James Adam, the fabulous collection of Old Master drawings of Cardinal Alessandro Albani. Both collections arrived in London in the following February, making the Royal Collection one of the choicest in Europe. Though Smith had acquired many Italian paintings from the fifteenth century until his own day, the collecting of books, including illuminated manuscripts and incunabula, was his first love. This was also true of George III, whose collection was supposed by some to be opened to selected members of the public, for an announcement was made, probably not at his command, that 'as soon as the grand Collection of Drawings, etc. . . . arrive in Town, they will be deposited in the Queen's Palace, which with those already there, will make the finest Collection in Europe; and that Tickets will be given to the Nobility and Gentry to admit them to see it.'[29]

In addition to acquiring collections already assembled by other hands, the King was active as a patron of contemporary painters and draughtsmen. One of his striking creations was the Warm Room in the King's suite at Buckingham House, where on three walls he hung seven paintings which he had commissioned from Benjamin West.[30] The King was early interested in neo-classical painting, having admired Nathaniel Dance's *Death of Virginia* when exhibited in 1761.[31] Painted in 1759 by an artist who was the son and brother of distinguished architects, the elder and younger George Dance, this is probably the earliest dated classical history painting by a British artist at work in Rome.[32] This stoical portrayal of death preferred to dishonour takes place in a setting crowded with temples and public buildings, all in the Doric order, which was chosen for its stern, manly character. The King had learned from Chambers, his architectural tutor as Prince of Wales, that, according to Vitruvius, the Doric was the order appropriate for military heroes.

---

29 *Public Advertiser*, 20 December 1762.
30 See Postle, 'A Taste for History'.
31 See Millar, *Later Georgian Pictures*, p. xiii.

32 See D. Goodreau, ed., *Nathaniel Dance 1735–1811*, London, Kenwood House, 1977 (exh. cat.). *The Death of Virginia*, now lost, is known from a sketch in Sir John Soane's Museum.

The King acquired from Dance in 1765 his painting of *Timon of Athens* (fig. 48), the fifth-century BC misanthrope, for his austerely designed apartment at Buckingham House.[33] This moral essay on the theme of the rejection of society and wealth, an early statement of the eighteenth-century *Exemplum Virtutis*, was his first purchase of a neo-classical history painting, though he also commissioned family portraits, particularly from Gainsborough, Ramsay, Zoffany, and West. George III's acquisition of neo-classical paintings blended with his strong religious and moral feelings as well as an enthusiasm for the classical virtues of heroism and

33 Millar, *Later Georgian Pictures*, no. 725 and pl. 18. See *Shakespeare in
Art*, Arts Council of Britain, 1964 (exh. cat.), p. 3.

self-sacrifice, especially as deployed in the interests of patriotism. This was a common topic of the Enlightenment cult of patriotic or civic virtue, which was later subsumed in England into a monarchical nationalism, a process heightened by the Revolutionary and Napoleonic Wars.

The Pennsylvanian-born Benjamin West had arrived in England in 1763 and was introduced to the King by Robert Hay Drummond (1711–76), the Archbishop of York, who had preached the King's coronation sermon in 1761. In 1766 Drummond commissioned from West a painting of *Agrippina landing at Brindisium with the Ashes of Germanicus*[34] as part of his belief in the value of exemplars of ancient virtue for modern imitation. This stern Poussinesque painting had an archaeological background based on Diocletian's palace at Split, as recently published by Robert Adam, in *Ruins of the Palace of the Emperor Diocletian at Spalatro* (1764).[35]

FIG. 49 Benjamin West, *The Departure of Regulus*, 1769. Oil on canvas. RCIN 405416

---

34 Now in Yale University Art Gallery, New Haven.
35 Its title-page was designed by Thomas Hollis, who devised the iconographic programme of George III's Gold State Coach.

Failing in his attempt to raise money by subscription to enable West to turn from portraiture to history painting, Drummond suggested in 1768 that West should show his painting of Agrippina to the King. As a result, the King commissioned a group of history paintings at intervals, beginning with *The Departure of Regulus* in 1768 and subsequently agreeing to give West an annual stipend of £1,000 to free him from the necessity of painting portraits. Two of the early history paintings – *The Family of the King of Armenia before Cyrus* and *The Wife of Arminius Brought Captive to Germanicus by Segestes* [36] – were on the theme of the relationship between parents and children in princely families, while West was doubtless aware of the King's belief that the Hanoverian dynasty descended from Thusnelda, daughter of the German chieftain, Segestes.[37]

We know how the King hung these paintings at Buckingham House from a series of picture-hanging plans for his and the Queen's apartments for which the rough drafts and some emendations on the final drawings are in the King's hand.[38] *The Family of the King of Armenia before Cyrus* and *The Wife of Arminius Brought Captive to Germanicus* were to be hung in the Warm Room on the ground floor with West's *Departure of Regulus from the Senate and his Return to Carthage* (1769; fig. 49) and his *Oath of Hannibal* (1770).[39] According to Galt, who was writing virtually at West's dictation, the King read out to West the story of Regulus from classical literature, now thought to be *Punica*, the epic by Silius Italicus of the first century AD. A Roman consul of the third century BC, Regulus was admired by ancient Romans as a frugally living martyr who heroically gave the senate advice which inevitably led to his death. Regulus was, of course, a prominent part of republican history, so he was an unexpected hero for George III, who may perhaps have been attempting to defuse republicanism by assuming any merits it might possess. The King will certainly have appreciated the impressive background buildings in the Doric order in West's painting of Regulus, which are close to those in Poussin's *Rape of the Sabine Women* (Paris, Musée du Louvre).

West's scenes from the lives of Cyrus and Germanicus were commissioned as overdoors so as to fit the hang of the Warm Room. The other paintings by West in this room were the second, 1771, version of his *Death of Wolfe* (1770) and two smaller scenes of heroic deaths, *The Death of Epaminondas* (1773) and *The Death of the Chevalier Bayard* (1772).[40] The subject of the death of Bayard in 1524 was apparently suggested to the King by West as an appropriate accompaniment to the depictions of the heroic deaths of the Greek and modern

36 Millar, *Later Georgian Pictures*, nos. 1154 and 1155.
37 Galt, *West*, p. 51.
38 In the Royal Library at Windsor. See Russell, 'King George III's

Picture Hang at Buckingham House'.
39 Millar, *Later Georgian Pictures*, nos. 1152 and 1153.
40 *ibid.*, nos. 1167, 1156, and 1157.

generals, Epaminondas and Wolfe, as it 'would serve to illustrate the heroism and peculiarities of the middle ages'.[41]

The Warm Room at Buckingham House was an extraordinary shrine to the King's single-minded dedication to West, the Quaker with a strong moral sense who was curiously close in outlook to the King. His mixture of sophistication and simplicity also seemed to reflect the eighteenth-century concept of the noble savage. Indeed, West often pointed out that 'though he socialised with courtiers and kings, he had been raised in the Pennsylvania wilderness'.[42] John Adams, successor to George Washington as President of the United States, sought out West as a fellow countryman on his visit to London in 1783. Adams recorded that when West asked the King permission to show them his 'Wolf, Bayard, Epaminondas, Regulus, &c.' at Buckingham House, 'The gracious answer of the king and queen was, that he might show us "the whole house".'[43] As we shall see in Chapter 4, the King established the Royal Academy in the year in which he commissioned the painting of Regulus from West and discussed with him at Buckingham House the plans for the Academy, doubtless showing him the room for which his *Regulus* was destined.

THE QUEEN'S APARTMENTS AND ZOFFANY

It is now appropriate to consider the paintings which Queen Charlotte commissioned from Zoffany. The King and Queen chose to divide Buckingham House horizontally with his apartments on the ground floor, hers on the first. This was, once again, a domestic not a courtly disposition. From contemporary descriptions, and from Pyne's views of the Queen's Apartment and of the King's libraries, we may gain some impression of these interiors. The King's rooms, terminating in the libraries at the southern end, were in marked contrast to the Queen's apartments above, which boasted much more colour and ornament. Her most elaborate interior was the two-storeyed Saloon (fig. 50) in the centre of the east-facing entrance front where the Baroque doorcases, chimneypieces, and ceiling paintings by Laguerre were replaced with up-to-date neo-classical work. The refurbishment of the room is normally attributed to Chambers, but because the work was carried out at the King's own expense and the documentation has not survived, it is possible that other architects were involved, possibly including James 'Athenian' Stuart, who was a serious rival to Adam and Chambers in the 1760s.[44] He may also have contributed to the design of a sedan chair made

41 Galt, *West*, p. 50.
42 Abrams, *Valiant Hero*, p. 35, and Galt, *West*, pp. 189–90.
43 C. F. Adams, *Works of John Adams*, vol. I, p. 405.
44 See Worsley, 'Out of Adam's Shadow'.

FIG. 50 James Stephanoff, *The Saloon, Buckingham House*, 1818. Watercolour and bodycolour over pencil. RL 22141

for Queen Charlotte in 1763 with large-scale ornament, partly inspired by the Greek anthemion.[45] The King may well have deliberately set these three architects to work on the same room. The coffered coves of its ceiling were a form favoured by Stuart in several interiors such as the Boudoir at Holdernesse (later Londonderry) House, Park Lane, of about 1760–5.[46] This was commissioned by the 4th Earl of Holdernesse (1718–78), whom George III appointed governor to his two eldest sons in 1771.

Above the coving, possibly the work of Stuart, the actual ceiling of the Saloon at Buckingham House was painted in the antique style with scroll work and rinceaux by Cipriani, while the massive chimneypiece at the north end was designed in 1761 by Adam in the same style.[47]

45 RCIN 31182 (*George III and Queen Charlotte*, no. 274).

46 Watkin, *Athenian Stuart*, pl. 46. Londonderry House was demolished in 1964.

47 Illustrated in R. and J. Adam, *Works in Architecture*, vol. 1, part 5, pl. IV. The chimneypiece (with marble clock above) is now in the Queen's Presence Chamber, Windsor Castle (fig. 56).

FIG, 51   James Stephanoff, *The Crimson Drawing Room, Buckingham House*, 1817. Watercolour and bodycolour over pencil. RL 22142

FIG. 52   George III, *Design for a doorcase, c.1763*. Pen and ink and wash. Private collection

Initially, the room had a fairly sombre character for it was dominated by the seven great Raphael cartoons purchased by Charles I, but these were removed to Windsor Castle at the end of the 1780s,[48] and the walls were remodelled in a lighter neo-classical fashion. They were now articulated with pilaster-like strips filled with scrollwork, which framed large panels containing oval pier glasses below paintings in grisaille of neo-antique figures by Cipriani or Pergolesi.[49]

The centre room on the first floor of the west or garden front of Buckingham House, the Crimson Drawing Room (fig. 51), was provided with a handsome ceiling designed in his personal neo-antique manner by Robert Adam, who illustrated it in his *Works in Architecture*.[50] The fact that this and the chimneypiece in the Saloon were the only interior works by him at

---

48   They are today on loan to the Victoria and Albert Museum.

49   A highly finished drawing for the south wall (in the collection of the Royal Academy) has been attributed by John Harris to John Yenn after a design by Chambers, in *Buckingham Palace. A Complete History*, *Apollo*, August 1993.

50   R. and J. Adam, *Works in Architecture*, vol. I, part 5, pl. VII.

Buckingham House which he included in this book is a clear indication that his contributions did not involve anything else on a substantial scale. The Second Drawing Room, adjacent on the north, contained an elaborate ceiling designed by Chambers in a style similar to that by Adam in the Crimson Drawing Room. The ceiling was painted by Cipriani and the room also contained a bold chimneypiece by Chambers, carved with prominent rams' heads.[51]

We know the Second Drawing Room from the illustration of it in Pyne's *Royal Residences* (1819) and, in its first incarnation as the Queen's Dressing Room, in a painting which the Queen commissioned from Johann Zoffany in 1764, *George, Prince of Wales, and Prince Frederick, later Duke of York*.[52] Zoffany had probably been introduced to the King and Queen in 1763 by the Earl of Bute, who had employed him to paint portraits of his own children. In his portrait of the Prince of Wales and Prince Frederick, and in the accompanying portrait of *Queen Charlotte with her Two Eldest Sons*,[53] Zoffany concentrated as much on depicting the interiors as their occupants. As a result, he showed with great clarity the architectural articulation of the rooms, the chimneypiece and its fire-irons in the Queen's Dressing Room, and the exquisite contents of both rooms, much of it commissioned by the King and Queen, including furniture made to harmonise with the wall decoration. As has recently been observed of the portrait of the Queen and her sons, it 'makes one feel as if one is in the room and can breathe its air', for 'the setting has become the focus of interest, and the image in the mirror is more real than the sitters.'[54]

The paintings form part of the new eighteenth-century production of art objects for the market which allowed members of the educated middle class to express their personality through the design, arrangement, and furnishing of domestic interiors. Before this time, interiors had been representational symbols within the power structures of the court, the Church, and the aristocracy. As Blanning has stated, the 'economic forces which began the erosion of the feudal public sphere' meant that culture 'was transferred from something which was representational into a commodity which could be desired for its own sake'; he goes on to argue that the more that art objects 'became accessible to all, the more they lost their aura, their sacramental character'.[55] The Zoffany portraits remind us that in a number of spheres, George III and his Queen had the gift of identifying and so taking the sting out of forces which had the potential for undermining the status of hereditary monarchy.

These rooms also provide the clearest evidence of the King's personal involvement in the

51 Now in the King's Bedroom, Windsor Castle.

52 Millar, *Later Georgian Pictures*, no. 1200.

53 *ibid.*, no. 1199.

54 C. S. Smith, *Eighteenth-Century Decoration*, p. 222.

55 Blanning, *Culture of Power*, p. 9, in the course of an interpretation of the key work by Habermas, *Structural Transformation of the Public Sphere.*

design of Buckingham House in the form of a measured drawing of around 1763 for the design of a doorcase (fig. 52). Inscribed *Invenit, designavit, dedit Georgius III*, this was given by the King to Thomas Worsley, who was Surveyor General of the King's Works from December 1760. Worsley described it as 'A drawing of a door etc. Done by the King and given me to execute at the Queen's House'.[56] As would be expected, it is in the style of Chambers, notably the frieze with its festoon of hanging swags below a full architrave and dentil cornice. It is a close parallel to doorcases by Chambers such as that surviving in the former library at Parksted (later Manresa House), Roehampton, of around 1761. Worsley took his instruction seriously, so that the craftsmen under him and Chambers at the Office of Works made doors of this design throughout the Queen's suite at Buckingham House. One of them can be seen reflected in the mirror in Zoffany's portrait of the royal children in the Queen's Dressing Room; many others are seen in the interior views published by Pyne.

In 1769 Zoffany become a Royal Academician, not by election but by the personal nomination of the King, who then asked him to paint a group portrait of all the Academicians in 1771–2 (fig. 71).[57] The success of this led Queen Charlotte to give Zoffany the remarkable commission in 1772 of painting the celebrated Medici collection as arranged in the Tribuna at the Uffizi in Florence.[58] At the time when the King and Queen were arranging their own paintings and objects at Buckingham House, it seems that they were anxious for information about the Grand Duke of Tuscany's collection, which was then considered to be the finest in Europe. The Queen even paid for Zoffany's visit to Florence in 1772, but when he returned in 1779 with the completed picture it seems that neither she nor the King approved of his inclusion in it of so many portraits of living Grand Tourists.[59]

CLOCKS AND FURNISHINGS

The King's identification with the navy and its activities, combined with his close friendship with Bute, helps explain his interest in timepieces and weathervanes, objects which at this time combined high science with art. Over the chimneypiece in the East Library (fig. 46) was an impressive wind-dial with a convex glass made by the royal clockmaker, Benjamin Vulliamy.[60] With an associated weathervane, high above the roofs of the libraries, the King was thus enabled to conjecture how his fleet was faring. On the great octagonal desk in the Octagon Library (fig. 47) stood a four-sided astronomical clock, made of mahogany and

---

56   J. Roberts, 'Chambers', p. 48 and pl. 69.
57   Millar, *Later Georgian Pictures*, no. 431.
58   *ibid.*, no. 1211.
59   Millar, *Zoffany and his Tribuna*, p. 33.
60   *George III and Queen Charlotte*, no. 307.

FIG. 53 Christopher Pinchbeck, Sir William Chambers, and others, *Astronomical clock*, 1768. Tortoiseshell, oak, gilt bronze, silver, brass, steel, and enamel. RCIN 2821

FIG. 54 Matthew Boulton, Sir William Chambers, and Thomas Wright, *Mantel clock (King's Clock)*, 1770–1. Blue john, gilt bronze, enamel, brass, steel. RCIN 30028

mounted with open-work silver panels incorporating the lion and unicorn. It was constructed for the King in 1765 by Eardley Norton for the enormous sum of £1,042, possibly to the design of Robert Adam.[61]

The second astronomical clock commissioned for Buckingham House was made in 1768, from designs by Chambers with the help of the King himself, according to Lady Mary Coke who went to the shop of the jeweller, Pinchbeck, to see it in January 1768 (fig. 53).[62] Veneered in tortoise shell with gilt-bronze mounts including Corinthian columns at the corners, it resembles a domed temple or garden building such as Chambers's unexecuted temple at Wanstead and especially his Casino at Marino which was being built at this time.[63] The mechanism was constructed by Christopher Pinchbeck the younger (1710–83), a friend and supporter of the King,[64] with John Merigeot and John Monk. The four dials with chased silver faces show the time of the day with an extra hand for solar time, the tides at 43 ports, a planetarium with a dial thermometer, and the signs of the zodiac and sidereal time.[65]

This led to further commissions from the King and Queen in 1770–2 for objects with gilt-bronze mounts by the great industrialist, Matthew Boulton (1728–1809), who had begun to make ormolu in 1768 with his partner, John Fothergill, at their Soho manufactory near Birmingham. Boulton spent three hours in discussion at Buckingham House with the King and Queen in March 1770, after which the Queen showed him the chimneypiece in her bedroom on which she displayed china vases, asking him, 'how many [of his] vases it would

61 *ibid.*, no. 300.

62 Home, *Letters and Journals of Lady Mary Coke*, vol. II, p. 181; *George III and Queen Charlotte*, no. 302.

63 A point made by Young, 'Silver, Ormolu and Ceramics', in

Harris and Snodin, *Chambers*, p. 155.

64 See his entry in the *Dictionary of National Biography*.

65 Young, 'Silver, Ormolu and Ceramics', p. 216 n. 36, and J. Harris, *Chambers*, p. 219.

take to furnish it'.[66] Following a meeting with Chambers, Boulton produced two pairs of blue-john vases with gilt-bronze mounts, known as the King's Vases, and a further clockcase for the King (fig. 54). Made in 1770–1, Chambers's architecturally conceived table-clock and vases, the latter serving as four-branched candelabra, are finely decorated with classical swags, rams' heads, and Greek key friezes. The King thus gave his architect an opportunity to develop an ornamental vocabulary for small-scale objects, incorporating decorative details which he had drawn in Paris in 1749–51 and in Rome in 1751–5.[67]

In 1772 George III acquired from Matthew Boulton an allegorical Titus clock (fig. 55) with a figure of the Roman Emperor Titus standing by a pedestal inscribed *Diem Perdidi* (I have wasted the day).[68] The King would have enjoyed this moral message, for the words were those which Titus was supposed to have uttered when he had spent a day without performing any good deed. Altogether, the King acquired from Boulton two clocks, a pair of perfume burners, and at least six vases, including two pairs of King's Vases. Royal patronage on this scale was important because it set a pattern for the fashionable world to follow. Indeed, Boulton replicated some objects from the King's order in the hope of encouraging the King's loyal subjects to follow his example.

To adorn the chimneypiece by Robert Adam in the Saloon, George III commissioned from

FIG. 55 Matthew Boulton, *The Titus Clock*, 1771-2. Kenwood, English Heritage

FIG. 56 John Bacon, *Mantel clock for the Saloon, Buckingham House*, 1789. Marble. Now at Windsor Castle. RCIN 30009

FIG. 57 Robert Adam, *Design for an illumination for the King's birthday*, 1763. Pencil, pen and ink, and watercolour. RL 17643a

66 Matthew Boulton to Anne Boulton, 3 March 1770, cited in Goodison, *Ormolu*, p. 165.

67 See Barrier, 'Franco-Italian Album' in Snodin, *Catalogues of* *Architectural Drawings …*, *Sir William Chambers*, pp. 20–6. See *George III and Queen Charlotte*, nos. 275–7.

68 Goodison, *Ormolu*, pl. 183.

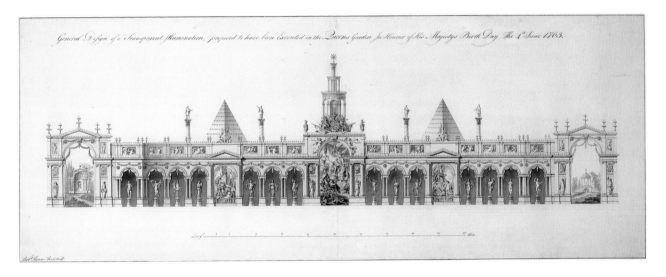

General Design of a Transparent Illumination, proposed to have been Executed in the Queens Garden In Honour of His Majestys Birth Day The 4th June 1763.

him a massive marble clock in 1789,[69] which was carved by John Bacon the elder (1740–99) and exhibited at the Royal Academy in the same year (fig. 56). Somewhat solemn for a drawing-room clock, it is supported by figures representing Vigilance and Patience which make it almost as monumental as a tomb, though these virtues probably appealed to the King's sense of duty.[70]

We might note here the absence from the activities as collectors of both George III and his son, the Prince of Wales, later George IV, of the acquisition of antique sculpture. This is surprising because, as has recently been pointed out, 'almost every other sovereign in Europe either owned a gallery of antiquities or had agents in Rome buying on his or her behalf.'[71] It may be that George III was following the example of Lord Bute, who was not a collector in this field, but it is striking that he did not include a gallery of antiquities at either Buckingham House or at his proposed palace at Richmond, nor did he at Windsor Castle. However, Chambers had built the Gallery of Antiques at Kew Gardens in 1757 which contained statues of gods and goddesses by Joseph Wilton.

ADAM'S ILLUMINATION AND TRANSPARENCY

Robert Adam also provided for Queen Charlotte the enchanting design for the 'illumination and transparency' (fig. 57) in the gardens of Buckingham House to celebrate the king's twenty-fifth

69 Clifford, 'John Bacon', p. 296 and fig. 34.
70 See above, n. 47. The Bacon clock case is inscribed with lines from Cowper's Latin Poems which in translation read: 'The long-expected hour that slowly draweth nigh how swiftly when tis here,

it passeth by. Be patient for its coming and be watchful too, that thou may'st catch and use it well.'
71 Scott, *Pleasures of Antiquity*, p. 115.

birthday in June 1763.[72] Doubtless representing her taste rather more than her husband's, this was a built fantasy of the kind created at the French court from at least the reign of Louis XIV onwards.[73] Adam and Chambers were perhaps more familiar with the related tradition in Rome, where similar temporary structures or painted backcloths were created as the *macchine* for numerous firework displays, notably the biennial firework festivals known variously as the *Festa della Chinea* and the *Fuochi Farnesiani*. In Rome in the 1750s, Adam and Chambers had seen designs for these, especially those by the students of the Académie Française in which they helped create the style we know as Neoclassicism.

Transparencies, popular at Vauxhall Gardens, have been described as 'pictures made with translucent paints on materials like calico, linen or oiled paper and lighted from behind in the manner of stained glass . . . [and] a favourite form of eighteenth-century public art, much seen on occasions of national rejoicing, such as military victories and royal weddings and births, when they were placed in the parks and in the windows of shops and dwellings as part of general "illuminations".'[74] Like the *Chinea* festival backdrops, the Queen's Buckingham House transparency was designed to be seen at night, lit artificially by 4,000 glass lamps, an effect well conveyed in the dramatic engraving of the full scheme, only partially executed, which Adam published in *The Works in Architecture*.[75] The Queen arranged that stage carpenters should erect 'all these machines, paintings, lights, &c.' during the temporary absence of the King at St James's Palace, so that it came as a surprise to him when the shutters were thrown open on his arrival around nine o'clock in the evening. Surprise was also a feature of many of the parallel festivities at courts in France.

Adam's transparency was a hemicycle of arches forming 'a temple of fortune', behind and above which rose two pyramids and four Corinthian columns capped with statues. The largest of the transparencies, probably painted on linen, were those in the central arch and in the arches in the middle of the sides; smaller ones were in the numerous panels in the attic. The central transparency represented the King giving peace to all parts of the earth with falling figures representing the vices at his feet.[76] Its triumphal theme was intended to celebrate not only the King's birthday in 1763 but also the Treaty of Paris which had ended the Seven Years War in the same year. It was the perfect expression of the mood of optimism, political as well as cultural, at the start of the reign, before problems such as the loss of the American colonies, the King's illness, and the threat from Napoleon

---

72   The executed design was rather simpler than that shown in fig. 57 (Oppé, *English Drawings*, no. 19).

73   For an illustrated survey of the architectural background, see DeLorme, *Garden Pavilions*.

74   Altick, *Shows of London*, p. 95.

75   R. and J. Adam, *Works in Architecture*, vol. 1, part 5, pl. V, where he caused confusion by misdating it to 1762 rather than 1763.

76   *Gentleman's Magazine*, vol. XXXIII, 1763, p. 300.

cast their shadows. Adam's 'illumination and transparency' formed a close parallel in theme and character to the Gold State Coach designed three years before by his principal rival, Chambers.

We shall shortly see a similar scheme built by Chambers in the form of a pavilion to receive the King of Denmark in 1768. Further research might show that such festival decorations were not as rare in England as might be supposed. For example, the Countess, later Duchess, of Northumberland provided illuminated festivities at Northumberland House for the Queen's brother, Prince Ernest of Mecklenburg-Strelitz in July 1762, for the King's birthday in 1764,[77] and for the King of Denmark in 1768, on which occasion an 'inexpressible variety of emblematic devices were illuminated with more than 15000 lamps and the temple erected in the inner court, was ornamented with transparent paintings'.[78] Adam might have been involved with the designs of these displays.

It is possible that Chambers contrived to ensure that Adam did not receive the commissions he might have expected as Joint Architect to the King. If so, Adam's transparency for Queen Charlotte must have come as some compensation, though he might also have expected a reward from the King for the fact that he, and especially his brother James, had spent six months negotiating on his behalf for the purchase of Cardinal Albani's collection of drawings, one of the finest collections of seventeenth-century drawings in the world. It has even been supposed that Robert Adam raised the question of their acquisition when he kissed hands with the King on his appointment as Royal Architect in November 1761.[79]

The combination of Chambers's close relationship with the King, and the King's preference for simpler design than Adam's, meant that Adam was probably content to relinquish his royal office, which he did in 1769 on becoming Member of Parliament for Kinrossshire. Chambers was throughout the central figure, though the King seems also to have been content with William Robinson, who was acting Clerk of Works at Buckingham House under Chambers. In April 1769 it was decided by the Treasury that maintenance of Buckingham House would become the responsibility of the Office of Works. Robinson was now formally appointed Clerk of the Works, in which capacity he would have been involved in the architecturally undemonstrative wing which the King commissioned to be built at the north end of Buckingham House for the Prince of Wales, the future George IV, in 1776.[80]

---

77   See Baird, *Mistress of the House*, pp. 160–2.

78   *Gentleman's Magazine*, vol. XXXIII, 1768, p. 490.

79   Fleming, *Robert Adam and his Circle*, p. 297.

80   Colvin, ed., *King's Works*, vol. V, pp. 137–8.

Richmond and Kew

Since the King's mother continued to live in the White House, which Kent had built for her at Kew, George III considered building a new residence for himself at Richmond, which would also serve to replace the long-vanished great palace at Richmond of Henry VII. In March 1763 the widespread expectation that the King was about to build a palace at Richmond led Robert Adam to write a letter to Henry Home, Lord Kames, about the character of the orders, in which he expressed the hope that 'If the King builds a palace in a magnificent and pure style of architecture, it will give a great push at once to the taste of this country.'[81] Lord Kames (1696–1782), the Scottish judge and philosopher, had recently dedicated his book, *Elements of Criticism* (1762) to the King.[82] Indebted to Locke's philosophy of association, this book was one of the most important statements of the Picturesque aesthetic in architecture and garden design. Kames argued in his Dedication that royal patronage should not celebrate the glory of kingship but that the arts should be encouraged 'for their beneficial influence in society'. He believed that 'By uniting the different ranks in the same elegant pleasures, they promote benevolence: by cherishing love of order, they enforce submission to government, and by inspiring a delicacy of feeling, they make regular government a double blessing.' He argued further that 'a flourishing commerce begets opulence . . . [which] is commonly vented on luxury, and on every sensual gratification,' so that it 'extinguishes the *amor patriae*, and every spark of public spirit.' By contrast, 'riches employed, instead of encouraging vice, will excite both public and private virtues. Of this happy effect, Ancient Greece furnishes one shining instance and why should we despair of another in Britain?'

These will have been golden words to the King who issued a 'Proclamation for the Encouragement of Piety and Virtue, and for the Preventing and Punishing of Vice, Profaneness, and Immorality'.[83] Patronage of architects and artists was to be for him, as for Kames, an act of civic virtue. Indeed, his architectural activities can be set in the wider context of *Improvement*, for example in agriculture, manufacture, and commerce, which is characteristic of the age in which he lived.

Literally hundreds of unsigned and undated architectural drawings are related to the King's ambition to build a palace at Richmond,[84] for his increasing family made a larger residence than Richmond Lodge desirable. The project seems to have grown out of the process of his training under Chambers, but continued to preoccupy him into the 1770s and, as we

81 Adam to Kames, 3 March 1763, quoted in Bolton, *Architecture of Robert and James Adam*, vol. I, pp. 50–4.

82 A point noted in Brewer, *Pleasures of the Imagination*, pp. 23–5.

83 *Gentleman's Magazine*, vol. LVII, 1787, i, pp. 534–5; and see *Annual Register*, 1760, p. 241.

84 J. Harris, *Chambers*, named the design of 1762, Richmond I; that for which the model was presented to the King in 1765, Richmond II; the palace on which construction was begun in 1769, Richmond III; and the design of 1775 of which a model was also made, Richmond IV.

have seen, must also briefly have concerned Adam. Designs by Adam for a new palace at Richmond are more in the manner of Chambers than in Adam's own more fanciful Piranesian mode (fig. 58).[85] Chambers had exhibited a design, of which we know nothing, for a palace at Richmond in 1762 at the Society of Arts, but the project was temporarily abandoned on the King's purchase of Buckingham House in that year. Designs for a palace in the Royal Library at Windsor, attributed to this date and to the King's own hand, are related to large Palladian country houses such as Wanstead House, Essex (*c.*1714–20), by Colen Campbell (d. 1729), and Wentworth Woodhouse, Yorkshire (*c.*1735–70), by Henry Flitcroft. The King was inspired by plates in *Vitruvius Britannicus*, to which he had doubtless been directed by Chambers, so that one design features corner towers in the manner of Wilton or Houghton. A sectional drawing (fig. 59)[86] includes a large picture gallery in which the pictures are shown *in situ*, a technique pioneered by William Kent in two drawings of 1725 for the saloon at Houghton Hall. In the British constitutional monarchy, noblemen have typically set architectural fashions which the monarch follows. It was not the King but the Duke of Norfolk who built a palace on a royal scale in 1763–7, the neo-Palladian north wing of Worksop Manor, Nottinghamshire, designed by James Paine and the Duchess of Norfolk.

Since these drawings of *c.*1762–5 for the palace which we call Richmond II were inspired by the great country houses of 30 or 40 years earlier, the initial design concept can be attributed to George III, for it is inconceivable that Chambers himself would have adopted such a

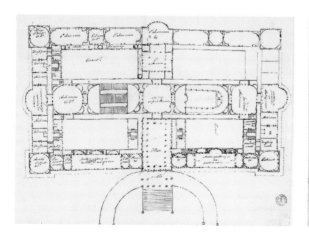
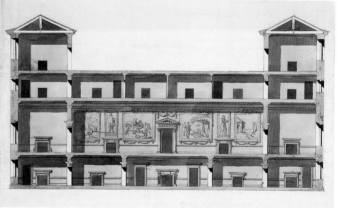

85 On Adam's designs for palaces for George III, see Tait,
Robert Adam, pp. 51–5.
86 J. Roberts, 'Chambers', pl. 61.

style in the 1760s unless it was at the express command of the King. However, Chambers and his Office worked up the King's designs into the many project drawings which have survived. Richmond II, for which drawings also survive in the British Architectural Drawings Collection, had a monotonous façade, no fewer than 23 bays long (fig. 61), and two court-yards divided by a large, centrally placed, apsidal hall (fig. 60), a little like the entrance hall at Holkham Hall.

The largest of all the palaces proposed for George III at Richmond, it is also known from a wooden model, made in 1765, but destroyed in the early twentieth century.[87] The fact that, at this time, it cost as much to make a large model as to build a small house, is evidence that the project was taken very seriously. It may have been inspired by the royal palace designed by William Kent in a more vigorous Palladian style for King George II and Queen Caroline, which we know from a pearwood model made in 1735 (fig. 11).

Chambers intervened in the process by producing more sophisticated designs in his own Franco-Italian manner. Known as Richmond III and IV, these include many beautiful and highly finished drawings which are neither in the hand of the King nor, probably, in that of Chambers, who can hardly have found time for such labour (fig. 62). However Chambers's office was expanding with the presence of James Gandon (1743–1823) and John Yenn in the 1760s and '70s. Another possible candidate for the authorship of some of these drawings is the architect and gardener William Robinson, who was described

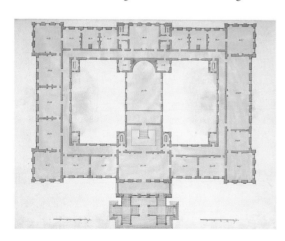

in a letter of 1765 by the 6th Earl of Findlater as 'the person who works about the king in all the designs in architecture which the king invents or directs himself.'[88] A neo-Palladian architect of moderate ability, Robinson was appointed Clerk of the Works at Whitehall, Westminster, and St James's, in 1754, and Secretary to the Board of Works and Clerk Itinerant in 1762. He was Clerk of the Works at Buckingham House from 1762, working directly for

87   *ibid.*, pl. 70, and J. Harris, *Chambers*, fig. 12.
88   Fraser, *Chiefs of Grant*, vol. II, *Correspondence*, p. 445.

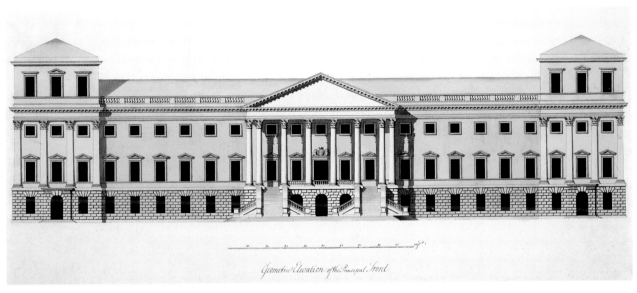

Geometric Elevation of the Principal Front

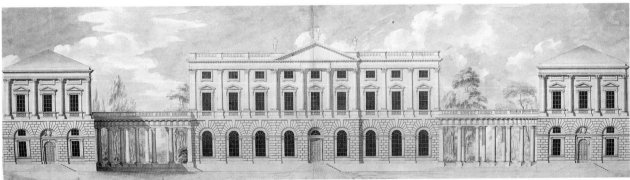

George III, and also Clerk of the Works at Somerset House; from 1763 onwards he made alterations to Carlton House for Princess Augusta.

Richmond II was abandoned, perhaps because of the vast scale and expense involved, though George III was content to spend many large sums from the Privy Purse on other projects. Indeed, construction was begun in 1769 on the central block of a palace by Chambers, Richmond III. However, work did not proceed beyond the ground floor. This building can

FIG. 63 Sir William Chambers, *Design for Richmond Palace: side elevation, c.1770*. Pen and ink and wash. RL 30302–4

FIG. 64 Sir William Chambers, *Elevation of a pavilion for the King of Denmark in Richmond Gardens*, 1768. Pen and ink and wash. RL 30374

be related to a later and more attractive design by Chambers, Richmond IV, in which a central nine-bay block was linked to lower three-bay pavilions by quadrant Doric colonnades, two columns deep (fig. 63).[89] This bears some resemblance to the language which Chambers had absorbed on his visit to Paris in 1774 to study recent public buildings in preparation for the commission for building Somerset House. Indeed, we know this design from a drawing probably made in 1775, of which a copy, together with the plan, was sent to Thomas Worsley as Surveyor of the King's Works. The whole project, of which the cost was estimated at nearly £90,000, was eventually abandoned altogether.

PAVILION FOR THE KING OF DENMARK

It remains to consider the buildings, both permanent and temporary, which the King built at Richmond Gardens. The first was an elegant temporary pavilion (fig. 64) built for the reception in September 1768 of his cousin and brother-in-law, King Christian VII of Denmark and Norway, who travelled to London and Paris between May 1768 and January 1769. In 1766 he had married George III's favourite sister, Princess Caroline Matilda (1751–75), but she remained at Frederiksborg, near Copenhagen, during his travels. She was divorced by her deranged husband and died in exile at Celle in Germany.

Though one-storeyed, the pavilion at Richmond Gardens was a vast rectangular structure of fifteen bays by eight, in which the entrance front, 200 feet long, boasted a pedimented centre in the form of a triumphal arch, 40 feet high, linked by rusticated arcades to canted bays with pyramidal roofs. Articulated with a Doric order with triglyph frieze, the King's favourite order, its exterior was a perfect expression of the King's tastes at this time. Its dynamic interior

89   Also known from a drawing at the Royal Institute of British Architects (J. Harris, *Chambers*, pl. 112), and from a now lost model (J. Roberts, 'Chambers', pl. 71).

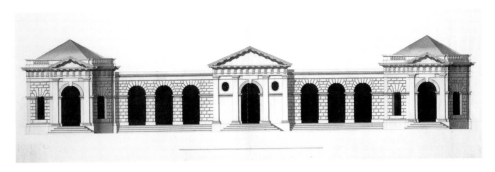

planning was more typical of the work of Adam than of Chambers, so that it is no surprise to hear that it supposedly incorporated an earlier pavilion built for Queen Charlotte by Adam, from whom she had commissioned the transparency and illumination for the King at Buckingham House in 1763. The pavilion at Richmond of 1768 was similarly rooted in the continental tradition of temporary festival architecture to which, in France, an entire department in the royal household, the *Menus-Plaisirs du Roi*, was devoted.[90] There is no precise English translation for the name of this important department which was established by François I and even survived, reorganised, the Revolution of 1789. Its extensive responsibilities in the pageantry of court life included the costumes, structures, and music for court ceremonies and ephemeral events such as firework displays, and even the king's jewellery and wardrobe.

Constructed of wood and canvas, Chambers's painted and gilded pavilion of 1768 contained transparent illuminations painted by Cipriani and John Richards. These were linked by nymphs and satyrs, holding festoons of flowers, to the arches at either end of the entrance front which contained 'emblematical pictures alluding to the arts and sciences'; the principal reception rooms were arranged on a cruciform plan, centring on a domed circular hall defined by eight free-standing columns 'wreathed with flowers, and ornamented with gold'.[91] With its music, supper, and fireworks, this magical and temporary extravagance was a product of the world of Chambers's French friends such as the architects Charles de Wailly and, especially, François-Joseph Bélanger (1744–1818), who was appointed *Dessinateur* to the *Menus-Plaisirs* in 1767. An admirer of the work of Adam and Chambers, Bélanger made tours of English buildings and parks at some point between 1769 and 1773, and again in 1778.[92] This was probably at the invitation of Chambers to whom he dedicated a drawing of the elevation

90 Separate from the *Bâtiments du Roi*, the *Service des Menus-Plaisirs* was under the direction of four key figures at the court, the *Premiers Gentilhommes de la Chambre*. See de Chennevières, *Les Menus-plaisirs du roi*.

91 *Gentleman's Magazine*, vol. XXXVIII, 1768, p. 490.

92 Woodbridge, 'Bélanger en Angleterre'.

of the Pavillon des Bains which he built at his Hôtel de Brancas in Paris of 1768.[93] With its unpedimented Ionic portico surmounted by statues, this elegant bathing pavilion is closely paralleled by the Casino, or *pavillon*, which Chambers built in up-to-date French taste at Marino House, near Dublin, for the 1st Earl of Charlemont. He had designed this in 1757, the year in which he was appointed tutor in architecture to the Prince of Wales, and it was built slowly between 1758 and 1776. The interior elevation of Bélanger's Pavillon des Bains is similarly close to designs by Chambers such as the Gallery of Antiques at Kew, also designed in 1757.

FIG. 65   The Royal Observatory, Richmond Gardens

FIG. 66   George Adams the elder, *Silver microscope, c.*1763. Science Museum (inv. no. 1949-116)

THE ROYAL OBSERVATORY AND THE WEATHER REGISTER

The Royal Observatory in Richmond Gardens (fig. 65) was built from designs by William Chambers in 1769 for George III to observe the transit of Venus on 3 June that year when, for a few minutes, the planet could be seen in silhouette as it passed across the face of the sun.[94] It was an important occasion as it provided an opportunity to measure the size of the solar system, including the distance between the earth and the sun. British interest was stimulated by a rivalry with France and other nations in viewing the transit.[95] Paid for by the King's mother, the Dowager Princess of Wales, the Observatory was built to the west of Richmond Lodge, which the King was to demolish three years later after moving into the White House in Kew Gardens. The Observatory was designed by Chambers in association with the King's astronomer, Stephen Demainbray, who provided the King with detailed notes on the transit of Venus which he stayed up late to watch. Demainbray had earlier been the King's tutor in mathematics and natural history and had lectured him on astronomy and electricity. The King visited his Observatory frequently, introducing his guests to Demainbray, whose home it became.

Perhaps as a result of the Swedish links of William Chambers, the Observatory is indebted to the mid-eighteenth-century observatories at Uppsala and Stockholm where the housing of instruments in a turret or cupola, rather than an open tower, had been pioneered.

93   The inscription reads *Dédié a Monsieur William Chambers: par son très humble serviteur Bélanger … architecte des menus: Plaisirs du Roy* (Royal Institute of British Architects Drawings Collection).

94   Woolf, *Transit of Venus.*

95   'Sir Joseph Banks and his Abiding Legacy', in *London Papers in Australian Studies*, no. 2, King's College, London, 2001, p. 4.

FIG. 67 James Adam,
*Elevation and plan of a
design for a weather
register, Richmond
Gardens*, 1770. Pen and
ink and wash. London,
British Library
(K.Top.XLI.16-y, 16-s)

Chambers also evidently aimed at reflecting the Palladian style which appealed to the King, so that his building unexpectedly resembles a Palladian villa with canted bays. Its two octagonal rooms were fitted by the carpenter, James Arrow, with handsome glazed bookcases and cupboards for models, since the rooms housed the King's collection of scientific instruments, many of which were of the kind then used to give demonstrations in lectures on natural philosophy (fig. 66). With his passion for machinery and scientific instruments, the King had created on 15 December 1760, at the very start of his reign, the unusual royal office of Mathematical Instrument Maker. This was for the leading London instrument maker, George Adams, who, as we have seen, had made Kirby's architectonic sector. The Observatory also contained 'a collection of ores from his Majesty's mines in Harz in Germany'.[96]

The King was doubtless emulating Lord Bute who had assembled a notable 'cabinet of mathematical and philosophical apparatus' at Luton Hoo.[97] Nonetheless, one philistine critic

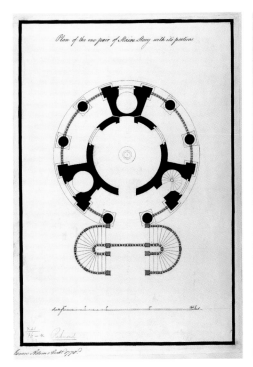

96 D. Lysons, *Environs of London*, 1796–1800, vol. I, Surrey, p. 446.
   The Harz is properly not a place but a range of hills.

97 Morton and Wess, *Public and Private Science*, p. 17, and see Turner,
   'The Auction Sales of the Earl of Bute's Instruments, 1793'.

complained in 1774 that 'The Observatory is a bauble of extravagance ill placed: it contains a great collection of useless books and instruments.'[98] The octagonal room in the west wing was used for transit observations, and that in the east wing for quadrant observations. From the gallery, with Chinese fretwork balustrades by James Arrow, a staircase led up to the viewing room surmounted by a cupola with a sliding opening to accommodate the telescopes in the moveable dome.[99]

In 1770 the King commissioned a further scientific building for Richmond Gardens in which to make meteorological observations, a 'weather register' which was never executed (fig. 67). This is to be regretted, for the surviving designs by James Adam are for a circular colonnaded building of exceptional elegance, resembling a garden temple or supper pavilion with a flat balustraded roof from which rise three circular turrets.[100] The order chosen for its six columns and their antae was that of the novel leaf capital published by James's brother, Robert Adam, in his *Ruins of the Palace of the Emperor Diocletian at Spalatro* (1764), a work dedicated to the King. James received the commission for the 'weather register' in his capacity as Architect of the King's Works, in which post he had succeeded Robert in 1769.

FIG. 68 Queen Charlotte's Cottage, Kew

FIG. 69 The drawing room on the first floor of Queen Charlotte's Cottage, Kew

---

98   *London Magazine*, vol. XLIII, August 1774, p. 361.

99   Cloake, *Richmond and Kew*, p. 49. Its appearance was altered by the addition of an upper storey to the two wings in the 1880s.

100 See Cloake, *Richmond and Kew*, pp. 49–50.

THE QUEEN'S COTTAGE

Pursuing the King's interest in astronomy has led us beyond the earlier years of his reign and its products at Richmond. We should therefore conclude this chapter with the Queen's Cottage of *c.*1771 which survives in Kew Gardens (fig. 68). The principal front of this *cottage orné* is a simple but subtle composition in which the gabled centrepiece, flanked by lower side bays with pyramidal roofs, distantly recalls Palladio's Venetian churches with their inter-locking pediments. Despite its brick and half-timbered construction below a thatched roof, it is thus less like the cottages of the eighteenth-century English Picturesque tradition than the more formalised *chaumières* which appear in French *jardins anglais*. A contemporary observed that 'The queen's cottage in the shade of the garden is a pretty retreat . . . The design is said to be her majesty's',[101] but it is likely that Chambers had a hand in a building which is close to those surviving in the *hameau* at Chantilly, begun in 1775, and even that of Marie-Antoinette at the Petit Trianon at Versailles.

The principal ground-floor room is treated as a print room, its walls hung with engravings by Hogarth, mounted on canvas and stretchers, while the main room above is prettily

painted as a floral arbour composed of convolvulus and nasturtium twined round a trellis of bamboo canes (fig. 69).[102] When the Queen's brother, Prince Ernest of Mecklenburg-Strelitz, came to stay at Richmond in the summer and autumn of 1771, Queen Charlotte described the cottage as having four or five rooms and recommended him to build a similar one on his own estate where it would look well and also provide a discreet setting for 'une Amie'.[103]

The varied architectural expressions of George III's artistic and scientific tastes which we have seen in this chapter represent the sunniest side of our story early in his reign before his illness. It will be necessary in due course to consider the possible influence on his architectural endeavours of other dark clouds on the horizon: those of the threat of Napoleonic invasion.

---

101 *London Magazine*, vol. XLIII, August 1774, p. 361.
102 Attributed to the hand of George III's third daughter, Princess
      Elizabeth, in *c.*1805 (Croft-Murray, *Decorative Painting*, vol. II, p. 204).
103 Hedley, *Queen Charlotte*, p. 308.

OPPOSITE Johann Zoffany, *The Royal Academicians*, 1771–2 (detail of fig. 71)

FIG. 70 William Hogarth, *Masquerades and Operas*, 1724. Engraving with etching, first state. RCIN 811358

The Royal Academy

The involvement of King George III in the foundation and continuing life of the Royal Academy was a remarkable expression of his belief in the importance of a professional artistic body to promote British art. An early attempt to establish such an institution had been made in 1711 by Sir Godfrey Kneller, former Principal Painter to King William III, when he founded an Academy of Painting and Drawing in Great Queen Street, London, with himself as first Governor.[1] On his return from Italy in 1719, the Earl of Burlington turned Burlington House, Piccadilly, into a kind of private academy of the arts in which he housed a group of artists, sculptors, musicians, painters, including Guelfi, Bononcini, and Kent. It is supposed that he had in mind an arrangement in which Colen Campbell would teach architecture, Kent painting, and Guelfi sculpture. In a satirical scene with Burlington House in the background, Hogarth provided Campbell's ambitious Doric entrance gateway with the inscription 'Accademy of Arts' (fig. 70).[2]

Frederick, Prince of Wales, the father of George III, also believed in the importance of establishing an academy.[3] The antiquary and engraver, George Vertue (1684–1756), claimed of the Prince in 1749 that he 'spoke much concerning the settlement of an Accademy For

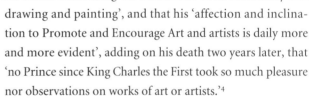

drawing and painting', and that his 'affection and inclination to Promote and Encourage Art and artists is daily more and more evident', adding on his death two years later, that 'no Prince since King Charles the First took so much pleasure nor observations on works of art or artists.'[4]

This belief that contemporary British art was in need of the kind of reform which could be brought about by a professional body, with the intellectual and educational role of representing artists and of promoting their interests, quickened in the middle years of the century. Products of this mood were the *Essay upon Design including Proposals for erecting a Public Academy* (1749) by the architect John Gwynn, a member of the St Martin's Lane Academy which had been founded by Hogarth in 1735. Gwynn has been mentioned in connection with the architectural education of

Could new dumb Faustus, to reform the Age,
Conjure up Shakespear's or Ben Johnson's Ghost,
They'd blush for shame, to see the English Stage
Debauch'd by foolries, at so great a cost.

What would their Manes say? should they behold
Monsters and Masquerades, where usefull Plays
Adorn'd the fruitfull Theatre of old,
And Rival Wits contended for the Bays.
Price 1 Shilling 1724.

---

1 For the art institutions in London from 1698 to 1768, see Bignamini, 'George Vertue'.

2 Paulson, *Hogarth's Graphic Work*, pp. 47–9 and pl. 44.

3 Rorschach, 'Frederick, Prince of Wales', p. 21.

4 Vertue, 'Notebooks', pp. 8 and 14.

George III, while the scholar Robert Wood wrote to the Earl of Bute in October 1759 suggesting that William Chambers should be invited to 'throw upon paper some loose hints' for an academy in a building 'costing at least £100,000'.[5] Wood was the author of the popular and influential archaeological books, *Ruins of Palmyra* (1753), and *Ruins of Balbec* (1757), the former used in the architectural instruction of George III, doubtless at the suggestion of Chambers (figs. 28, 29).

Reynolds, Chambers, Wilton, and Paine founded the Society of Artists of Great Britain, which held its first public exhibition in 1761 in Spring Gardens. Chambers exhibited architectural drawings at this and at subsequent exhibitions until 1768. Benjamin West joined the Society in 1765 and was a Director by 1768. In 1765 it changed its name to the Incorporated Society of Artists of Great Britain and was granted a royal charter. George III's librarian, Richard Dalton, who owed his royal appointment to the recommendation of Lord Bute, was its Treasurer, while his tutor, Joshua Kirby, became its President in 1768.

The establishment of the Royal Academy had evidently been a topic of serious discussion in royal circles since mid-1767.[6] Joshua Kirby was among those hoping that the Incorporated Society of Artists would become the Royal Academy. He was shocked to learn from the King, to whom he supposed he was close, that the painting the King commissioned from West in 1768, *The Departure of Regulus* (fig. 49), which we saw in Chapter 3, would not be exhibited at the Incorporated Society. While West was painting *Regulus*, the King told him of his proposal to create a Royal Academy which would be independent of the Incorporated Society of Artists.[7] Kirby, who was present when West handed over the painting to the King, praised it, expressing the hope that it would be sent to his exhibition. "'No," interposed the King, "it must go to my exhibition – to the Royal Academy."'[8] West's *Regulus* was, of course, the kind of high-minded statement of public and private virtue which the King hoped the Royal Academy would promote.[9]

Kirby had become President of the Incorporated Society in 1768, just as its rival was about to be founded. It seems that, unknown to Kirby, Chambers had persuaded Benjamin West, Francis Cotes (1725?– 70), and George Michael Moser (1704-83) to join him in signing a petition to the King on 28 November 1768 in which they asked him to grant a royal 'instrument of foundation' to establish a Royal Academy.[10] This tore the Incorporated Society apart; seventeen of its Directors left to become members of the King's new academy.

5   J. Harris, *Chambers*, p. 165.

6   For a tart account of these years see Strange, *An Inquiry*. The hostility of Sir Robert Strange to the Academy was aggravated by his own exclusion from it as an engraver and a Jacobite.

7   Erffa, *West*, p. 51 and pl. 48.

8   Galt, *West*, p. 40. West's *Regulus* was duly shown in the first Royal Academy exhibition in the spring of 1769.

9   See Taylor, *Art for the Nation*, ch. 1, 'In the image of the King. Toward the Royal Academy of Arts', pp. 1–28.

10 Savage, 'The "Viceroy" of the Royal Academy', in Harris and Snodin, *Chambers*, p. 193.

THE FOUNDING OF THE ROYAL ACADEMY

With the founding of the Royal Academy in 1768, instruction in architecture featured as a more central activity than in the earlier attempts at establishing an academy. In 1768 Chambers wrote the foundation document for the future Royal Academy, which was largely based on what he had prepared for Bute a decade earlier. The document was written with the close co-operation of the King, who signed it on 10 December 1768. George III was, to some extent, following in the first, tentative footsteps of his gifted father, Frederick, Prince of Wales. It has been speculated that, but for Frederick's premature death in 1751, the Royal Academy might have been founded as early as 1760, which would have been the first year of Frederick's reign.

The document known as the Instrument of Foundation explains that, 'There shall be a Treasurer . . . who, as the King is graciously pleased to pay all deficiencies, shall be appointed by His Majesty.' It went on to announce that the King 'doth hereby nominate and appoint William Chambers, Esquire, Architect of his Works, to be Treasurer.' Describing the King as 'the patron, protector, and supporter' of the Academy, the Instrument emphasises that he is required to give his personal approval to the appointment of the Secretary and of the painters and sculptors who teach in the Schools of Design. The Instrument concludes with the smack of firm government: 'I approve of this Plan; let it be put in execution. GEORGE R.'[11]

One of the last academies of art to be founded in Europe, the Royal Academy of Art was inspired by the French Académie Royale d'Architecture. This had been established by Colbert in 1671 for Louis XIV as part of a system of total control of architecture, the arts, and manu-facture. The world of the French Academy was one in which Chambers was completely at home, for he had been trained as an architect in 1749–50 at the École des Arts in Paris by Jacques-François Blondel who became Professor at the Académie Royale d'Architecture in 1762. Chambers became a corresponding member of the Académie Royale in 1763 and main-tained close friendships with French architects such as Julien-David Leroy and Charles de Wailly, both products of the Académie, where Leroy also became a Professor in 1762.

In France a tradition of royal and public buildings in a grave classical style, though retaining the high mansard roofs of the sixteenth century, survived into the late eighteenth century. Like the Crown it served, it was transmitted in an hereditary fashion through dynas-ties of architects, notably François Mansart (1598–1666) and his great-nephew, Jules Hardouin-Mansart (1646–1708), and Jacques-Jules Gabriel (1667–1742) and his son, Ange-

---

11   Hutchinson, *The History of the Royal Academy, 1768–1968*,
     Appendix A, pp. 209–13.

Jacques Gabriel (1698–1782). The twin palaces in what is now the Place de la Concorde, built in 1755–74 by Ange-Jacques Gabriel, were among the recent buildings which Chambers drew on his visit to Paris in 1774 to prepare himself for designing Somerset House.

It can be appreciated from Chambers's *Treatise* that he saw himself as a broad central figure handing down an established tradition beyond the range of passing fashion and of the narrow whims of those whom he regarded as fanatics. These included the theorist Marc-Antoine Laugier (1713–69) and the proponents of the superiority of Greek architecture over Roman. It was the grand conservative system of French architecture which Chambers admired and which he hoped to echo in England by encouraging the King to set up an Academy. It is likely that, as Chambers's pupil, the King would have shared this ambition of achieving a royal and national style. Indeed, Chambers persuaded him to assume the responsible role of 'patron, protector, and supporter' of the Royal Academy. Providing the large sum of £5,000 from his Privy Purse to establish it and pay the salaries of its officers, he oversaw the details of its constitution as well as the selection of its membership. By contrast, the Incorporated Society of Artists, which it replaced, had a more democratic constitution.

As 'quasi servants of the crown', the Royal Academicians (fig. 71) 'occupied positions analogous to Chambers's own existing office of Architect to the King.'[12] This, again was a parallel to the French Académie where all Royal Academicians were *architectes du roi*, the Director being the *premier architecte du roi*. However, Chambers was Treasurer of the Royal Academy, not President, an office occupied by Sir Joshua Reynolds. It must be confessed that, as the dominant figure in the Councils of the Academy for nearly 30 years, Chambers did not play a very generous role, blocking the appointments of his rivals, notably Robert Adam. Indeed, as Nicholas Savage has observed, 'the only architects elected to the Academy during Chambers's active participation in its affairs' were Adam's rival, the young James Wyatt, two of Chambers's own pupils, Edward Stevens (*c*.1744–75) and John Yenn, and Joseph Bonomi (1739–1808).[13] However, this is to overlook Chambers's vital support at the Royal Academy of the young John Soane, which led him to show to the King Soane's winning Gold Medal designs for a Triumphal Bridge in 1776. This resulted in the King approving straightaway the award to Soane of the three-year travelling scholarship to Rome which the Gold Medal carried with it, even though Sir Joshua Reynolds insisted on the Academicians themselves making the formal

---

12   Savage, 'The "Viceroy" of the Royal Academy', p. 196.

13   *ibid.*

election in the following year, 1777. The greatest British architect of the early nineteenth century, Soane professed life-long devotion to George III for personally approving his award and enabling him to travel abroad, for it was in Italy that he established the network of patronage on which his future career rested.[14] He was elected an Associate of the Royal Academy in 1795, during the Treasurership of Chambers, and a full Academician in 1802.

Soane was also indebted to Thomas Sandby, Professor of Architecture at the Royal Academy from 1770, whose annual series of lectures made a profound impression on him. However,

14   See Watkin, *Soane*, ch. 2, 'Soane's Relations with the Royal Academy',
     pp. 65–97, and Hoock, *The King's Artists*.

the Academy did not play a leading role in the architectural culture of England: it did not hold the meetings for academic discussion which were a central part of its opposite number in Paris, while its members had less of a role in representing particular branches of the arts than did their French counterparts, and tended simply to serve the institution.

The Building and Decoration of Somerset House

In 1771 George III arranged for the Royal Academy to be moved from Dalton's Print Warehouse in Pall Mall to a more dignified, indeed royal, home in the dower house of the Queen, Somerset House, in the Strand (fig. 72). An Act of Parliament of 1775 confirmed the transference of the Royal Academy to Somerset House, but in 1780 it moved into purpose-

FIG. 72 Thomas Sandby,
*The Garden or River Front
of Old Somerset House,*
*c.*1760. Watercolour, pen
and ink, and pencil.
RL 14698

FIG. 73 Thomas Malton,
*The Great Court, Somerset
House,* 1796. Etching.
RCIN 703074

GREAT COURT, SOMERSET PLACE.

built new premises designed by Chambers in the Strand block of 1776–80 at his new Somerset House. This vast new building, not completed till 1796, was an outcome of the notion of uniting the various government offices in a new building on a single site (fig. 73). The idea was first proposed in 1771, the year in which the King gave the Royal Academy a home in the old Somerset House. To unite government offices in this way was a concept completely novel either on the continent or in England. The construction of a complex of government buildings on the site of the Tudor and early Stuart Somerset House was also daring since it involved replacing a royal palace with a public building. The approval of the King was thus necessary.

On 6 May 1774 the Board of Works confirmed that the existing buildings were in a poor state of repair; four days later, the future of the palace was discussed by the King and Lord

North, his First Minister; and on 17 May, the King authorised demolition. This was part of a deal by which Buckingham House became the Queen's official dower house in place of Somerset House. The arrangement was formalised by an Act of Parliament in April 1775, which reimbursed the King for the cost of buying Buckingham House and adapting it as a royal residence.

The architect first appointed by the Treasury in 1774 for Somerset House was William Robinson, Secretary to the Board of Works and a close architectural accomplice of the King. William Chambers, as Comptroller of the Board, had a better claim than Robinson to the prestigious commission for what would be 'the largest building operation carried out at public expense during the Georgian era'.[15] A keen francophile, Chambers was out of the country in May 1774, studying the new public buildings in Paris by architects such as Gabriel, Gondoin, Antoine, and Chalgrin. On his return, Chambers began a campaign of denigrating Robinson whose unexpected death in October 1775 enabled Chambers to take over the commission.

Chambers, as we have seen, was an admirer of Parisian public buildings such as the École de Chirurgie (School of Surgery) of 1769–75, by Jacques Gondoin, who published a handsome monograph on this much-visited building, *Description des écoles de chirurgie* (Paris 1780). Here, Gondoin explained its role as a modern Temple of Aesculapius, a piece of narrative architecture which, through its deployment of the orders and ornament, explained its purpose at every turn. Chambers ensured that Somerset House was fully described in various newspapers in 1778,[16] and that these accounts were brought together by Giuseppe (Joseph) Baretti (1719–89), Secretary for Foreign Correspondence to the Royal Academy from 1769 to 1789, in his pamphlet, *Guide through the Royal Academy* (1781).[17]

Chambers had absorbed the doctrine of appropriate character in architecture from his master, Jacques-François Blondel, who had taught Gondoin as well as most of the leading French architects of the day. In his *Treatise on Civil Architecture* (1759), to which Blondel was a subscriber, Chambers developed the theory of architecture as language, explaining how 'materials in architecture are like words in phraseology . . . they actuate the mind with unbounded sway.'[18] At Somerset House he put this into practice in a number of ways. To begin with, in the design of its Strand front, Chambers echoed a much-admired element of old Somerset House. This was the New Gallery (seen to the left in fig. 72), then attributed to Inigo Jones, though today known to have been built in 1662–3 by Jones's pupil, John Webb,

15   Colvin, ed., *King's Works*, vol. v, p. 363.
16   *ibid.*, p. 372, n. 1.
17   See Jenkins, 'External sculptural decoration of Somerset House'.
18   Chambers, *Treatise*, 1791 edn., p. 3.

for Queen Henrietta Maria. Chambers chose this Jonesian building as a source of inspiration for it had, reluctantly, to be demolished to make way for the new Somerset House. He and George III had already used the New Gallery as a theme in their third and fourth projects for the new Richmond Palace (figs. 62, 63).[19]

Somerset House was interpreted as a royal building in Baretti's learned, 32-page account, bristling with references to writers such as Vasari, Baldinucci, and Winckelmann. The Strand block with its premises for the learned societies, he described as 'that part of the design which Royal Munificence has appropriated to the reception of polite Arts, ancient knowledge, and modern philosophy'.[20] Chambers gave the building appropriate resonance through the use of carved symbolical ornament, including, on the attic of the Strand front, four male figures symbolising the stoic virtues: 'Justice, Prudence, Valour and Moderation; Qualities by which Dominion can alone be maintained'.[21] Baretti wrote of the head of the old man representing the Ocean over the central arch that 'round his temple is bound a regal Tiara, adorned with crowns, tridents, and other marks of Royalty.' Tablets spreading over the architrave and frieze contain 'basso-relievo medallions of the King, Queen, and Prince of Wales, supported by lions', while centrally placed above this is a colossal group of the Arms of the British Empire by John Bacon, RA, flanked by Fame and the Genius of England with a festoon of laurel and the insignia of the Order of the Garter. The colonnaded entrance is adorned with the 'cyphers of their Majesties and the Prince of Wales'.[22] Previous Palladian architects had not ornamented their buildings with sculpture in this way, but Chambers brought welcome commissions to the principal sculptor members of the Royal Academy. He seems to have commissioned this costly work without formal reference to the Treasury but in consultation with Lord North and the King.

Trained at the newly established Royal Academy schools in 1769, Bacon was a favourite sculptor of George III (fig. 74), particularly following the sittings at Buckingham House for the bust which he made of the King in 1770 for Christ Church, Oxford. The King admired this so much that he ordered several copies to be made, including one for presentation to the University of Göttingen. It will thus have been with royal approval that Bacon was chosen as the sculptor for the monumental statue of George III in the centre of the courtyard at Somerset House. Carved by Bacon in 1778–83 at a cost of £2,270 5s, it was – unusually for this period – cast in bronze. Based on a drawing of around 1775 by Giovanni Battista Cipriani (fig. 75),[23]

19 Newman, 'Somerset House and Other Public Buildings', in Harris and Snodin, *Chambers*, p. 118.

20 Baretti, *Guide*, pp. 4–5.

21 *ibid.*, p. 6.

22 *ibid.*, pp. 6–7.

23 Royal Library, Windsor Castle. See Oppé, *English Drawings*, no. 120.

FIG. 74 John Bacon,
George III, 1775. Marble.
RCIN 31610

FIG. 75 Giovanni Battista
Cipriani, *Design for the
monument to George III in
the courtyard of Somerset
House*, c.1775. Pen and
ink and wash.
RL 13248

it forms the centrepiece of an ambitious group that includes a fountain. In 1755 Chambers
and Joseph Wilton had brought Cipriani from Rome to London where he became a founder
member of the Royal Academy and taught in its Schools from 1769 to 1779.

    The King encouraged Bacon and promoted his neo-classical style so that in the statue of
the King conceived by Cipriani and Bacon, he wears ancient Roman dress.[24] This was in
accordance with the precepts of Sir Joshua Reynolds who informed the students at the Royal
Academy that 'the familiarity of the modern dress by no means agrees with the dignity and
gravity of Sculpture.'[25] It is presumed that he was referring to the modern military uniform
worn by the Duke of Cumberland in Henry Cheere's statue of him (1770) in Cavendish
Square. Queen Charlotte did not share her husband's enthusiasm for Bacon, for she is
supposed to have asked him of his statue at Somerset House, 'Why did you make so frightful
a figure?' Bacon replied obscurely, 'Art cannot always effect what is ever within the reach of
Nature – the union of beauty and majesty.'[26]

24   The only other statue of George III in London, the handsome bronze
    equestrian monument (1836) by Matthew Cotes Wyatt in Cockspur
    Street, depicts him in modern dress.

25   Reynolds, *Discourses*, p. 187.

26   Blackwood, *London's Immortals*, pp. 42–4.

In his statue of George III, the ample folds of the King's toga are reflected in the rich curls of his hair, while he holds a large rudder in his left hand and a laurel sprig in his right. At his feet are the lion of England and the ornamental prow of a Roman ship. In front of the tall pedestal on which this group stands is a bearded figure of Father Thames, seated on a rock against a cornucopia and discharging water from an inverted urn. The models are the famous figures of the Nile and of the Tiber in the Vatican and the Louvre respectively. A fairer judgement of Bacon's statue than Queen Charlotte's might be to see it as a figure of strength yet also of benevolence, uniting the virtues of ancient Rome with those of modern England, and combining harmoniously with its architectural setting.[27]

Benjamin West, shortly after succeeding Reynolds as President of the Royal Academy in 1792, proudly commemorated his association with the King and the Academy in a self-portrait in which he holds the instrument of its foundation, signed by the King in December 1768.[28] Also included as a demonstration of his personal artistic programme are a volume called *History of England*, possibly by David Hume, and a Bible. But the most prominent feature is a large portrait of George III in profile as a Roman emperor, crowned with a laurel wreath. It was in such a mood that Joseph Baretti, hailing Somerset House as a 'new Seminary of Arts', and, describing the casts of antique sculpture which it contained, wrote, 'Let us confidently hope in the present hour of Royal Patronage, that productions of equal perfection will soon be added to them by the rising genius of the British School.'[29] As a palatial building with representations of the King and his realm in sculpture and symbolical ornament, Somerset House is almost a substitute for the palace at Richmond which he and Chambers planned for so many years. Indeed, it is architecturally extremely reminiscent of the later designs for that palace (figs. 62, 63).

---

27 However, modern critics have followed the opinion attributed to Queen Charlotte: John Harris describes 'Bacon's unfortunately mundane statue of George III, rising like a mechanical *Tableau* from the Piranesian vaults' (J. Harris, *Chambers*, p. 102), while Howard Colvin dismisses it as 'rather insipid' (*King's Works*, vol. v, p. 373).

Neither author makes any reference to the other figures in the group as a whole as designed by Cipriani.

28 The property of the Society of Dilettanti. See Erffa, *West*, pp. 452–3 and plate on p. 3.

29 Baretti, *Guide*, p. 32.

5

THE ARCHITECTURE OF CHIVALRY AND THE RETURN TO WINDSOR

FIG. 76 James Fittler after George Robertson, *South-east view of Windsor Castle (with the Queen's Lodge and the Royal Family on the South Terrace)*, 1783. Engraving. RCIN 700380

The first two Hanoverian monarchs had been indifferent to Windsor Castle, but in the 1770s George III conceived the idea of returning to take up residence there. Together with his interest in chivalry from the late 1780s, this not surprisingly encouraged a shift to a Gothic style akin to that which Paine and Adam had employed at Alnwick. Unable to use the decaying royal apartments at Windsor, George III had a plan made in 1776, probably by William Chambers, for turning the south range of the Upper Ward into convenient apartments, linked with a new west range. When this was rejected as too expensive, he enlarged Queen Anne's 'Garden House', a redbrick house of around 1690, just to the south of the castle, renaming it the Queen's Lodge (fig. 76). To serve as a subsidiary residence during the royal family's visits to Windsor, he remodelled the nearby Burford House, naming it Lower Lodge. With Chambers as the executant architect, these emerged in 1776–82 as somewhat bleak, castellated blocks for which the King is believed to have drawn up the first designs. The Queen's Lodge was faced in grey stucco except for the porch which was in stone and adorned with Garter imagery – stars and garters.

George III's initial step in rehabilitating medieval England, chivalry, and the Gothic style was the commissioning of a cycle of history paintings for Windsor Castle from Benjamin West who, as we have seen, had become his favourite painter. The King subsequently emphasised the ceremonies of the Order of the Garter, elaborating their setting at Windsor, St George's Chapel, with new Gothic work. He went on to rebuild part of the Upper Ward at Windsor in the Gothic style, then being hailed as the national style. Carried out when the country was under the threat of a Napoleonic invasion, this work was successful in reinventing the image of the monarch and the castle as historic symbols of nationhood.[1]

The King's Audience Chamber, Edward III, and Chivalry

The King's interest in chivalry and Gothic architecture was stimulated by his friendship with Richard Hurd, whose passion for books and for book collecting he also shared. In 1774 he appointed Hurd Bishop of Lichfield and two years later to the important office of tutor, or preceptor, to the Prince of Wales and Prince Frederick, the future Duke of York. It seems that it was on the strength of Hurd's two

---

1   See Colley, 'Apotheosis of George III', and *Britons*.

Dialogues 'On the Constitution of the English Government', which were included in his *Moral and Political Dialogues* (1759), that the King chose him for the tutorship of his sons. The antiquary Francis Kilvert, nephew of Hurd's chaplain, Richard Kilvert, claimed that these Dialogues were seen as making Hurd 'eminently qualified to direct the education of a future sovereign'.[2] Another of Hurd's chaplains, the Revd William Arnald, was also appointed subpreceptor to the two Princes.

Hurd had praised chivalry as early as 1759 in his *Moral and Political Dialogues*, while in his *Letters on Chivalry and Romance* (1762; 3rd edn. 1765), he became an important early vindicator of medieval literature and Gothic art from imputations of barbarism. Kenneth Clark wrote that, 'Hurd, "the last man to wear stiff-topped gloves", was perhaps the most curious of those unconscious Romantics, at once the most "donnish" and the most revolutionary,'[3] while Dr Johnson declared, 'Hurd, Sir, is a man whose acquaintance is a valuable acquisition.'[4] In his *Letters on Chivalry and Romance*, Hurd praised what he called Gothic chivalry as well as Spenser, Shakespeare, and Milton, drawing parallels between the epics of Homer and chivalric romances, and claiming that 'Greek antiquity very much resembles the Gothic.'[5] Parallels of this kind had been made in *Amadis of Gaul*, the chivalrous romance from medieval Spain or Portugal, which was popular in translation in England in the seventeenth century. It would almost certainly have been known to Hurd.

Attracted in the late 1780s by the close connection between chivalry and kingship, the King commissioned Benjamin West to paint a cycle of seven great history paintings which glorified the military and chivalric career of Edward III, Queen Philippa, and the Black Prince.[6] In venerating the Black Prince, George III was following the example of his father who, as we have seen, had commissioned marble busts of him and of King Alfred for his gardens at Carlton House.[7] In the contemporary political propaganda of the anti-Walpole Whigs, King Alfred was hailed as the founder of the English constitution and in particular of English liberty, and the Black Prince as a model of bravery, clemency, and generosity.

Born in Windsor Castle in 1312, Edward III, the Black Prince's father, was known as Edward of Windsor and takes his place with Charles II and George IV as the earliest of the great builders at the Castle. It was he who built much of what George III inherited, paying for it out of the proceeds of his wars in France where he defeated the French at Crécy in 1346 and took Calais in the following year.[8] In 1348 he founded the Most Noble Order of the Knights

2   Kilvert, *Memoirs of … Richard Hurd*, pp. 120–1, and see Eddy, *Bibliography of Richard Hurd*.

3   Clark, *Gothic Revival*, p. 80.

4   Mowbray Morris, *Boswell's Life of Johnson*, p. 598.

5   Hurd, *Moral and Political Dialogues*, 3rd edn, vol. III, p. 237.

6   See Vale, *Edward III and Chivalry*.

7   Rorschach, 'Frederick, Prince of Wales', p. 24.

8   Packe, *Edward III*, pp. 158–61.

FIG. 77 Benjamin West,
*The Institution of the
Order of the Garter*, 1787.
Oil on canvas.
RCIN 407521

of the Garter, about which it has been debated 'Whether it was a throwback to the Arthurian chivalry and the Crusades, or a calculated move in the world of fourteenth-century *Realpolitik*, designed to ensure . . . the loyalty of twenty-four knights'.[9] The founding of the Order formed part of the cycle of paintings commissioned from West (fig. 77). Edward III's son, the Black Prince, captured the King of France at Poitiers in 1356, in which year William of Wykeham was put in charge of the King's Works and began extensive building for Edward III at Windsor.

The 26 foundation Knights of the Garter had all been with Edward III on his campaigns in France. The French motto of the Order, *honi soit qui mal y pense* (Shame to him who thinks ill of it), may have been directed to those who disputed Edward's claim to France, while the dark blue chosen for the mantle worn by the Knights was the colour of the royal coat of arms of France. It has been supposed that the Garter was a strap adopted by the King's party, perhaps at the battle of Crécy. Their patron saint, St George of Antioch, was a warrior saint who, according to tradition, was martyred in Palestine in the third century AD.

The Order acquired tremendous prestige, holding an annual three-day feast including

9   Patterson, *Royal Insignia*, p. 88.

celebrations on 23 April, the feast day of St George. These took place in St George's Hall, a great south-facing room in the Upper Ward of Windsor Castle built by Edward III and later remodelled. To provide a setting for the services of the Order, he also partly rebuilt the chapel which had been begun in 1260 by Henry III in the Lower Ward. Queen Elizabeth I declared that the Garter ceremonies need not take place exclusively at Windsor, while they were revived by Charles I who restored the ancient statutes and the blue mantles of Edward III which had been replaced with red ones. However, the ceremonies were not performed annually under the Stuarts, while the early Hanoverians visited Windsor infrequently. George III was one of the monarchs most committed to Windsor Castle and to its associations with the medieval ceremonies of the Knights of the Garter. 'From the fifteenth century, the bestowal of the Garter on foreign rulers has been used as a way of marking and securing alliances,'[10] though George III used it more to stress the role of the British royal family, especially of his German princely relatives, a point to which we shall return.

The cycle of medieval history paintings commissioned by George III from Benjamin West was to be hung in the King's Audience Chamber (fig. 78) in the suite of rooms in the Upper Ward at Windsor Castle which had been remodelled by Hugh May for Charles II in 1675–84.[11] It was a monumental commission, for three of the paintings measure over fourteen by nine feet. As with the Warm Room at Buckingham House, the scheme was a kind of *Gesamtkunstwerk*, for the paintings were commissioned to be of the right sizes to fit the different spaces and were hung in chronological order. In other words, they were treated as tapestries, another archaising element, for Charles I had proposed a scheme for tapestries on the same theme for his Audience Chamber in Whitehall, now known as the Banqueting House.

Identifying the monarchy with national myth and history, these remarkable paintings reflected the discussions which the King had enjoyed with Hurd and with West who, according to his biographer, Galt, complained that Italian painters had painted 'monkish legends in which no one took any interest, while the great events in the history of their country were but seldom touched.' Galt explained how 'the King, recollecting that Windsor-Castle had, in its present form, been erected by Edward the Third, said that he thought the achievements of his splendid reign were well calculated for pictures, and would prove very suitable ornaments to the halls and chambers of that venerable edifice.'[12]

To execute this ambitious and prestigious commission, which West did remarkably quickly,

10 Patterson, *Royal Insignia*, p. 88, and for George's own spectacular Garter regalia, see pls. 52–3 and 63–4.

11 Erffa, *West*, pp. 192–203. See, too, Girouard, *Return to Camelot*,

pp. 21–6; Strong, *And When did You Last See Your Father?*; and Greenhouse, 'Benjamin West and Edward III'.

12 Galt, *West*, pp. 51–2.

FIG. 78 Charles Wild,
*The King's Audience
Chamber, Windsor Castle,*
1818. Watercolour and
bodycolour over pencil.
RL 22109

he bought a house in Park Street, Windsor, and was given a room in the Castle in which to work. The seven paintings, all completed in 1787–9, are *Edward III Crossing the Somme* [in 1346], *Edward III with the Black Prince after the Battle of Crécy* [in 1346], *Queen Philippa at the Battle of Neville's Cross* [in 1346], *The Institution of the Order of the Garter* [in 1348], *Edward III entertaining his Prisoners at Calais* [in 1349], *Queen Philippa interceding with Edward III for the Burghers of Calais* [in 1349], and *Edward, the Black Prince, receiving King John of France after the Battle of Poitiers* [in 1356].[13] West exhibited the paintings at the Royal Academy between 1787 and 1794, after which they were all hung in the Audience Chamber.[14]

In the scene of Edward III after the Battle of Crécy in 1346, the helmet of the dead King of Bohemia, who had unwisely chosen to fight on the French side, is clearly shown by West with

13 Millar, *Later Georgian Pictures*, nos. 1158–64. For an interesting, if rather exaggerated attempt to relate the paintings to the King's relations with members of his family and to contemporary events

such as the American War of Independence, see Greenhouse, 'Benjamin West and Edward III', pp. 185–8.

14 Knight, *Windsor Guide*, p. 32.

its ostrich feathers and the motto *Ich Dien*. These were the emblems taken for his own use by the Black Prince and his heirs as Prince of Wales, and which he wears in West's depiction of him taking the French King prisoner. To help West, George III lent him a drawing of the sword which had reputedly been surrendered by King John of France to Sir John La Warr, in whose family it had descended. The drawing had been given to the King by his ADC, Lieutenant Colonel William Dansey, who wrote in a letter of 7 October 1788 to John Robinson, Surveyor General of Woods and Forests, that 'on Sunday morning walking the Terrace [of Windsor Castle] Mr West told me he had got the drawing of the sword, which I had given the King, with which he is very much pleased, and will put it in the picture of the Battle, and beg'd I would write to you for the crest of the Warre family which he is very anxious about.'[15] A further reason for West's concern for historical accuracy in the depiction of this scene was that he had convinced himself that he was descended from the Sir Thomas West who had fought at the battle of Crécy and from whom the family of the Earls De La Warr was also descended.[16]

One of the most significant paintings, *The Institution of the Order of the Garter*, takes its place with the other paintings in the cycle as the most important on medieval subjects to be carried out in Europe during the eighteenth century. This and two other large canvases[17] have been on loan from the Royal Collection since 1968 to Barry's Palace of Westminster, an appropriate home since they inaugurated the grandiose manner of romantic history painting which flourished in the nineteenth century. West took advantage of his office as Historical Painter to the King, to which he had been appointed in 1772, to make full use of the royal armouries, heralds, and the King's library, and, like his nineteenth-century successors, he carried out much research into archival and other sources to ensure accuracy. He also had advice from the King himself, who followed the process with his characteristic attention to detail, of which Henry Angelo[18] gives us a vivid description.

> Mr. West had found it necessary to depart from his first plans as he obtained new historical facts, particularly in the armorial bearings. 'But, in no instance,' said Mr. West, 'nor even for the most minute alteration that I made, ever escaped the vigilant memory of His Majesty.' 'I perceive, West,' he would say, 'that you have altered this – ay – and that. It stood so-and-so; I thought you

15   Quoted in White, *Gentleman of Fine Taste*, p. 15.
16   Galt, *The Life and Studies of Benjamin West*, 1816, p. 2.
17   Millar, *Later Georgian Pictures*, nos. 1162–4.
18   Angelo, *Reminiscences*, vol. I, pp. 198–9.

were wrong.' Indeed, the king was learned in heraldry, and often set the heralds themselves right, in certain questions upon their own science.

The books West studied included the *History of England* (1754–62) by David Hume who stressed the modest bearing of the Black Prince in taking the King of France prisoner. For the painting of the inauguration of the Garter, West used Elias Ashmole's book, *The Institution, Laws and Ceremonies of the most Noble Order of the Garter* (1672), and, for the Garter robes, Joseph Strutt's *The Regal and Ecclesiastical Antiquities of England* (1773), a book which was itself part of the reinvention or rehabilitation of medieval England. West shows the altar flanked by kneeling figures of the King and the Prince of Wales, with Edward's wife, Queen Philippa, in red, kneeling near the centre. In the canopied oratory or King's Closet, taking the form of a balcony over the altar, is the King of Scotland, captured at Neville's Cross. Despite his historical study, West made an error with the architectural setting of the painting, for the Gothic interior of the present St George's Chapel was begun by Edward IV in 1478, 130 years after the founding of the Order of the Garter. Also, to associate himself with the pageantry, legitimised by his supposed descent from the De La Warr family, West included the figures of himself and his wife in the painting on the extreme left-hand side.[19]

The significance of this painting is made clear when we realise that the King envisaged the Audience Chamber in which it hung as a Garter Throne Room, where new companions of the Order could be installed.[20] As we have already noted, the room was conceived as a total decorative and iconographical entity. The King chose to retain the ceiling which Verrio painted for Charles II showing the re-establishment of the Church of England at the Restoration in 1660, with personifications of England, Scotland, and Ireland, attended by Faith, Hope, Charity, and the Christian Virtues, but he now fitted the walls with Garter-blue silk hangings sporting flowered borders, gilded the cornice and the mouldings, and added a new chair of state below a grandiose canopy. The canopy was hung with dark blue valances adorned with garlands of flowers which had been executed from designs by Mary Moser at Mrs Pawsey's school of needlework.[21] It contained portrait medallions by West of George III and Queen Charlotte, while the background to the throne was flanked by broad gilded pilasters painted in arabesque by Biagio Rebecca. No less striking was the elaborate chimney-piece, flanked by entwined tridents surmounted by wreaths, which was inserted in 1786,[22]

19 See Abrams, *Valiant Hero*, pp. 32–4 and fig. 13.
20 The King's Audience Chamber was remodelled and reduced in size by Wyatville in the 1820s to serve as the Ante-Throne Room. For a full account of the new fittings made for George III, see H. Roberts,

'Neoclassical Episode at Windsor'.
21 It is probably the one now in the Garter Throne Room (RCIN 35805).
22 Colvin, ed., *King's Works*, vol. VI, p. 374.

possibly to the designs of James 'Athenian' Stuart.[23] The King also commissioned West to paint *St George Slaying the Dragon*[24] to hang over this chimneypiece. In 1787 he proposed the production of an ambitious book on the institution and progress of the Order of the Garter which would include 'large graphic illustrations'.[25] These were to be by Benjamin West with help from the King, but the project was abandoned following the King's illness in 1788.

West and the Chapel of the History of Revealed Religion

The King conceived an even more ambitious project in 1779 of transforming the seventeenth-century Royal Chapel at Windsor Castle as a Chapel of the History of Revealed Religion which was to be hung with 35 large canvases by West on the theme of revealed religion.[26] This formed part of the King's sympathy with the new move to introduce art into Anglican churches, which was first expressed in 1773 when he supported the controversial proposals of the Dean and Chapter of St Paul's to adorn the Cathedral with a great cycle of paintings by six leading members of the Royal Academy: Sir Joshua Reynolds, Benjamin West, Angelica Kauffman, Giovanni Battista Cipriani, James Barry, and Nathaniel Dance. In a petition doubtless drafted by Reynolds, the Academicians argued that 'the art of painting . . . would never grow up to

FIG. 79   Benjamin West, *Design for the altar wall for the King's Chapel, Windsor Castle, c.1779–81*. Bodycolour, pen and ink, and wash on brown paper. RL 17863

FIG. 80   Benjamin West, *Design for a wall for the King's Chapel, Windsor Castle, c.1779–81*. Watercolour, pen and ink, and wash. RL 18992

23   It is no longer in the room, from which it was probably removed by Wyatville, but an almost identical chimneypiece, possibly the same one, is now in the Admiral's Study at Greenwich. See H. Roberts, 'Neoclassical Episode at Windsor', n. 7, and Worsley, 'Out of Adam's Shadow', p. 102 and fig. 7, where it is attributed to 'Athenian' Stuart in c.1765–9.

24   Millar, *Later Georgian Pictures*, no. 1151.

25   According to the *Morning Post* (Whitley, *Artists and Their Friends*, vol. II, pp. 72–3).

26   Erffa, *West*, pp. 577–81, Meyer, 'Benjamin West's Chapel of Revealed Religion', and Pressly, *Revealed Religion*. There are various estimates of the number of paintings and their proposed location.

maturity and perfection, unless it could be introduced into churches, as in foreign countries.'[27] However, despite the King's support, the scheme was abandoned when the Bishop of London, Dr Terrick, declared in fury that 'whilst I live, and have the power, I will never suffer the doors of the Metropolitan Cathedral to be opened for the introduction of Popery.'[28]

Nonetheless, the King 'began to think that the tolerant temper of the age was favourable to the introduction of pictures into the churches',[29] and he expressed his support for images in a Protestant church in his proposed Chapel of the History of Revealed Religion. He commissioned illustrations for this from West of 'subjects from the Bible, susceptible of pictorial representation, which Christians, of all denominations, might contemplate without offence to their tenets'.[30] When objections were made to the fact that West was a Quaker, the King replied that he would undoubtedly be a Quaker himself but for the accident of his birth. In the presence of West, the King consulted church dignitaries, notably Bishop Hurd, at Windsor about the programme for this commission.[31] According to one account, West

> was a good deal startled, upon being shown into a room there, to find it filled with bishops . . . [but] The King kept smiling whilst the painter was speaking, and, at the conclusion, said, with an air of triumph, 'You see how well *he* understands these things, for whilst you bishops have been spending your time amongst heathen fables, he has been studying his Bible![32]

West worked between 1779 and 1801 on what was one of the most extensive projects in the history of British art, largely inspired by *The Divine Legation of Moses Demonstrated* (1738) by Hurd's friend, Bishop Warburton. The classical treatment with which it was proposed to transform Hugh May's Baroque interior of the 1670s and '80s with its paintings by Verrio is known from a number of drawings from around 1780 which are attributed to Benjamin West (figs. 79, 80) and William Chambers.[33] One of the drawings (fig. 80) shows the walls divided by classical pilasters with stylised plant ornament in the manner of Chambers or Stuart; another has more conventional coupled Corinthian pilasters separating arched niches which are flanked by large figures of angels revealing the paintings by drawing back simulated drapery. A drawing for the altar wall (fig. 79) shows it dominated by a vast canvas of *Moses Receiving the Laws on Mount Sinai* with, below it, a small painting of the Last Supper hung immediately over the

27 Newton, *Works*, vol. I, 'Life and Anecdotes', pp. 105–6.
28 Leslie and Taylor, *Life and Times of Sir Joshua Reynolds*, vol. II, p. 38.
29 Galt, *West*, p. 52.
30 *ibid.*, p. 53.
31 See Dillenberger, *Benjamin West*, pp. 44–94, where it is claimed that 'the paintings would have dominated the total space …

like the Sistine Chapel or like the Arena Chapel in Padua.'
32 Fletcher, *Conversations of James Northcote*, pp. 154–5.
33 The most important are four in the Royal Library, Windsor Castle, and one at the Yale Center for British Art, New Haven. See Meyer, Benjamin West's Chapel of Revealed Religion', figs 1–4 and 6, Erffa, *West*, Appendix I, pp. 577–81, and Pressly, *Revealed Religion*.

altar.[34] The niches flanking the painting of Moses, left blank in the drawing, were to contain canvases of *The Call of Isaiah* and *The Call of Jeremiah*.[35] The disposition of this wall, with its flanking doors below arched niches, retained that of the altar wall of the late seventeenth-century Royal Chapel.

The Royal Academicians drew up an address to the King congratulating him on a scheme in which 'you have directed the arts to their true end, the cultivation of religion and virtue; for it is by such means only that they have risen to perfection in Greece and Italy.'[36] It seems that when James Wyatt succeeded Chambers as architect at Windsor in 1796, he proposed that West's paintings should be incorporated into a new chapel to be formed on the site of the internal courtyard in the Upper Ward known as Horn Court. However, the whole scheme was abandoned in 1801, partly because the classicising paintings no longer fitted into the Gothic castle as conceived by George III and James Wyatt. It also seems that the King had been worried by West's move from his earlier and calmer Raphaelesque mood to something

34 These two paintings are today respectively at the Palace of Westminster and the Tate Gallery.

35 According to the *Catalogue Raisonné of the … Historical Papers … [of] the late Benjamin West … which will be Sold By Auction,* 22, 23 and 25 May 1829, pp. 27 and 38–9. The two paintings are in the Musée des Beaux-Arts, Bordeaux.

36 Leslie and Taylor, *Life and Times of Sir Joshua Reynolds*, vol. II, p. 39.

FIG. 81 Benjamin West,
*George III resuming power
in 1789*, 1789. Oil on
canvas. New York,
Hirschl & Adler Galleries

approaching a Burkean sublime.[37] The eighteen completed paintings were eventually returned to West's sons, and Horn Court was converted by Wyatville as the Waterloo Chamber. The commissioning by George IV of portraits of the victors of the Napoleonic Wars for this newly formed room turned it into a secular counterpart to what his father had proposed.

The King's recovery in 1789 was made the subject of a remarkable emblematic painting which West painted in that year to celebrate his resumption of power (fig. 81).[38] The composition is also recorded in an attractive preparatory drawing in the Royal Collection.[39] In the finished painting, a burst of divine light appears from heaven, as in an icon, above the King's head as he marches confidently towards the throne on which rest the crown and sceptre. Most unusually, the composition is dominated by three large columns which bear shields carrying inscriptions. In front of the columns stand three groups of figures whose virtues the columns represent in a reference to the supposed anthropomorphic origin of the classical orders. Going back to Vitruvius, this is a tradition which West and the King will have known. At the same time, the symbolic columns recall Masonic iconography, as in the frontispiece to Batty Langley's *The Builder's Jewel* (1741) where three columns are hung with symbolic labels, while the Doric column is also marked W for Wisdom, the Tuscan S for Strength, and the Corinthian B for Beauty.[40]

To the left of the throne stand the President of the Privy Council and the Lord Chancellor; on the right, William Pitt. The left column, in the richest order, the Corinthian, represents the members of the House of Lords who had supported the King's cause during his illness. Inscribed 'Honour', it bears the number of those voting on the side of the King and Queen. Next to it is a stern Doric column, inscribed 'Virtue', representing the Members of the House of Commons, and similarly bearing the relevant number of votes. The right column, also Doric, is inscribed 'Science' and refers to the doctors who cured him. In the background is the Round Tower of Windsor Castle with the Royal Standard flying, for it was to Windsor that the King returned in triumph on his recovery on 14 March 1789. West is supposed to have displayed a transparency of this subject outside his own house in March 1789. The King's recovery was also marked by a transparency designed by Biagio Rebecca. Mrs Charlotte Papendiek (1765–1839), 'Assistant Keeper of the Wardrobe and Reader to Her Majesty', recorded in March 1789 that the Queen, 'from her privy purse, gave private orders for a splendid illumination at this palace; Rebecca painted a beautiful transparency.'[41] She also

37 *Farington Diary*, vol. VI, 1 December 1804, p. 2461.

38 See Erffa, *West*, p. 220 and pl. 107, and Lloyd, *Quest for Albion*, pp. 12–13 and fig. 5.

39 RL 17721, and Oppé, *English Drawings*, no. 641, where the subject is misidentified.

40 E. Harris and N. Savage, *Architectural Books*, pp. 264–5.

41 Barrett, *D'Arblay Diary*, vol. III, Tuesday, 10 March 1789, p. 171.

described the elaborate transparencies which illuminated public buildings in London for three nights later in the month, including the Bank of England, East India House, and the Army Pay Office in Whitehall, and a triumphal arch erected at Hyde Park Gate. Thomas Jefferson's young friend, Thomas Lee Shippen, wrote to him enthusiastically from London that, 'the illuminations here last Thursday were so universal brilliant and beautiful that I cannot help mentioning them to you . . . It was a wonderful display of wealth luxury and population beyond all example and not a little taste in the decoration of the houses graced the shew.'[42]

Mrs Papendiek described a celebratory banquet in St George's Hall at this time with 'several ornamental dishes such as I had never seen before. Temples in barley sugar, four feet high, and other devices introducing the motto and emblematic of peace and joy.'[43] Ephemeral art of this kind, making striking use of architecture and architectural ornament, was clearly an important feature of the reign of George III, but it seems to have left little visual record.

Royal Visits to Historic Houses

It is not always appreciated that George III and his Queen were the first British monarchs since King James I who travelled frequently in their kingdom. The country houses they stayed in or visited in the 1770s and '80s included Thorndon Hall, Essex; Wilton House and Tottenham Park, Wiltshire; Lulworth Castle and Sherborne Castle, Dorset; Cotehele and Mount Edgcumbe, Cornwall; Bulstrode Park, Buckinghamshire; Nuneham Courtenay, Oxfordshire; and Hartlebury Castle and Croome Court, Worcestershire. There is documentary evidence showing the King's passion for touring country houses, leading almost to a revival of the progresses of Stuart monarchs. The visits of relevance to us in the context of his attitude to Windsor are those he made in 1789 to three historic houses, Cotehele, Lulworth, and Sherborne.[44] Though standard biographies of George III do not mention these visits, these houses, which were rich in association, may well have had an influence on his own building activities in the Gothic style at Windsor and Kew Palace.

One friend from whom George III derived an interest in the romance of chivalry was Bishop Hurd, whose closeness to the King was evidenced in his role in the proposed cycle of paintings representing revealed religion at Windsor. This was followed by Hurd's visits to Windsor to confirm Prince Edward and Princess Augusta in May and December 1785 respectively, and to preach on Christmas Day in 1785 and 1786. When Dr John Thomas, Bishop of

42   Boyd, *Jefferson*, vol. IX, p. 666.

43   Papendiek, *Court and Private Life*, vol. II, pp. 69–72 and 101.

44   On these visits, known partly from Queen Charlotte's diary for August

to December 1789 in the Royal Archives (her only other diary being for 1794), see John Cornforth, 'Fit for a King', *Country Life*, 21 May 1992, pp. 54–7.

HARTLEBURY CASTLE

Winchester, died on 1 May 1781, the King immediately decided to offer the see of Winchester to the Hon. Brownlow North, Bishop of Worcester, thus leaving Worcester free for his friend, Hurd. Indeed, Hurd received a personal letter from the King offering him the bishopric of Worcester the morning after Dr Thomas's death. Accepting the appointment enabled Hurd to take possession of the noble residences in which the bishop was housed: a palace in Worcester, a massive eleven-bay early Georgian pile built onto a thirteenth-century core, as well as Hartlebury Castle, a romantic moated palace in an historic deer park (fig. 82).

In 1781–2 Hurd added to Hartlebury a magnificent library, 84 feet long, following his purchase in 1779 of the library of William Warburton (1689–1779), chaplain to George III, Dean of Bristol, and Bishop of Gloucester. An admirer of Hurd and a Shakespearean scholar, Warburton had been a close friend of Alexander Pope. George III gave Hurd several hundred books for his library at Hartlebury from at least as early as 1782.[45] In 1790 the King gave Hurd versions of the Gainsborough portraits of himself and Queen Charlotte to hang in his palace at Worcester. The paintings were made in different sizes, three enormous and three more modest, to match the wall spaces. The King, in turn, owned two portraits of Hurd by Gainsborough, one of which was commissioned by the Queen in 1781 and hung in her

45 Hurd wrote to the King from Hartlebury Castle on 16 July 1782, noting that he had received 'the German Latin books, which Your Majesty was pleased to order for me' (Fortescue, *Correspondence of King George the Third*, vol. VI, p. 87).

FIG. 83 James Ross, *View of the Royal China Manufactory in the City of Worcester*, 1795 (V. Green, *The History and Antiquities of Worcester*, vol. II, 1796, plate facing p. 19). Engraving. RCIN 1140643

bedroom at the Queen's House.[46] The other was moved from the King's Closet at the Queen's House to the Council Room in the King's Private Apartments at Windsor Castle in 1804.[47]

In 1783 George III attempted unsuccessfully to persuade Hurd to accept the archbishopric of Canterbury and paid him further tributes by staying with him in 1788 at Hartlebury Castle from 2 to 4 August and at Bishop's Palace, Worcester, from 5 to 7 August.[48] Accompanied by Queen Charlotte, the Duke of York, the Princess Royal, and Princesses Elizabeth and Augusta, the King took breakfast with Hurd in the library. This was by no means a wholly private visit for, later in the day, the King showed himself to as many as 8,000 of his loyal subjects 'ranged row on row up the natural amphitheatre formed by that corner of the park'.[49]

While staying with Bishop Hurd at Worcester in August, the King heard the *Messiah* at the

46 See Rosenthal, *Art of Thomas Gainsborough*, p. 101 and pls. 74 and 96.

47 Millar, *Later Georgian Pictures*, pp. 41–2 and pls. 71–2.

48 For accounts of their visit, see Green, *History and Antiquities of … Worcester*, vol. I, pp. 296–300, and *Gentleman's Magazine*, vol. LVIII,

1788, ii, pp. 755–7, 757–9, and 1075–6, which includes their visits to Cheltenham and Tewkesbury.

49 Pearce, *Hartlebury Castle*, p. 306.

Three Choirs Festival at Worcester Cathedral, visited country houses, and walked through the streets of Worcester and Cheltenham arm in arm with the Queen, accompanied by only one soldier. In Worcester they visited Flight's celebrated porcelain shop and manufactory, leaving orders for many pieces and granting the firm a Royal Warrant (fig. 83).[50] They also inspected Michael and Watkins's carpet manufactory, again making orders.[51] They visited ordinary people in their houses, as at Windsor, but here 'his doings were reported in the newspapers and the whole country learnt about them.'[52] The crowds grew ever greater, the Queen being told by magistrates that at one point between fifty and sixty thousand people had gathered to see them.

One reason for the royal expedition of August 1788 was that the King's doctors thought that his intermittent bouts of illness would be cured by taking the waters in Cheltenham, but, unhappily, his most serious attack of porphyria began in October that same year. However, the King brought Hurd to Windsor on Saturday 15 March 1789 as part of the events celebrating his return to Windsor that day, following his recovery from his illness. After fireworks that evening, he 'renewed his public service at church [next morning], by taking the Sacrament' at a service at which 'Bishop Hurd preached an excellent sermon, with one allusion to the King's recovery, delicately touched and quickly passed over.'[53]

Thinking his convalescence would be promoted by sea air and sea-bathing, the King embarked on a prolonged visit to the West Country in June 1789. The journey was made the subject of a popular booklet, 112 pages long, called *A Diary of the Royal Tour, in June, July, August, and September, 1789*, of which one of the aims was evidently to reassure the public that he had returned to sanity. He spent the first five days in June at the King's House at Lyndhurst. Fanny Burney, who had been appointed Second Keeper of the Robes to the Queen in 1786, described how, on entering the New Forest, the King was given by custom a pair of milk-white greyhounds, specially decorated, at a ceremony attended by 'The bowmen and archers and bugle-horns [who] are to attend the King while he stays here, in all his rides'.[54] The King's House was a royal hunting lodge enlarged by Charles II and incorporating the late-Elizabethan redbrick Verderer's Hall.[55] During his stay here the King allowed the crowds of well-wishers to come up to the house to watch him eating. The royal party spent much time at Weymouth as well as staying in a succession of country houses, not returning to Windsor until mid-September. During precisely these months in the summer of 1789, while the King was being welcomed everywhere by vast crowds of cheering subjects, the dramatic

50 The firm changed its name to Flight and Barr in 1792.

51 Green, *History and Antiquities … of Worcester*, pp. 298 and 300. On the significance of the King's promotion of the porcelain and carpet industry, see Sandon, *Flight and Barr*, pp. 16–21.

52 Brooke, *George III*, p. 323.

53 Barrett, *D'Arblay Diary*, vol. III, p. 173.

54 *ibid.*, p. 188.

55 Colvin, ed., *King's Works*, vol. v, *1660–1782*, pp. 205–7 and fig. 11.

events of the French Revolution were unfolding across the Channel.

While staying at Saltram in Cornwall, the royal party visited Cotehele, the romantic early-Tudor manor house which had been in the possession of the Edgcumbe family since the mid-fourteenth century (figs. 84, 85). Sir Richard Edgcumbe, who had fought at the side of Henry Tudor at the Battle of Bosworth in 1485, had remodelled the house, while his son Piers, created knight-banneret by Henry VIII, completed the building, including the great hall, in the 1530s. At the time of George III's visit in 1789, the owner of Cotehele was George Edgcumbe (1720–95), Viscount Mount Edgcumbe, a member of the Society of Dilettanti, a Fellow of the Society of Antiquaries, and a friend of Sir Horace Mann, with whom he had stayed in Florence.[56] The King raised him to the rank of earl to mark his visit to Cotehele.

The royal party arrived at Cotehele via the River Tamar in the private barge of the 19-year-old Lord Boringdon, the owner of Saltram. Having been conveyed from the river in 'Triumphal cars . . . , On their arrival at the outer gate twenty-one pateraroes were fired.' After viewing 'the ancient curiosities of the castle, amongst which are several pieces of old armour', they took breakfast in the present Old Drawing Room, with its Gothic porch and linenfold panelling. The consciously historic display of furniture at Cotehele, as well as the antiquarian flavour of some of the interior decoration, may have been due to the medieval-ising tastes of the King's host, the Earl of Mount Edgcumbe, for both he and his wife were close friends of Horace Walpole.[57] In 1769 Lord Mount Edgcumbe had restored the Chapel on the Cliff at Cotehele to commemorate the family hero, Sir Richard Edgcumbe, who had died in 1489, and also commissioned an antiquarian painting of Sir Richard's tomb at Morlaix in Brittany.[58]

The importance of the royal visit is suggested by the fact that Queen Charlotte kept a surprisingly detailed account of it in her diary, where she described 'a large Hall full of Old Armor & Swords & Old Carved Chairs of the Times', and elsewhere 'Old Tapestry . . . [and] Chair Seats made of the Priests Vestments'. She recorded that 'At Breakfast we Eat off the

FIG. 84 Nicholas Condy, *The Quadrangle, Cotehele, Cornwall*, 1857 (N. Condy, *Cothele*, facing p. 6). Lithograph by Day and Haghe. RCIN 1140763

FIG. 85 Nicholas Condy, *The Hall, Cotehele, Cornwall*, 1857 (N. Condy, *Cothele*, facing p. 12). Lithograph by Day and Haghe. RCIN 1140763

56   Ingamells, *Dictionary*, p. 329.

57   For a discussion of this, see Cornforth, 'Cotehele'.

58   Probably intended for the Chapel, this is today kept in the house.

Day & Haghe Lith.rs to the Queen.

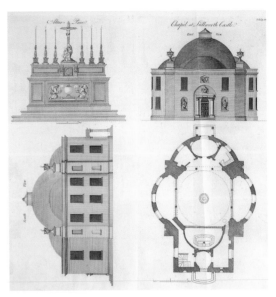

FIG. 86 James Fittler, *Lullworth Castle, Dorset*, 1789 (J. Hutchins, *The History and Antiquities of Dorset*, vol. 1, 1796, facing p. 227). Engraving. RCIN 1070421

FIG. 87 *The Chapel at Lulworth*, 1796 (J. Hutchins, *The History and Antiquities of Dorset*, vol. 1, 1796, facing p. 228). Engraving. RCIN 1070421

Old Family Pewter, & used Silver knives Forks & Spoons which have been Time immemorial in the Family & have always been kept at this place.'[59]

In August 1789 the King and his party moved on to Lulworth Castle, a romantic sham castle with no defensive function, built in 1608 as an echo of Spenser's *Faerie Queene* (fig. 86).[60] They were received in this crenellated essay in nostalgia by Thomas Weld (1750–1810), who had helped found the Jesuit College at Stonyhurst, and his wife, both from ancient Catholic families. The King was on friendly terms with several of his Roman Catholic subjects and gave a generous life pension to Prince Henry Benedict, the Cardinal Duke of York, Henry IX, in 1799. However, on his visit to Lulworth, the Prince of Wales's illegal marriage in 1785 to the widow of Thomas Weld's brother might have caused some embarrassment.[61] Fanny Burney noted that 'They show one room in which two of our Kings have slept; Charles II. and poor James II.' Describing the Castle as 'built with four turrets . . . and fitted up with great elegance', she found the chapel 'truly elegant, – a Pantheon in miniature', and containing 'superb' vestments (fig. 87). Built for Thomas Weld from designs by John Tasker in 1786–7, this was the first free-standing Catholic chapel built for public worship since the Reformation.[62] According to a family tradition, when Thomas Weld wanted to build a chapel at Lulworth, George III said to him, 'Build a family mausoleum and you can furnish the inside as a Catholic chapel if you wish.' It is interesting that the King saw this building on completion, since it was illegal to build a Catholic chapel before the Catholic Relief Act of 1791. Designed by James Wyatt, who became the King's own favourite architect, this domed, centrally planned chapel at Lulworth owed something to Wyatt's famous Pantheon in Oxford Street (fig. 17). Its magnificent altar was designed by

---

59 Cornforth, 'Cotehele', p. 68.

60 Manco, *et al.*, 'Lulworth Castle'.

61 After Edward Weld's death in 1775, his widow, Maria, married Thomas Fitzherbert who also predeceased her. As Fanny D'Arblay pointed out, it was a 'singular circumstance, that their Majesties should visit a house in which, so few years ago, *she* might have received them'.

62 Manco and Kelly, 'Lulworth Castle from 1700', where the visit of King George III and Queen Charlotte is not mentioned.

Giacomo Quarenghi for the Jesuit college at Bruges. Fanny Burney described how 'The altar is all of finest variegated marbles, and precious stones are glittering from every angle.'[63]

During the same stay in Weymouth, the King and the Royal Family visited Lord Digby at his historic seat, Sherborne Castle, Dorset. This would have been of particular interest to the King as it was in origin a hunting lodge built in the 1590s on land bought from Elizabeth I by her favourite, Sir Walter Raleigh. It was briefly a residence of William of Orange during the Revolution of 1688 when, according to tradition, his first proclamations following his accession as William III were printed in the castle. Partly to prepare for the visit of George III, Lord Digby had added a wing to the castle to match the Elizabethan and Jacobean style of earlier parts. It has recently been suggested that, 'Only three weeks before, England had received with disbelief news of the fall of the Bastille . . . [so] the sight of England's constitutional monarch mingling happily with the crowd in his inspection of the Digbys' ancient seat and their modern improvements, was a moment of thought-provoking thanksgiving.'[64]

Like many of his generation, Bishop Hurd made the shift from Whig to Tory during the Terror following the French Revolution. Indeed, when the country was under threat from invasion by French forces, the King wrote to the 74-year-old Hurd to say that 'it has been thought by some of my friends' that, in the event of an invasion, he and his family should take refuge with Hurd in the episcopal palace at Worcester or at Hartlebury Castle.[65] Hurd swiftly wrote a letter of acceptance,[66] though this rather improbable plan was not adopted. Instead, a remarkable set of barracks was built in 1803 at Weedon, Northamptonshire, containing three pavilions to house the King in case of invasion. The site was selected as the furthest point from any coast.

In the context of the appreciation of a medieval and chivalric past provided by the King's friendship with Hurd and his visits to historic houses, we should mention the tastes of his chaplain from 1769, Dr Thomas Percy (1729–1811), editor of *Reliques of Antient English Poetry* (1765), and *Northern Antiquities* (1770). Dr Johnson, who stayed with him for some weeks in his rectory in 1764, described Percy in 1778 as 'a man out of whose company I never go without having learned something'.[67] With Percy's *Reliques*, antiquarianism enters into the mainstream of British writings, for he established 'a genealogy for English poetry that was native rather than grafted from Greece and Rome, seeing the true roots of English verse, as of Englishness and Britishness, as bedded in gothic soil'.[68]

63 Barrett, *D'Arblay Diary*, p. 201.
64 Smith and Hall, 'Sherborne Castle', p. 46.
65 Fortescue, *Correspondence of King George the Third*, vol. VI, 30 November 1803, p. 143.
66 *ibid.*, 3 December 1803, pp. 143–4.
67 Mowbray Morris, *Boswell's Life of Johnson*, p. 462.
68 Brooks, *Gothic Revival*, p. 109.

Percy, whose real name was Piercy, was the son of a grocer but claimed descent from the Percys, Earls of Northumberland. Indeed, he became chaplain to the 1st Duke of Northumberland (1714–86) and was subsequently appointed to the bishopric of Dromore by George III. The Duke of Northumberland, born Hugh Smithson, was created Earl of Northumberland in 1750 and Duke of Northumberland in 1766. A key figure in the court of George III, he was a close friend of the Earl of Bute, whose daughter married his eldest son, though they were later divorced. The King made him a member of the Privy Council and Chamberlain of the Queen's Household in 1762, raised him to the Dukedom in 1766, and appointed him Master of the Horse in 1778.[69] The Duchess of Northumberland was a Lady of the Bedchamber to the Queen.

In 1770 Dr Thomas Percy published for the Duke a manuscript which the Duke had recently acquired, *The Household Book of the Earl of Northumberland in 1512 at his Castles of Wressle and Leconfield in Yorkshire.* Obsessed by the antiquity of the family of his wife who was the heir to the Percys, Earls of Northumberland, the Duke kept up a great neo-feudal state at Alnwick Castle, Northumberland, Syon House, Middlesex, and Northumberland House, Charing Cross. James Boswell, attending a rout at Northumberland House in December 1762, described his hosts as 'a noble family in every respect. They live in a most princely manner, perfectly suitable to their high rank. They keep up the true figure of old English nobility.'[70] In *The Household Book*, the Duke and Duchess could find an historical justification for this splendour for, as Percy wrote in his Preface

> Here we see the great magnificence of our old nobility, who seated in their
> castles, lived in a state and splendour very much resembling and scarce infe-
> rior to that of the Royal Court. Their Household was established upon the
> same plan, their Officers bore the same titles, and their Warrants ran in the
> same form and stile. This remarkable resemblance to the Royal Establishments
> will strike the Reader the moment he opens this Book.

The Earls of Northumberland had been absentee landlords at Alnwick from the sixteenth century, allowing the medieval castle to fall into a dilapidated condition while they used Syon and Petworth as their country residences. However, the 1st Duke and especially his Duchess

---

69   See Greig, *Diaries of a Duchess*. A biography of the Duke is a
     desideratum, but in the meantime see Lomas, *Power in the Land*,
     pp. 165–72.
70   Pottle, *Boswell's London Journal*, p. 71.

FIG. 88 William Watts after Lord Duncannon, *Alnwick Castle, Northumberland*, 1783 (W. Watts, *The Seats of the Nobility and Gentry*, pl. LVII). Engraving. RCIN 1076103

FIG. 89 Henry Emlyn, *Design for a new building, Lower Ward, Windsor Castle*, 1786. Pen and ink and wash. Dean and Canons of Windsor (P 79)

had a romantic vision of returning to Alnwick as their main seat and of restoring the keep as a residence (fig. 88). They fulfilled this ambition by employing James Paine to adapt it in the Gothic style (*c.*1754–68) and by then switching to the King's architect, Robert Adam, to complete the process as a piece of chivalric Gothick romance (*c.*1770–80). Though George III never travelled so far north as Alnwick, it is inconceivable that he did not know of his friends' achievement there, which was something of a model for what he was to do at Windsor.[71]

St George's Chapel, Windsor

Henry Emlyn, who was employed at Windsor as carpenter, builder, and architect to the Office of Works from 1761 and to the Dean and Chapter from 1784 to 1791, made a design for George III in about 1780 for a large neo-Palladian building in the Lower Ward (fig. 89).[72] This building, which would have replaced the Dean's Cloister, Canons' Cloister, Deanery, and Dean's Library, boasted Emlyn's remarkable British order in which the foliage of the capital consisted of knightly plumes with the star of the Order of the Garter between the volutes. With this chivalric gesture, published by Emlyn to coincide with the coming of age of the Prince of Wales,[73] he hoped to tempt the King, whose wishes to live in the castle were confirmed following his dramatic recovery from his illness in 1789. The King is supposed to have allowed Emlyn to erect an example of the British order at Windsor, which has since been removed.

71 On the Duchess as a keen and well-informed country-house tourist with a sensitive eye, see Percy and Jackson-Stops, 'Exquisite Taste and Tawdry Ornament'. For her important role at Syon and Alnwick, which has not previously been appreciated, see Baird, *Mistress of the House*, ch. 10.

72 Reproduced in S. M. Bond, 'Henry Emlyn of Windsor'.

73 Emlyn, *Proposition*, pl. XXV, and *Gentleman's Magazine*, vol. LII, 1782, p. 77.

 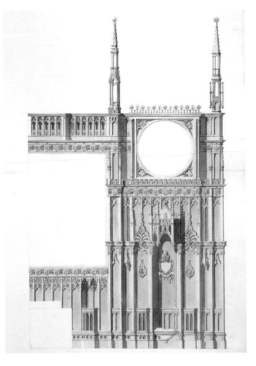

FIG. 90 James Stuart, *A design for the east end of St George's Chapel, Windsor Castle*, 1771. Watercolour and pen and ink. Dean and Canons of Windsor (F 21)

FIG. 91 Thomas Sandby, *Design for reredos, St George's Chapel, Windsor Castle*, c.1787. Pen and ink and wash. Dean and Canons of Windsor (E 36)

FIG. 92 Charles Wild, *The Quire of St George's Chapel, Windsor Castle*, 1818. Watercolour and bodycolour over pencil. RL 22115

In St George's Chapel, the King took a decisive step towards the Gothic Revival as an appropriate background for the Garter ceremonies. He not only reaffirmed the role of the chapel as the seat of the Order of the Garter but also went some way into turning it into a chapel royal. James 'Athenian' Stuart had designed a new east window for St George's Chapel as early as 1771, which incorporated the arms of the Knights of the Garter in a vast circle centred on a Garter badge enclosing the royal arms.[74] Below was an elaborate reredos designed in a clumsy and ill-informed Gothic, Stuart's only known attempt in that style (fig. 90). It seems that this work was not executed and that Stuart was instructed to design a reredos in the classical style, for in 1785 that reredos was removed on the King's orders because it was 'of Grecian architecture, & not of course corresponding with the stile of the Chapel'.[75] It was replaced with a neo-Perpendicular panelled screen by Thomas Sandby which was similar to Stuart's, though more elegant (fig. 91). This was executed in slightly altered form by Henry Emlyn who,

---

74 Watkin, *Athenian Stuart*, pp. 55–6 and pl. 80.
75 St John Hope, *Windsor Castle*, p. 426.

surprisingly for this date, acquired considerable skill in working in a convincing fifteenth-century style. The episode sheds an instructive light on the King's change of taste in the 1780s.

In 1782 the King commissioned Benjamin West to design a depiction in stained glass of the Resurrection to fill the great east window of St George's Chapel (fig. 92).[76] Its installation in 1786 unfortunately involved removing the Gothic tracery but this was reinstated by George Gilbert Scott in 1863 when West's stained glass, executed by Thomas Jervais, was removed.[77] The original proposal, as in 1771, was that this window should incorporate the arms of the Knights but this arrangement was abandoned on the King's orders. He persuaded the Garter Knights, including his friends Lord Bute and the Duke of Northumberland, and his brother-in-law, Charles William Ferdinand, Duke of Brunswick, to contribute to its cost of over £4,000.[78] Below this was West's altarpiece of the Last Supper, nearly twelve feet long, painted in 1786 and put in place that December in the neo-Gothic reredos by Sandby and Emlyn. The King also gave a carpet for the altar as well as a set of lamps, all designed by Emlyn.

The popularity of glass painting in the eighteenth century owed much to its promotion by the first two Presidents of the Royal Academy, Sir Joshua Reynolds and Benjamin West, who from the 1770s designed schemes of painted glass in major buildings. A recent scholar has argued of George III that 'As a patron of contemporary glass-painting on a bold and monumental scale the King certainly had no equal.'[79] This claim was based on West's Resurrection in the east window at St George's, on his three large windows relating to the Nativity in the aisles, and on his never-completed Crucifixion in the west window.[80]

With Henry Emlyn as architect and carpenter, the King remodelled and enriched the eastern half of the chapel from the choir screen to the high altar. He began by elaborating, presumably for the King's use, the Queen's Closet, the famous first-floor chamber behind an oriel made for Catherine of Aragon. Characteristic of Burgundian court ritual, such a feature had been created for Henry VII in the chapel of his palace at Richmond. Emlyn's additions to this closet at Windsor included a charming curved Gothic canopy as well as Gothic furniture. In 1786–91 came the enlargement and restoration of the richly carved stalls, originally 21 on each side, constructed under Edward IV and his successors in 1477–84.[81] Emlyn added four new stalls, two on the north and south sides at the east end, with new canopies to the knights' stalls which are brilliantly successful facsimiles of the medieval originals. The reason for this expansion was that from 1786 the King increased the number of the Knights, partly in order to

FIG. 93 Henry Emlyn, *Garter Stalls in St George's Chapel: Procession to St Paul's Cathedral in 1789*, c.1790. Oak. Dean and Canons of Windsor

FIG. 94 Henry Emlyn, *Garter Stalls in St George's Chapel: Thanksgiving ceremony in St Paul's Cathedral in 1789*, c.1790. Oak. Dean and Canons of Windsor

FIG. 95 Henry Emlyn, *Garter Stalls in St George's Chapel: Attempted assassination of George III in 1786*, c.1790. Oak. Dean and Canons of Windsor

76 For a critical account of the work of West at Windsor, see Tighe and Davis, *Annals of Windsor*, pp. 340–2.

77 For a photograph of the east end with the work of West and Emlyn still *in situ*, see J. Roberts, 'Henry Emlyn's Restoration of St George's Chapel', pl. I.

78 For a list of the subscribers, see St John Hope, *Windsor Castle*, vol. II, p. 390. The King contributed £1,525 to the cost of this window.

79 Baylis, 'Absolute Magic', p. 25.

80 See Meyer, 'Benjamin West's Window Designs for St George's, Windsor'.

81 James, *St George's Chapel, Windsor*.

accommodate his seven surviving sons, each of whom he appointed a member of the Order.[82]

Emlyn's carving is an extremely successful essay in the style of the original, though it has a modern iconography including scenes from George III's life on the desk fronts. No fewer than six scenes depict the events surrounding the Service of Thanksgiving for his Recovery held at St Paul's Cathedral on St George's Day 1789. These include the carriage procession to St Paul's (fig. 93) as well as the scene inside with the King and Queen in their traverse, a canopied stall which is a recreation of medieval royal ritual (fig. 94). Three further scenes depict the attempt of Margaret Nicholson to assassinate the King on 2 August 1786 (fig. 95). These graphic images of the King were an imaginative and unconventional way of weaving his person into the fabric of this great statement of medieval chivalry, almost anticipating some aspects of the use of the media in the modern world.

Emlyn also provided a door to the King's stall at St George's, Windsor, depicting George III in Garter robes inspecting a design for a window. More importantly, he also added a large Gothic tester and brought the adjacent stalls forward slightly to allow for a huge new screen (fig. 96). This supported a lavish new organ in 1788–91 by Green, also given by the King, and featuring an elaborate Gothic case designed by Emlyn but since rearranged. The monumental new screen which he commissioned from Emlyn in 1787 extends across the whole width of the nave and is over six feet deep.[83] The King had become interested in the possibilities of the new technology by which Mrs Coade manufactured artificial stone from 1769 so that the new screen, remarkably, is of Coade stone. Completed in 1790, it is also a brilliantly accurate essay in Tudor Gothic inspired by elements of the chapel itself so that it deceives most visitors today, though it is just a giant piece of pottery.[84] The fan vaulting inside the screen is inspired

---

82 In 1786 he appointed William, Edward, Ernest, Augustus, and Adolphus. Since the Order has consisted of the sovereign and 25 companions from its foundation, George III's increase of its numbers in 1786 and 1805 was deplored by Sir Nicholas Harris Nicolas in *History of the Orders of Knighthood*, vol. II, pp. 287, 291–3, and 296–9.

83 Emlyn illustrated it in the 3rd edn (1797) of his *Proposition*, pl. XXX.

84 However, the front of the screen, except for the balcony, was replaced with natural stone in the 1920s by the Surveyor of the Fabric on the mistaken grounds that Coade stone was a kind of unstable plaster.

FIG. 96 Henry Emlyn, *Design for Organ Screen, St George's Chapel, Windsor Castle, c.1789.* Pen and ink and wash. Dean and Canons of Windsor (E 24)

by that in the side aisles of the chapel but, unlike those, the fans on the east side spring not from the wall but from slender, free-standing colonnettes, an imaginative touch in which Emlyn successfully entered into the spirit of late Perpendicular architecture.[85] He also included in the screen devices of the sovereign and the current Knights, while in the north aisle of the chancel he added a standing wall-monument to Edward IV in 1789–91. With a stone tester and Gothic panelling, it incorporates two small columns and a tablet, all in black marble, from earlier monuments. George III paid for all this work at Windsor, including Garter-blue velvet for the sovereign's and prince's stalls and for the Communion table, out of the Privy Purse. It amounted to nearly £14,000.

As part of his remarkably extensive patronage of the Coade stone manufactory at Lambeth, the King commissioned an ambitious font as well as three statues for the west front of St George's Chapel. The octagonal font with small figures in niches below panels framing quatrefoils was a neo-Perpendicular essay of which Mrs Coade was so proud that she exhibited a duplicate of it in Coade's Gallery in Westminster Bridge Road, which she opened in 1799. She boasted

85   See Kelly, *Mrs Coade's Stone,* p. 217.

FIG. 97 John Yenn,
*Design for the Music
Room, Windsor Castle:
elevation of organ and
wall*, 1794. Pen and ink
and wash. RL 18690

FIG. 98 John Yenn,
*Design for Queen
Charlotte's Drawing
Room, Windsor Castle:
elevation of east wall*,
1795. Pen and ink and
wash. Royal Academy of
Arts (B.14d)

that the font had been shown at the Royal Academy and that the King had asked for it to be
sent to Buckingham House so that he and his family could inspect it at their leisure.[86]

The Coade stone statues to fill existing niches on the west front of the Chapel represent
Edward the Confessor, St George and the Dragon, and, surprisingly for George III, the Virgin
and Child at the top of the façade. This replaced the figure which had been smashed at the
Reformation but is rather incongruously based on the Coade representations of the Vestal
Virgin and is accompanied by a putto. The figure of Edward the Confessor, by contrast, is
convincingly early sixteenth-century in character.

All this work at St George's, Windsor, was carried out during years of crisis in France: the
Revolution in 1789, the arrest of Louis XVI in June 1791, and his execution in January 1793.

The Upper Ward Restored and Rebuilt

In the Upper Ward of Windsor Castle, George III restored St George's Hall, retaining Verrio's
mural paintings of the Foundation of the Order of the Garter. In addition to work in the
King's Audience Chamber, during the 1790s, following the King's decision to take up residence
at the castle itself, numerous small alterations and modernisations were effected in the Upper
Ward apartments.[87] So long as Sir William Chambers was Surveyor General and Comptroller
of the King's Works, these were still mostly in the classical, not the Gothic style, which the
King had already adopted for the chapel on associational grounds. The principal change was
the construction in 1794–5 of an elegant Music Room and Drawing Room for Queen
Charlotte from designs by John Yenn, a pupil and close associate of Chambers (figs. 97, 98).[88]

---

86 *ibid.*, p. 218. The font was destroyed *c.*1880.

87 Expenditure amounted to around £3,200 annually in the 1790s
    (Colvin, ed., *King's Works*, vol. VI, p. 374).

88 See H. Roberts, 'Neoclassical Episode at Windsor' and *King's Pleasure*,
    pp. 5–7 and figs. 4–5.

This Office of Works commission was doubtless passed to Yenn by Chambers, who died in 1796. Yenn's drawings of 1794–5 are in an elegant Chambersian style, somewhat old-fashioned for their date. The King paid for this work out of his Privy Purse, though Yenn was already a royal architect who had been Clerk of the Works at Buckingham House, Kensington Palace, and the Royal Mews, from 1782. He had also always played an active role in the Royal Academy. His new Music Room and Drawing Room were, unusually, in the east range of the Upper Ward, not the north range where the royal apartments had been from the twelfth century. George III thus set a precedent which was followed even more completely by George IV, who remodelled the entire east range as private apartments from designs by Wyatville in 1824–8, destroying Yenn's work in the process.

George III made his most extensive changes to the Castle in 1800–14, when the immense sum of around £150,000 was spent on Windsor, by both the Office of Works and the Privy Purse.[89] The mood is well conveyed by Miss Lucy Kennedy, a resident in the Castle, who recorded in her diary in January 1804 that the King is intending to reside 'constantly' in the Castle. She added that 'His Majesty plans all the alterations himself; it is his great amusement.'[90]

FIG. 99 Charles Wild, *The Upper Ward, Windsor Castle, looking west towards the Round Tower* (detail), 1819. Watercolour and touches of bodycolour over pencil. RL 22096

---

89 For the first notice of this work, see *Gentleman's Magazine*, vol. LXX, 1800, ii, p. 892, where Wyatt is described as having been commissioned 'to alter and decorate a wing'.

90 MS diary in Royal Library, RCIN 1180580 (Colvin, ed., *King's Works*, vol. VI, p. 376).

FIG. 100 Charles Wild,
*The Grand Staircase,
Windsor Castle*, 1818.
Watercolour and touches
of bodycolour over
pencil. RL 22097

FIG. 101 The ceiling of
the Grand Vestibule,
Windsor Castle, with
plasterwork by Francis
Bernasconi

The King's principal aims were to Gothicise the exteriors and to create greater convenience internally.[91] His architect was James Wyatt, who had succeeded Sir William Chambers as Surveyor General and Comptroller of the King's Works in 1796, posts he held till his own death in 1813. His appointment was partly due to the success of his first royal commission, which was the remodelling of Frogmore House at Windsor for Queen Charlotte. As early as 1791 he made designs in the Gothic style, for which he was now best known, for Little Frogmore House which stood to the north-west of the surviving (Great) Frogmore House. Little Frogmore was demolished soon after the purchase in 1792 of Great Frogmore, which Wyatt built from that year in the classical style.[92] However, he did build Gothic ruins in the grounds of Frogmore in the 1790s, based on designs by Princess Elizabeth.[93]

By 1798 Wyatt was repairing the ceiling of the Queen's Audience Chamber and working on a number of staircases in the Castle. More importantly, he created a new battlemented entrance tower from the quadrangle in the Upper Ward (fig. 99). Flanked by semi-octagonal bays, all ornamented in Bernasconi's patent stucco, this led to an imposing new State Staircase of 1800–4 on the site of that by Hugh May of the 1670s (fig. 100). This was in the tradition of royal planning of which a famous example is Bernini's Scala Regia at the Vatican Palace, leading up to the Sala Regia, the papal throne room. Stylistically, Wyatt's stair was a Gothic extravaganza in his Fonthill Abbey manner, rising in two straight flights from an aisled Gothic entrance hall to the King's Drawing Room. The stair was lit by a high octagonal lantern, visible externally, and supported on a superbly detailed fan vault, the work of the gifted stuccoist, Francis Bernasconi (fig. 101). This survives today as the ceiling of the

---

91 Some of the changes effected in the interiors by James Wyatt can be
    seen in the illustrations to Pyne's *Royal Residences*.
92 For the Gothic designs, see J. Roberts, *Royal Landscape*, pp. 216–18 and pl. 218.
93 *ibid.*, p. 225 and pl. 223.

Grand Vestibule, though Wyatt's staircase was destroyed by Wyatville, who also replaced Wyatt's entrance tower.

The King's scheme of around 1779 for creating the Chapel of Revealed Religion was now abandoned. Instead, Wyatt improved circulation by constructing a gallery or cloister round Horn Court in 1805–6. In the meantime he began Gothicising the exterior façades of the north range of Upper Ward to match his new entrance tower and the façades of Edward III.[94] This involved replacing many of the round-headed windows which dated from Hugh May's remodelling of the Upper Ward for Charles II in a subdued classical style in the 1670s and '80s. Wyatt had altered the six lower windows of the range by December 1800, and worked on the others from 1801 to 1809. His tall, two-light transomed windows in Portland stone were close to those he provided at Fonthill Abbey, though it is clear from the engraving by Wenceslaus Hollar in Elias Ashmole's history of the Order of the Garter of 1672 that Wyatt largely reinstated Edward III's work. He also added tall octagonal towers at the north-east and north-west corners.[95]

James Wyatt's new work in the Upper Ward was continued in 1804 during the summer visit of the Royal Family to Weymouth, whence George III wrote to Wyatt on 5 September. The passage gives the clearest indication of the King's exceptional memory and attention to detail, the more remarkable since he wrote away from the Castle.

> The King is much pleased with Mr. Wyatt's report of the state of the works in hand in Windsor Castle and has nothing to remark but that he feels the reasons are conclusive why the opening cannot be made in the middle of the Musick Room, and approves of Handel's bust being placed in that pannel on a bracket as was intended over the chimney, but sufficiently high that the harpsichord may remain in its present place; the chimney in this case need not be altered. The door into the old Confectionery from the Withdrawing to it must be now executed as well as a passage at the back of that side of the room from whence the communication will come to Mrs. Egerton's Tower.[96]

While at Weymouth, the royal family became familiar with James Wyatt's Pennsylvania Castle, Portland, Dorset, built in the Gothic style in 1800 on the suggestion of the King for

---

94 For the renewal of the Upper Ward in 1357–68, see Wilson, 'Royal Lodgings of Edward III at Windsor Castle'.

95 For further details on this work, see H. Roberts, *King's Pleasure*, pp. 5–8 and fig. 9.

96 Aspinall, *Correspondence*, vol. v, p. 228. The Queen's Music Room, designed for her by John Yenn in 1794–5, was in the east range of Upper Ward, next to the Chester Tower in which lived Mrs Egerton, one of her ladies-in-waiting.

his friend, John Penn, and officially opened by the King's daughter, Princess Elizabeth. It served a political purpose since Penn supposedly had a mission to watch the English Channel and receive information from sea-captains and others who acted as secret agents as to the movements of French ships. Pitt rewarded him with the governorship of Portland in 1805 and command of the local militia.

On the King's return from Weymouth in September 1804, the Castle was described as 'the future residence of the King, Queen, and the Princesses', though it was considered that, despite the 'repairs and improvements, under the direction of Mr. Wyatt, [it] has still to undergo many changes suggested by his Majesty, who has long made Antient and Modern Architecture his peculiar study . . . The intended improvement, it is supposed, will take six years to complete.'[97] Nonetheless, 1805 was the King's *annus mirabilis* at Windsor where on 25 February he triumphantly displayed Wyatt's new apartments at a party on the kind of lavish scale more usually associated with George IV. It was explained that 'During the time Mr. Wyatt was fitting up the rooms, his Majesty had the entertainment in mind'; this entertainment was described as a 'house-warming', which was estimated to have cost not less than £50,000 – surely a wild exaggeration – and included a supper for 500 guests.[98]

The threat from Napoleon which lent force to this defiant display of confidence had been given tangible expression by the invasion of Hanover by his armies in May 1803. As a result, Hanoverian silver furniture and dining plate were shipped in crates to London where they arrived five months later. These included the magnificent silver service commissioned by George III in the 1770s for use in his palaces in Hanover. The survival of 120 pieces of this commission represent 'the largest surviving tranche of a unique Franco-German commission, and is one of only a handful of royal, neo-classical services to have survived anywhere in the world.'[99] The grand party at Windsor in February 1805, which included a concert of German music, was a patriotic celebration with a German theme, intended to attract popular support for the campaign against Napoleon. The Hanover chandeliers, the silver side tables and mirrors acquired by George II, and the dining silver commissioned by George III, were now seen for the first time by the English court, while 'Wedgwood figures celebrating patriotic themes adorned the centre of the tables.'[100]

Two months later, on St George's Day, 23 April 1805, the most magnificent Garter ceremony since the days of Charles II was held.[101] According to contemporary accounts, it was

---

97   *Gentleman's Magazine*, vol. LXXV, 1805, i, p. 130.

98   *ibid.*, pp. 262–4. The King's long-standing and well-known veneration for Eton led to the presence at the party of 80 boys from the school. He even went there in person to invite them.

99   Glanville, 'A George III Silver Service'.

100 *ibid.*

101 For a detailed full account of the ceremonies, see *Gentleman's Magazine*, vol. LXXXV, 1805, i, pp. 374–6 and 470–4.

'the king's particular wish that as many as of the old customs should be kept up as possible', including a baron of beef, a Tudor tradition, and the 'Horse Guards band playing "Britons strike Home!"' in ceremonies noted for the 'chivalrous spirit and majesty of the scene, during a space of seven hours'.[102] Another commentator noted that 'Knights sat down at the sovereign's table, wearing the caps of state . . . [and] gorgeous mantles of blue velvet [which] would do their best to bring back the days of King Edward and his Knights of the Round Table and thus hurl a chivalric defiance to the mushroom court of the Tuileries.'[103] It was also stressed of this ceremony that 'Its revival, therefore, at a moment of danger like the present . . . is an act of sound policy . . . [so as] to inspire an elevated idea of their rank and importance [in noblemen], but also to fan the flame of loyalty and patriotism which pervades every class of His Majesty's subjects.'[104]

The splendour of the ceremonies had not been equalled since the seventeenth century. It was the last Garter Feast on this grand scale, as well as the last Installation, until 1948, when the ceremony was again revived as a symbol of renewal after the war. The year 1805, chosen by George III for this patriotic celebration, was an important one: it was the year after Napoleon became Emperor – hence the reference to his 'mushroom court' – and had 90,000 men assembled near Boulogne as an invasion force, doubtless carefully watched over by Penn at Pennsylvania Castle.

Reference was made to this in an account of the King's annual visit to Weymouth in August 1804.

> Whilst crouching millions are compelled to join in the military cavalcade of
> an ambitious Tyrant on the Continent: what a striking contrast do we behold,
> in the mild and unassuming condescension of our beloved Sovereign in his
> delightful excursion to a favourite residence at Weymouth.[105]

In the same year, the grateful citizens of Weymouth commissioned a handsome statue of the King from the Coade stone manufactory. One of the most triumphalist of all images of him, it was set up in 1809 at the entrance to the town at the south end of the Esplanade to celebrate the golden jubilee of his reign. He is shown in Garter robes, holding the sceptre, with a huge crown behind him on a neo-antique table with monopodia legs in the form of winged lions. The royal arms feature on an oval shield, while the massive pedestal on which the King stands

102   Belsham, *Memoirs of the Reign of George III*, vol. ii, pp. 330–2.
103   Knight, *Passages of a Working Life*, vol. i, p. 64.
104   *Gentleman's Magazine*, vol. lxxv, 1805, i, p. 374.
105   *ibid.*, vol. lxxiv, 1804, ii, p. 1233.

FIG. 102 D. Havell after
F. Nash, *The Royal Vault,
St George's Chapel,
Windsor Castle,* 1817.
Hand-coloured aquatint.
RCIN 700729

is flanked by large representations of the lion and unicorn.[106] The inhabitants of Weymouth had good reason to be grateful for the trade he brought to the town where he and the royal party occupied Gloucester Lodge, or the King's Lodge, an ambitious mansion at the east end of the esplanade. Six bays long with a frontage to the sea of 80 feet, this had been built after 1780 by George III's brother, the Duke of Gloucester. The King added to it 'in a spacious entrance court . . . domestic offices', including stabling for sixteen horses, and elsewhere a 'range of brick buildings' with accommodation for a further fourteen horses.[107]

Meanwhile, building at Windsor went on, with work beginning around 1810 on the gothicising of the exteriors of the south and east fronts of the Upper Ward where the Queen and the younger unmarried members of the royal family had moved into first-floor lodgings. The Queen's private sitting room and bedroom, in the tower at the south-east corner of the

106 Kelly, *Mrs Coade's Stone*, pp. 182–3 and 232.

107 From the Sale Catalogue, 14 July 1820, of *The Marine Residence and Household Furniture, of His late Majesty, at Weymouth*. There was a suite of six reception rooms and a waiting room on the first floor, with ten bedrooms on the second floor and a further thirteen for servants in the attics.

Upper Ward, could scarcely have been further from the King's bedroom on the ground floor of the north range of the Upper Ward.[108] The separation of their quarters was related to the fear of a return of the King's malady, necessitating that, as before, he was kept apart from the Queen and the royal family. A noble surviving element of George III's work is the Royal Burial Vault which James Wyatt constructed for him in 1804–12 below the former Lady Chapel at the east end of St George's Chapel (fig. 102).[109] This was in keeping with much continental royal custom, notably the Habsburg vault at the Capuchin church in Vienna. These had been difficult years in the life of the nation: 1808 was the first peak of the economic war, with grave effects on English life; 1811 was the second, a year of bankruptcies all over Europe, with food shortages and a trade crisis in England with exports impeded. Thus Windsor was remodelled in Gothic in the opening years of the nineteenth century when the monarchy was seen as a revered symbol of national resistance to French ideas and French power.[110]

Gothic, the King, and Nationhood

The final stage in the story of the King's wish to build a palace at Richmond is the Gothic palace which was begun in 1801 from designs by James Wyatt on the banks of the Thames just west of the Dutch House, known today as Kew Palace (fig. 103). We first hear of it in 1794 when Farington noted that 'Wyatt lately shewed Hodges a set of designs for a Palace to be built at Kew, which the King has a serious intention of doing, – Kew is private property of the King which He may dispose of as He pleases.'[111] Its estimated cost in 1801 was £40,000 but £100,000 had been spent by 1806, for work proceeded quickly, the King reporting to his eldest daughter in late September 1803 that

> The body of the house is compleated, and now its floors and windows are preparing. The chief stairs cannot be built till the next summer. The east wing is nearly as forward, the entrance of the court is now building, and the other wing will be undertaken next summer; by this you may guess that I cannot as yet calculate how soon the stables, greenhouse and other appendages will be finished.[112]

The design of the Castellated Palace at Kew (fig. 104), with its central keep, four storeys high, surrounded by a high curtain wall, all crenellated, may have been determined by George III,

108   As shown in D. and S. Lysons, 'Plan of Windsor Castle. MDCCV' and 'Plan of the Upper Ward of Windsor Castle. MDCCV', in *Magna Britannia. Berkshire* (H. Roberts, *King's Pleasure*, figs. 8–9).

109   It was reported in December 1811 that 'The Mausoleum at Windsor, begun by Cardinal Wolsey, has lately been finished, agreeably to

the direction of his present Majesty' (*Gentleman's Magazine*, vol. LXXXI, 1811, ii, p. 651).

110   For a general and well-balanced overview, see Marilyn Morris, *British Monarchy and French Revolution*.

111   *Farington Diary*, vol. I, p. 141 (12 January 1794).

112   Aspinall, *Correspondence*, vol. IV, p. 135.

FIG. 103 John Greig, *The main block of George III's New Palace, Kew*, 1819. Engraving and etching. RCIN 702968

FIG. 104 C. Hullmandel after William Westall, *View from across the river of James Wyatt's New Palace, Kew*, 1823. Lithograph. RCIN 702960

for it represents a departure in Wyatt's style from the more Rococo Gothic flavour of Sheffield Place, Sandleford Priory, and Lee Priory. The King is recorded as having said of Wyatt that at Fonthill Abbey 'He had done a great work,'[113] but since Kew was a toy fort with a round tower at each corner, it seems to be the result of the King's wish to echo Lulworth Castle which he had seen twelve years earlier. We shall see later that his eldest daughter, the Princess Royal, Queen of Württemberg, declared that it would be 'Lulworth improved'.[114] The rigorous symmetry of the plan may also be related to the need of the court for two parallel suites of State Apartments, not easily fitted into an asymmetrical layout. The most spectacular feature would have been the grand staircase which, lit by a high tower, filled the centre of the main block as at Ashridge, the Gothic house Wyatt was shortly to begin.

The Palace at Kew was also unusual for its internal fireproof skeleton of cast iron, probably not including load-bearing supports, which James Wyatt had based on the incombustible system patented by his brother, Samuel, in 1800. Samuel Wyatt adopted it in his abortive scheme for rebuilding Albion Mills, Blackfriars, with an internal fireproof skeleton of hollow, tubular, units of cast iron.[115] Kew Palace was probably the first use of this material for a non-commercial or non-industrial building.

The shell had been almost completely roofed when work stopped in 1811 because of the King's illness. It was rumoured that half a million pounds had been spent but, despite the

113   *Farington Diary*, vol. VI, p. 2214 (8 January 1804).
114   Below, p. 199.
115   Colvin, ed., *King's Works*, vol. VI, pp. 356–9.

fact that he paid for it out of his Privy Purse, it was attacked by radicals. For example, Dance wrote to Soane in 1802 that 'the rascally democrats have made it their stalking horse.'[116] Indeed, with dry rot spreading through its empty carcase, it was demolished, partly with explosives, on the orders of George IV in 1827–8 at about the time of demolition of Carlton House. Nash and Wyatville reused much of its material at Buckingham Palace and Windsor Castle respectively.

In understanding the King's Gothic work, we should recall that Gothic had long been promoted as an English style on patriotic or nationalist grounds. Alexander Pope had argued in 1725 that Shakespeare resembles 'an ancient majestic piece of *Gothick* Architecture, compar'd with a neat Modern building: The latter is more elegant and glaring, but the former [Gothic] is more strong and more solemn.'[117] Batty Langley, author of *Ancient Architecture, Restored, and Improved . . . In the Gothic Mode For the Ornamenting of Buildings and Gardens* (1742), promoted Gothic 'as part of his patriotic campaign for English traditions, crafts and craftsmen',[118] a process in which, as we have seen, he preceded Emlyn in inventing a British order. One of the major monuments of the Georgian Gothic Revival, Arbury Hall, Warwickshire (*c.*1750–*c.*1790), has recently been interpreted as an expression of the belief of its owner, Sir Roger Newdigate (1719–1806), that Gothic symbolised the ideal of the historic British constitution.[119] With some Jacobite sympathies, Newdigate was one of those for whom the accession of George III brought hope that the Tories would be brought back from their 40-year-long banishment. He wrote memoranda around 1760 and in 1765 setting out his political views, which centred on the Crown, the parliamentary constitution, and the Anglican Church. His chief architect at Arbury from 1761 was Henry Keene (1726–76), Surveyor to the Fabric of Westminster Abbey and father-in-law of William Parry, Welsh harpist to George III.

Edmund Burke went on to draw a compelling political parallel between the preservation of historic institutions such as the monarchy in France, and the preservation of historic build-ings. This was in his influential book *Reflections on the Revolution in France* (1790), warmly admired by George III and a challenging opposition to the politics of contemporary France at a time when there were those in England who still sympathised with the Revolutionary ideals. In it, he also suggested that old buildings should not be demolished and that new ones should reflect the resonances of their predecessors.

---

116   Bolton, *Portrait of Sir John Soane*, p. 94.

117   'Preface to the Works of Shakespear' (1725), in *The Prose Works of Alexander Pope*, R. Cowler, ed., vol. II, Oxford 1986, p. 25.

118   E. Harris and N. Savage, *Architectural Books*, p. 267.

119   Hall, 'Arbury Hall'. See also Hall, *Gothic Architecture and its Meanings*, pp. 18–21.

The anti-Christian and anti-monarchical tone of Revolutionary France had shocked the majority of the English, and Wyatt's new Gothic work at Windsor had the 'strong and solemn' character admired by Pope. The antiquarian John Carter[120] published a major study of Gothic called *The Ancient Architecture of England* (1795–1814) in which he promoted Gothic as a bulwark against Napoleon and democracy.[121] He argued of 'the Roman and Grecian styles of architecture . . . [that] the admiration that has been conjured up in [their] support has necessarily turned the genius of Englishmen from their national architecture, to toil in an inglorious and servile pursuit to imitate a foreign manner.'[122] Elsewhere, he urged that

> In a day like the present, when 'the infernal dispensers of liberty and equality' are spreading their destroying power over so many realms . . . it behoves every Englishman to come forward in the general cause, to protect his king and country . . . and I know of no way that I can so well aid the general cause, as to stimulate my countrymen to think well of their own national memorials, the works of art, of ancient times, and not hold up any foreign works as superior to our own; and, in particular, the name of *France* should never be introduced, but to raise ideas of terror and destruction.[123]

The kind of architecture which goes with this can be seen in Wyatt's castellated Gothic at Windsor and later at Kew, though the materials and details at Windsor were insufficiently accurate to win praise from the demanding John Carter. He wrote ironically of Wyatt's staircase that he was 'in a manner "planet-struck" at the novelty and brilliancy of scene, in the various manufactures of stucco (or "Patent Compo"), brass and iron', finding the vault 'unexampled and extraordinary'.[124] By contrast, he praised Henry Emlyn's organ screen at St George's Chapel, Windsor (fig. 96), with its Coade stone details cast from original features in the chapels in the side aisles, as 'certainly the best imitation of our Antient Architecture that has yet been provided'. He also admired Benjamin West's Nativity windows in the north and south aisles.

Related architecturally and politically to Wyatt's work at Windsor was his creation for John Penn of Pennsylvania Castle, Dorset, which, as we have noted above, was an essay in castellated Gothic. In 1796 Penn had published a commentary on the contemporary threat to

120 See Crook, *John Carter and the Mind of the Gothic Revival.*

121 See Watkin, 'Greek and Gothic Country Houses', in Airs, *Regency Great Houses.*

122 *Gentleman's Magazine*, vol. LXIX, 1799, i, p. 92. See also Frew, 'Gothic is English'.

123 *Gentleman's Magazine*, vol. LXIX, 1799, i, p. 190.

124 *ibid.*, vol. LXXV, 1805, ii, pp. 724 and 924. This forms part of a series of waspish anonymous articles which Carter contributed to the *Gentleman's Magazine* between 1798 and 1817 under the title 'The Pursuits of Architectural Innovation' by 'An architect'. Criticisms of George III's Gothic work at Windsor can be found in vol. LXXV, 1805, i, pp. 529–30; ii, pp. 629–32, 723–6, 818–21 and 924–6.

English liberty by the French in the form of a blank verse drama in three acts entitled *The Battle of Eddington; or, British Liberty. A Tragedy.* On the theme of the defeat of the Danes by King Alfred, it was dedicated to William Pitt as 'the champion of law and order'. It was actually staged at Windsor in 1824. As we have seen, Pennsylvania Castle was opened in 1800 by one of the King's daughters, and it was subsequently visited by the King and Queen and their children. It may, indeed, have influenced the King's decision to build his own Gothic castle at Kew in the following year.

The King was supported in his promotion of Gothic by his daughter, Charlotte Augusta (1766–1828), the Princess Royal, who married in 1797 the Hereditary Prince of Württemberg. Thanks to Napoleon, he became King of Württemberg in 1806. In the following year Princess Catharine of Württemberg married the Emperor's youngest brother, Jérôme Bonaparte, leading to the great irony that the eldest daughter of George III, the greatest enemy of Napoleon, should become stepmother-in-law to Napoleon's brother. An architectural enthusiast for Gothic and landscape design, the Princess Royal wrote many letters to her father, encouraging him in his Gothic work at Windsor and Kew. The King's consciousness of the potentially daring nature of his switch to Gothic is clear in the almost embarrassed tone of the letter he wrote to his daughter about Kew Palace in 1803:

> I never thought I should have adopted Gothic instead of Grecian architecture,
> but the bad taste of the last forty years has so entirely corrupted the professors
> of the latter, I have taken to the former from thinking Wyatt perfect in that
> style, of which my house will I trust be a good example.[125]

This was indeed very different from the moment in 1784 when it was reported that he had especially asked that Downing College, Cambridge, should be designed in the classical, not Gothic style.

The novel iron frame of Kew recurred on a smaller scale in the remarkable Gothic conservatory which the King's son, the Prince of Wales, commissioned for Carlton House in 1807 from the architect Thomas Hopper (1776–1856). Rich with royal and national emblems, this ambitious Gothic structure was the scene of the banquet he gave to mark the establishment of his Regency in 1811 when the exiled Bourbon royal family of France was treated to a display

---

125   Aspinall, *Correspondence*, vol. IV, 1968, p. 135.

of British royal magnanimity and magnificence. British symbolism extended even to the ornamentation of the Coade stone candelabra, though the building was also remarkable structurally as an example of British industrial skills in its daring use of iron and glass.

From Kew depends Smirke's Lowther Castle, Westmorland, and Eastnor Castle, Herefordshire, but we should also note here the great Gothic Revival house of Ashridge, Hertfordshire, begun by Wyatt in 1806 for the 7th Earl of Bridgewater (1753–1823), a professional soldier who rose to the rank of general, and was a Tory MP in the years 1777–80 and 1783–1803. Becoming the fourth richest man in England in 1803, he was a man of grandiose character whose vast wealth enabled him to keep up a semi-royal state. In the entrance hall at Ashridge he put up a plaque with an inscription in Gothic lettering recording that the foundation stone was laid by Lady Bridgewater on 25 October 1808, and pointing out that this was the anniversary of the accession of George III to the throne. Since Lord Bridgewater chose both the national Gothic style and the same architect that the King had chosen at Windsor and at Kew, we can interpret Ashridge as his tribute to his sovereign.

Tory landowners in the later eighteenth century favoured the castle style because of its traditional and feudal associations. The fact that Gothic could be used for political ends is further demonstrated by the Whig 11th Duke of Norfolk (1746–1815) who, in remodelling Arundel Castle from 1787, adopted Gothic for reasons opposite to those of George III and the Tories. At Arundel it was hailed as a symbol of ancient liberties, trial by jury, and the moderation by the barons of the royal prerogative.[126] An amateur architect, the Duke of Norfolk was chairman of the Whig Club and a friend of the Prince Regent. Another Whig, the 3rd Duke of Portland (1738–1809), whose mother was close to Queen Charlotte, remodelled his Buckinghamshire seat, Bulstrode Park, in around 1806–9. He added an ambitious new wing in the castellated Gothic style from designs by James Wyatt, echoing his contemporary work at Windsor Castle which, just five miles away, terminated one of the extensive views from Bulstrode's hilltop site. The Duke of Portland, who was created the King's Lord Chamberlain in 1765 and served as Prime Minister in 1783 and 1807–9, shared the musical interests of the King and Queen, inviting Dr Charles Burney to spend many of his summers at Bulstrode Park. He also employed Humphry Repton to landscape the park at Bulstrode in the 1790s at a time when Repton may have been advising the Queen on the grounds at Frogmore.[127]

Returning to George III, we should note his interest in the Royal Entrance planned for his

126 See Robinson, *Arundel Castle*, p. 28.
127 J. Roberts, *Royal Landscape*, p. 122 and n. 136.

FIG. 105 Joseph Michael Gandy, *Design perspective for Sir John Soane's Scala Regia, the House of Lords*, 1800. Watercolour over pencil. London, Sir John Soane's Museum (P283)

ceremonial visits to the House of Lords (fig. 105). The existing House, medieval in origins, had no gallery for visitors on such occasions, and the royal approach to it was ramshackle and undignified. In response to an invitation to design a new House of Lords in 1793, John Soane prepared drawings for interiors in the classical style, richly ornamented with symbolic statuary and painting, which he described as commemorative of public actions and distinguished talents. The unusually placed statues of kings on his staircase create almost the impression of a living tableau at Madame Tussaud's. He claimed that when he showed the designs to George III at Windsor, the King gave them his 'entire approbation, and was particularly pleased with the idea of appropriating the two great rooms [Court of Requests and Painted Chamber] leading to the proposed new House of Lords as a depôt for Sculpture, commemorating great public actions, voted by Parliament, a better position than in Westminster Abbey, . . . [and] with the idea of the Great Scala Regia, to be decorated with statues of our Kings.'[128]

Soane was a passionate classicist who refused to bow to the rising tide of Romantic taste, which saw Gothic as appropriate for new work in the medieval Palace of Westminster. His new entry and stair were not built because of the war against France, but George III continued to complain bitterly of the inadequacies of the building to Wyatt in 1799.[129] Soane tried to create for George III a setting for royal ceremonial of a type new in England, or at least since the seventeenth century. The King gave his enthusiastic support to Soane's ambitious project which, had it been executed, would have contributed to the growth of the public ceremonies, rites, and festivals, which had become, from the later 1780s, a liturgy of nationalism, refocused on the person of the King. It was that message which Emlyn seemed to have understood when he created his remarkably graphic scenes of the King's life, including his procession to St Paul's.

The cult of the personality of the monarch had been hinted at by Edmund Burke in his celebrated eulogy of the person of Marie-Antoinette which was probably the best-known passage in his *Reflections on the Revolution in France*. Here, Burke seemed to suggest, perhaps unwisely, that the human face of the monarch as a person was as important as the hereditary principle itself: a dangerous path for an hereditary and constitutional monarch to pursue.

128 Soane Museum MSS, John Soane, 'Statement of Facts respecting the
     Design of a new House of Lords', 1799, f. 15.
129 *Farington Diary*, vol. IV, p. 1141.

6

LANDSCAPE, AGRICULTURE, AND ARCHITECTURE: RICHMOND AND WINDSOR

OPPOSITE After J. Gendall, *The east front of Cranbourne Lodge, Windsor Great Park* (detail of fig. 110)

As Prince of Wales, George III had been encouraged to take an interest in botany by the Earl of Bute, who had been involved with the Prince's parents in laying out the gardens at Kew with exotic trees and plants. Unlike other European capitals, London had no great botanical garden, so that in dedicating nine acres of the gardens to botanical purposes in 1759, the Dowager Princess of Wales laid the foundation of the Royal Botanical Gardens which could be seen as a rival to the celebrated *Jardin du Roi* in Paris under the direction of Georges-Louis Leclerc, Comte de Buffon (1707–88). The earliest purchases of the future George III, made at the age of 16, included 95 exceptional watercolours by Maria Sibylla Merian (1647–1717) of plants, fruit, and insects. In 1768, he acquired the no less striking 263 watercolours of flora and fauna made for *The Natural History of Carolina, Florida and the Bahama Islands* (1731–47), a handsome publication by Mark Catesby (1682–1749).

Oddly, the plant collector, Peter Collinson (1694–1768), complained in 1768 that 'I wish the King had any taste in flowers or plants; but he has none, there are no hopes of encouragement from him, for his talent is architecture.'[1] However, the King went on to support Sir Joseph Banks, the President of the Royal Society, in creating the Royal Botanical Gardens at Kew as the greatest centre for the study and conservation of plants in Europe.[2] As a court pursuit, botany became fashionable, natural history societies sprang up across Britain, and there were numerous botanical publications.[3]

Agricultural Improvements

For a true countryman like George III, landscape gardening was inseparable from the agricultural operations of the country estate.[4] He operated at a time when the rationalising and reordering of landed estates, often with model farmhouses by leading architects, made England the wonder of contemporary Europe and beyond, being admired by visiting Americans, French, Russians, and Swiss. George III established three farms on over 1,000 acres at Windsor, where he indulged his knowledge of agriculture, including crop rotation and especially sheep farming, so it was not for nothing that he was known as 'Farmer George'. He showed great interest in Arthur Young's *Annals of Agriculture, and other Useful Arts* from their inception in 1784, actually contributing two letters on crop rotation to them for which he adopted the pseudonym of Ralph Robinson, the name of one of the shepherds at Windsor.[5] A prominent 'agriculturalist, author, enthusiast for enclosure and dynamic promoter of the

1 Peter Collinson to William Bartram, 16 February 1768 (quoted in J. Roberts, *Royal Landscape*, p. 64).
2 See Desmond, *Kew, passim.*
3 See Uglow, *Lunar Men*, p. 268.
4 On the King and agricultural improvement in Britain, see Gascoigne, *Joseph Banks and the English Enlightenment.*
5 'On Mr. Ducket's mode of cultivation' in Young, *Annals of Agriculture*, vol. VII, pp. 65–71 and 332–6. The Duke of Grafton contributed essays to the same volume. The King must have enjoyed the conceit of signing both his letters, 'Your most humble servant'.

maximum net produce of British agriculture', Arthur Young (1741–1820) was 'marked by a lively commitment to "improvement" whether in picture collecting, agricultural science, architecture or landscape gardening'.[6] George Washington was in regular correspondence with him.[7]

Young's ambitions can be paralleled by William Donaldson who, describing himself as 'Late Secretary to the Government of Jamaica', published a fascinating book in 1775 called *Agriculture Considered as a Moral and Political Duty; in a Series of Letters, inscribed to His Majesty.* Adopting as one of his aims 'to illuminate the subject, with intellectual prospects, hitherto unobserved in the walks of agriculture',[8] Donaldson saw agriculture as rooted in antiquity and in the great periods of world history. With high ambitions, seemingly close to those of the King whom he mentioned constantly during the course of the book, Donaldson proposed the creation of a central body to regulate agriculture. He declared of this, 'let the temple be dedicated to industry, and named the Board, or Great Council of Agriculture. Here your Majesty will preside as the imperial citizen of your realms.'[9]

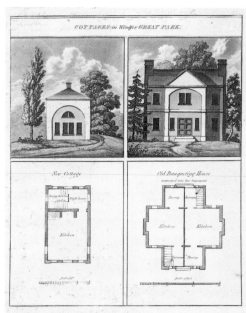

From the 1770s it became increasingly fashionable for landowners to build model farms, to develop an interest in farming techniques, and to commission portraits in which they were painted with their livestock.[10] Lord Kames, who had dedicated to the King his philosophical work, *Elements of Criticism*, in 1762, followed Donaldson's example by publishing *The Gentleman Farmer; being an Attempt to Improve Agriculture by Subjecting it to the Test of Rational Principles* (Edinburgh 1776). As we shall see in Chapter 7, Prince Franz of Anhalt-Dessau imported these ideals to his idealised landscape garden at Wörlitz, where he saw himself as the 'imperial citizen' of his realms.

George III was concerned not only with agricultural improvements but with the living conditions of those who worked on the soil. Indeed, a labourer's cottage was built in 1793 from his designs as part of the ongoing improvements of Windsor Great Park (fig. 106, left). Showing his continuing interest in architectural design well into his reign, it is a moderately elegant composition, if very simple, with an arched motif on its façade. It is, perhaps, hard to decide whether to be impressed that a monarch should devote attention to so trifling an improvement to the welfare of one of his humblest subjects, or to feel that such time was

FIG. 106 Cottages constructed in Windsor Great Park to George III's designs. Engraving. RCIN 700840

---

6   Watkin, *English Vision*, p. 2.

7   Robinson, *Georgian Model Farms*, p. 11.

8   Donaldson, *Agriculture Considered as a Moral and Political Duty*, p. 14.

9   *ibid.*, p. 170.

10   Uglow, *Lunar Men*, p. 343.

inappropriately spent against the background of major international events such as the Terror in France in 1794. In the year of the Terror, the revolutionary year II (i.e. 1793–4), the King also supervised the conversion into tenements for two labourers of a modest Banqueting House or tea-house, built in the mid-eighteenth century on Moat Island in the Great Park.[11]

'Capability' Brown at Richmond Gardens

Though, as we have seen, George III was enthusiastic in 1785 about the new, Rousseauesque flower garden at Nuneham Courtenay (fig. 19), he also retained an admiration for the more staid tastes of Lancelot 'Capability' Brown. The leading landscape architect in the country until his death in 1783, Brown had been appointed Royal Gardener at Hampton Court by the King in 1764. It is curious to note that the King later asked him why he had undertaken no improvements in his modern landscaped style at Hampton Court, and that, in an obscure reply, Brown 'excused himself "out of respect to himself and his profession"'.[12] In fact, the King took little interest in Hampton Court, a place where the court had last met in 1735, so that Brown's task was to retain, for the most part, its ancient formal gardens. At Richmond, by contrast, as we shall see shortly, George III commissioned Brown to carry out a major project in the new taste in 1764.

The King's promotion of the introduction of 'natural' elements into gardens and landscapes is testified in a letter of 1762–3 in which he returned designs by 'Capability' Brown for Kensington Gardens, objecting to an area which he thought 'should be more broke; by riding through the thickets I have seen many pretty, forest plants which I fancy will do extrem'ly well for the plantations here.'[13] Before the King transferred his attention to Windsor, he added some significant new buildings in the grounds of Richmond Lodge, where he also remodelled the gardens extensively in the 1760s. These were to form the setting for the palace with which he proposed to replace Richmond Lodge. Today the western part of Kew Gardens, these grounds had been laid out in the 1720s and 1730s for Queen Caroline by Charles Bridgeman,[14] who was already beginning to move away from the traditional formal garden in favour of the kind of open parkland with waving belts of trees which we associate with 'Capability' Brown.

It was in 1764 that the King and Queen began their annual summer migrations to Richmond Lodge. In that year the King commissioned Brown to relandscape Richmond Gardens, which included demolishing the eighteen houses of the adjacent hamlet of West Sheen to extend

11 J. Roberts, *Royal Landscape*, p. 66. The converted building is shown on the right of fig. 106.

12 Jacques, '"Capability" Brown at Hampton Court'.

13 Cited in Francis Russell's monograph on Lord Bute.

14 P. Willis, *Charles Bridgeman and the English Landscape Garden*, pp. 101–5.

the area of pasture for the King's cattle.[15] The King was probably inspired to employ Brown by seeing the work he was carrying out from around 1760 across the River Thames in the park at Syon for his friend Hugh Smithson, the future Duke of Northumberland. No less significantly, it was also in 1764 that 'Capability' Brown began work on one of the most ambitious projects of his career, the park for Lord Bute at Luton Hoo, a vast undertaking which occupied him for nearly sixteen years. The close relation of this scheme to royal projects at courts in England and Germany is clear from a letter in which Brown reported to Bute that 'We have got as many trees as we wanted this season from the Princess of Wales's garden [at Kew], on which acc[ount]t. I desired Mr. Haverfield to forward the trees for your Lordship as fast as possible'.[16] John Haverfield, as we shall see in Chapter 7, was sent to Germany by the Dowager Princess of Wales to help her nephew, Duke Ernest of Saxe-Gotha and Altenburg, in the creation of his garden at Gotha.

Brown's plan for Richmond, dated 10 December 1764, includes near the northern end the large palace which, as we have seen, Chambers and the King proposed in that year. The rural character at which Bridgeman had hinted at Richmond Gardens was now emphasised by Brown, who eliminated the few formal elements created for Queen Caroline such as the canal and most notably the great terrace which ran almost the whole length of the gardens along the River Thames. Supported by a brick wall, this was separated from the Thames by a public road which largely fell out of use following the construction of a wooden bridge over the river at Kew from designs by John Barnard in 1758–9. An Act of Parliament in 1766 allowed the King to close this road, provided he retained the towpath which was needed for river traffic.[17]

Brown was thus able to bring the Thames into visual association with the gardens of Richmond Lodge, an effect described in great detail by Arthur Young, who wrote:

> Richmond Gardens have been lately altered: the terrass and the grounds about it, are now converted into waving lawn that hangs to the river in a most beautiful manner: the old avenue is broken, and the whole clumped in some places with groves; in others with knots of trees, and a very judicious use is made of single ones: no traces of the avenue are to be seen, though many of the trees remain. The lawn waves in a very agreeable manner, the wood is so well managed, that the views of the river vary every moment. A gravel walk winds

15 Stroud, *Brown*, pp. 123–5 and pl. 26a.

16 'Capability' Brown to Lord Bute, 11 March 1767 (cited in Stroud, *Brown*, p. 133).

17 Desmond, *Kew*, p. 66.

through it, which commands the most pleasing scenes . . . a flock of sheep scattered about the slopes, add uncommonly to the beauty of the scene.[18]

There could be no better description of the effects at which Brown aimed, but not everyone approved of his destruction of the great terraced walk and avenue at Richmond Gardens. It was regretted, for example, by the anonymous author of a bitterly ironical article, 'On Gardens, and the false taste thereof, particularly of Kew and Richmond'.[19] The King followed the progress on site at Richmond Gardens with great interest, frequently discussing its details with Brown and presumably approving of the latter's demolition in 1766 of Merlin's Cave, the bizarre folly which William Kent built for Queen Caroline in 1730. In 1785 an Act of Parliament was passed, one of the numerous provisions of which enabled the King to unite Richmond Gardens and Kew Gardens by abolishing Kew Lane, popularly known as 'Love Lane', the walled road which had separated them.[20] He was thus able to create a single, delectable garden-estate, running roughly north–south along the banks of the Thames.

Richmond Park

On 23 June 1761 George III appointed Lord Bute Ranger of Richmond Park where many repairs and works costing £6,000 were carried out in 1761–4 under the King's personal supervision.[21] The Rangership of Richmond Park carried with it the occupancy of White Lodge (fig. 10), the hunting lodge built for George II in 1727–8 from designs by Roger Morris. In fact, Lord Bute rarely stayed at White Lodge as the Ranger and virtually shared it with the King and Queen, who visited frequently, entertaining the King of Denmark to breakfast there in 1768. Most remarkably, when Bute died in March 1792, the King decided to take over the Rangership himself, with the Hon. Stephen Digby as Deputy. The contemporary topographer Daniel Lysons (1762–1834) believed that despite the size and antiquity of Richmond Park, it 'has however some defects and deformities, which are now about to be removed, as some improvements are projected which promise to make it one of the most beautiful parks in the kingdom.' He went on to describe the King's ambitious plans for the estate.

It is said that his Majesty who, since the death of the Earl of Bute has taken it in to his own hands, has it in contemplation to cause all the swampy parts to

18 Young, *Farmer's Tour*, vol. II, pp. 247–8. The full account is considerably longer than this extract.

19 *London Magazine*, vol. XLIII, August 1774, pp. 359–61.

20 It also stipulated that the Vestry should build a new workhouse on Pesthouse Common. The King built this at his own expense (Cloake, *Richmond and Kew*, p. 127).

21 Board of Works, Accounts, 142; Letter Books, 3, p. 156; and *Calendar of Home Office Papers, George III*, 1760–5, 25 June 1761 (Cloake, *Richmond and Kew*, p. 116).

be effectively drained, the rough banks to be levelled, and the roads turned where beauty and advantage may be gained by so doing. The open parts, especially the large tract of ground towards East Sheen, are to be ornamented with plantations properly adapted to the elevation of the surface; and the vallies opened so as to carry [i.e. create] the appearance of greater extent, and to give additional grandeur to the old plantations.[22]

As a minor part of this improvement, the King in 1795 approved designs for new gates and a lodge at Richmond Gate on Richmond Hill (fig. 107) by John Soane, who had been appointed Deputy Surveyor of HM Woods and Forests in that year.[23] The rusticated gate piers shown in his drawing[24] may have survived from a design submitted in 1793 by Nathaniel Kent (1737–1810), the King's agricultural agent at Richmond and at Windsor Great Park, but the lodge, built on Richmond Hill in 1798–9, is a perfect miniature essay in the stripped style which Soane devised for economical and functional buildings. Thus its feature of an arch within an arch recalls his lodge and adjacent stables at the Royal Hospital, Chelsea, of 1809–17.

In 1801 the King granted White Lodge to Henry Addington (1757–1844), his new Prime Minister, later Viscount Sidmouth, together with the offer of 60 acres to form a park and gardens to insulate the house from Richmond Park itself. Addington was content with five acres, which were landscaped in 1805 by Humphry Repton.[25] On the King's orders James Wyatt also carried out extensive alterations at White Lodge in 1801–6.[26] This was in Wyatt's capacity as Deputy Surveyor of Woods and Forests, an office in which he had succeeded John Soane in 1799.

Virginia Water

Always at home on the land and with country pursuits, it was at Windsor that George III's interests in landscape design and associated buildings found their most natural expression. As Jane Roberts has shown in her definitive study of the landscape at Windsor, 'the King's major contribution to the history of the English Landscape must be the repair and recreation of Virginia Water, in which he was personally involved through much of the 1780s and 1790s.'[27] Virginia Water had been created in the southern area of the Great Park in 1753 for George III's uncle, William Augustus, Duke of Cumberland, in his capacity as Ranger of the Great Park, with the assistance of his Deputy Ranger, Thomas Sandby. Its great size, 150 acres, made it

22 Lysons, *Environs of London*, vol. 1, *Surrey*, pp. 456–7.

23 See Cloake, *Richmond and Kew*, pp. 118–19.

24 Sir John Soane's Museum 62/9/17.

25 Described by Repton in *Fragments*, pp. 83–5.

26 Colvin, ed., *King's Works*, vol. v, p. 355.

27 J. Roberts, *Royal Landscape*, p. 67.

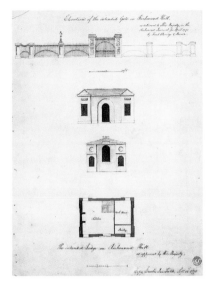

FIG. 107 Sir John Soane, *Design for gates and lodge at Richmond Gate, Richmond Hill*, 1795. Pencil, pen and ink, and watercolour. London, Sir John Soane's Museum (62/9/17)

FIG. 108 Thomas Sandby, *Design for the cascade and grotto at Virginia Water*, c.1788. Pencil, pen and ink, and watercolour. RL 14666

the largest piece of artificial water in the country, but the collapse in 1768 of the original dam or pondhead, constructed only of sand and clay, led to a disastrous flood in the course of torrential rainfall which caused much damage both inside and outside the Park. Though extensive repairs and remodelling were needed, these were not possible for nearly twenty years until the lengthy process of acquiring additional land was finally completed.

A memorable feature of the original Virginia Water was the giant cascade at its eastern end, 30 feet high with an ambitious rockwork grotto at its head.[28] The cascade was destroyed and the grotto damaged in the flood of 1768, but both were replaced by Sandby on George III's orders in the late 1780s (fig. 108).[29] The commissioning of this second cascade and grotto at Virginia Water, on a site 300 yards north of its original position, led to the creation of a sensational combination of sound, light, and darkness. George III's most dramatic venture into the world of the Burkean Sublime, it went beyond the calmer mood of his favourite landscape designer, 'Capability' Brown. The creation of the new cascade and the associated extension of Virginia Water were accompanied by a massive landscaping programme incorporating hills, woods, and lawns, from which unexpected views of the lake could be obtained.

28 It was known on the continent through the engraving of it in Georges Louis Le Rouge, *Jardins anglo-chinois.*

29 J. Roberts, *Royal Landscape*, pp. 475–84 and pls. 519–28.

The new cascade at Virginia Water is closely paralleled by the no less spectacular contemporary cascade which survives at Bowood, Wiltshire. This was created in 1785–7 for the Whig 2nd Earl of Shelburne whom we shall see inspiring Prince Franz of Anhalt-Dessau at Wörlitz. Apparently modelled on a painting by Poussin, the cascade at Bowood stands at the foot of the extensive lake which 'Capability' Brown had formed for Lord Shelburne in 1761–8.

Humphry Repton

As a figurehead in the world of horticultural and agricultural improvement, the King became a natural object of the attentions of Humphry Repton, who had succeeded 'Capability' Brown as the leading landscape designer in the country. Having heard of the King's favourable opinion of the 'Red Books' in which Repton presented his proposals for landscape design to his clients, he obtained permission to dedicate his first published book on his art, *Sketches and Hints on Landscape Gardening* (1795), to the King. After presenting a copy to him at a levée, Repton recorded that 'The King said, "Mr Repton I have been very patient to see this book, I have seen several of your manuscript books, and have read them" . . . pay[ing] me a compliment which many of his Majesty's liege subjects . . . apt to look at the pictures without reading the book . . . had never thought of.'[30]

Repton referred in the dedication of *Sketches and Hints on Landscape Gardening* to the 'gracious patronage of this Volume' by George III, who presided over 'the genius and industry of Great Britain, fostered by our glorious constitution'. Writing in 1794 during the Terror in France, Repton suggested a parallel between gardening and politics which he made more explicit in a letter to Uvedale Price of the same year. In this lengthy letter, which he chose to publish in full in *Sketches and Hints*, he claimed that

> The neatness, simplicity, and elegance of English gardening, have acquired the approbation of the present century, as the happy medium betwixt the wildness of nature and the stiffness of art; in the same manner as the English constitution is the happy medium between the liberty of savages, and the restraint of despotic government; and so long as we enjoy the benefit of these middle degrees, between the extremes of each, let experiments of untried theoretical improvement be made in some other country.[31]

---

30 Humphry Repton, MS Memoir, 213, British Library (quoted in
    Daniels, *Humphry Repton*, p. 191).
31 Repton, *Sketches and Hints*, cited from Loudon, *Landscape Gardening
    and Landscape Architecture*, p. 106.

The proposals made for the King's parkland by Nathaniel Kent, whom we have met as his agricultural consultant, followed many of the principles of Repton. The King owned the third edition (1793) of Kent's *Hints to Gentlemen of Landed Property* (1775) and also ordered for his library three leading publications on the Picturesque: *The Landscape* (1794) by Richard Payne Knight; *Essay on the Picturesque* (1794) by Uvedale Price; and a work by Repton himself. As we saw in Chapter 1, Uvedale Price's younger brother, Major William Price, was the guiding spirit behind Queen Charlotte's garden at Frogmore. Repton recorded that the King 'took my little book in his hand and said "I suspect Repton has the best of it".'[32] If this is so, it is doubtless because of the criticisms made by Uvedale Price and Payne Knight of what they regarded as the bland and outdated artificiality of the King's gardener, Brown. A letter by Uvedale Price has recently come to light which shows that as late as 1798 George III was still firmly on the side of 'Capability' Brown. He found 'great fault' with the extreme opinions on the Picturesque of Uvedale Price, whom he considered 'an enemy to all neatness & comfort; and professed himself a most zealous admirer of Mr Brown . . . I should like to see all Europe like a place of Mr Brown's.'[33] Price responded with a tart but perceptive verse 'On his Majesty's Improvements', partly inspired by his anti-Tory stance:

> Windsor! Thy injured towers, parks, forests, groan
> England! Thy wealth, power, freedom, all are flown
> What various ruin from his pretty tricks
> Whose taste was form'd by Brown; by Bute his politicks.[34]

We also have knowledge of George III's similar opinion of the art of William Gilpin (1724–1804), another leading Picturesque theorist. Gilpin recorded that 'The poor king, who had seen several of my drawings, was speaking of them lately to a friend of mine, only a little time before he was taken ill; Well, said he, I must confess, I like to see something more neat: & I believe nine in ten are of his Majesty's opinion.'[35] Nonetheless, Queen Charlotte and the Princesses were more sympathetic to the romantic aquatint views of landscapes and mountain scenery with which Gilpin illustrated his *Tours*, published between 1782 and 1802.[36]

---

32 Nonetheless, Repton was unsuccessful in his attempt to obtain the office of Deputy Ranger of Windsor Great Park on Sandby's death in June 1798 (J. Roberts, *Royal Landscape*, p. 67).

33 Uvedale Price to Sir George Beaumont, 2 February 1798, Coleorton MSS, Pierpont Morgan Library (quoted in Daniels, *Humphry Repton*, p. 134).

34 *ibid.*, 17 February 1798.

35 William Gilpin to Mary Hartley, 19 December 1788 (quoted in Barbier, *William Gilpin*, p. 171, n. 3).

36 See Bermingham, *Learning to Draw*, pp. 98–115.

The Lodges at Windsor

Cumberland Lodge, known as the Great Lodge till the end of the eighteenth century, is situated about three miles due south of Windsor Castle near the centre of the Great Park, in which it is the largest single building.[37] It had been the official residence of the Ranger of the Great Park from after the Restoration in 1660, at which point it was newly built, but it reverted to the Crown in 1790 on the death of the King's brother, Henry Frederick, Duke of Cumberland, though his widow lived in it until 1803.

In 1800 Wyatt had completely rebuilt the keeper's lodge at Sandpit Gate in Windsor Great Park in a modest castellated style,[38] and in 1803, after the Duchess of Cumberland had moved to Switzerland, the King employed him to remodel Cumberland Lodge, providing a new west (garden) front on an ambitious scale in the lean Gothic style which he was adopting at the Castle, though here carried out in a rather incongruous red brick (fig. 109). Featuring tall windows below a crenellated skyline, the composition is punctuated by slender turrets and a central towered entrance with only a shallow projection.[39] Work was suspended in July 1804 when there were outstanding bills for work costing around £2,000. In the next month, when the King's illness returned, he took an intense dislike to the Queen, declaring that he intended to fit up the Lodge for his own accommodation together with one of his wife's ladies, the Countess of Pembroke, and the two youngest Princesses. This ambition disappeared when

FIG. 109　The west (garden) front of Cumberland Lodge, 1981

37　Hudson, *Cumberland Lodge.*

38　J. Roberts, *Royal Landscape*, p. 363 and pls. 376–7.

39　The interior of Cumberland Lodge was extensively remodelled in the later nineteenth century and twice in the twentieth century.

FIG. 110 After J. Gendall, *The east front of Cranbourne Lodge, Windsor Great Park, c.1823.* Hand-coloured aquatint. RCIN 700926

CRANBURN LODGE.

the King's mind returned to stability in November so that the Royal Family was able to pay a visit at the start of the month 'to see the great improvements making there'.[40]

In 1804 the King turned his attention to Cranbourne Lodge in Windsor Forest. Two miles to the north-west of Cumberland Lodge, this was a handsome house of the 1660s which was the residence of the Keeper of Windsor Forest and the Warden of Cranbourne Chase. The King now commissioned James Wyatt to remodel the house for his bailiff, George Villiers, who had been his Groom of the Bedchamber from 1789. Wyatt transformed the plain building in a highly romantic way by adding a tall, octagonal Gothic tower à la Fonthill Abbey at the north-east corner in 1808, and a square tower at the south end, both in red brick (fig. 110).[41] The work was sufficiently extensive to provide apartments for the use of the King and Queen and their daughters, so that by 1815 the astonishing sum of over £20,000 had been spent on this comparatively modest house of which all that survives today is the octagonal tower.

40   *Gentleman's Magazine*, vol. LXXV, 1805, i, p. 67.

41   J. Roberts, *Royal Landscape*, pp. 289–90 and pls. 289–91.

7

ARCHITECTURE AND COURT CULTURE IN ENGLAND AND ON THE CONTINENT

In the Introduction to this book we noted how it was not until the late twentieth century that historians and art historians began to acknowledge the formative role of the court in early modern Europe. Moreover, from July 1917 when George V changed the name of the Royal House to Windsor,[1] the British were encouraged to forget the links of their monarchy with the courts of Europe, while hostility to Germany was understandably sustained by the Second World War. George III, by contrast, as well as being Elector (from 1814 King) of Hanover, also held the high office of Arch-Treasurer of the Holy Roman Empire, which made him a member of the Empire's Electoral College. Till the end of the Empire in 1806, when he ceased to be an Electoral Prince, it consisted of around 300 sovereign entities, a wider concept even than modern Germany. George III never forgot his dual allegiance to Britain and to the Empire, or at least to Hanover; indeed, according to one contemporary, he once 'laid his hand upon his breast with fine, manly frankness,' and exclaimed 'Oh! My heart will never forget that it pulses with German blood.'[2] British influence on German architecture in the eighteenth century was considerable, and in this chapter we shall concentrate on the princely courts of the Empire to which George III was connected by marriage.

Visitors to England from the Holy Roman Empire

The Seven Years War greatly reduced building activity in France and especially in the German principalities, but not in England. It has not generally been appreciated that, when the war ended in 1763, many foreign visitors came to England to see the latest developments in architecture and particularly in garden design.[3] It almost seemed for a time as though England were rivalling Italy as a Grand Tour destination. The royal gardens with their buildings by Chambers became a central attraction for German visitors to London in the second half of the eighteenth century when Kew was one of the most influential European gardens of the day. George III liked to show it to visitors from the Empire, notably those from Hanover, while Queen Charlotte entertained her relatives at Richmond, among them her brothers: Prince Ernest of Mecklenburg-Strelitz, Military Governor of Celle in George III's Hanoverian territories, and her favourite, Charles, who became Grand Duke Charles of Mecklenburg-Strelitz, Military Governor of Hanover. Visiting London, Prince Ernest discussed topics such as gardening and hunting with George III, sending him a book on trees in 1770. He laid out a garden, the Prinzengarten, on his estate near Celle in which he said that 'everything is in the true English taste,'[4] while

---

1   The previous name had been Saxe-Coburg-Gotha.

2   Hibbert, *George III*, p. 373.

3   For an overview of German interest in English literature

and culture in the Enlightenment, see Maurer, *Aufklärung und Anglophilie*.

4   Quoted in M. Köhler, 'The German Connection', n. 8.

the great garden historian Christian Hirschfeld (1742–92), praised it for features such as its 'aspect champêtre' and extensive cow pastures.[5] The U-shaped house at the Prinzengarten, one-storeyed, of timber construction, with a tall mansard roof, was suitably pastoral and modest for its setting. Queen Charlotte recommended Prince Ernest, on a visit to Richmond in 1771, to build a thatched cottage along the lines of hers at Kew.

Prince Charles of Mecklenburg-Strelitz, who visited the royal gardens at Richmond in 1771, wrote of them, 'that is my paradise,' and laid out a landscaped park in the style of 'Capability' Brown at his summer residence of Hohenzieritz, north of Neustrelitz.[6] This was probably designed by the Scottish botanist and gardener Archibald Thompson, who worked for the Earl of Bute at Luton Hoo.[7] Prince Charles, who was ruling Duke of Mecklenburg-Strelitz from 1794, introduced the question of the relation of the passion for the *jardin anglais* on the continent to the views of Rousseau on nature, morality, and sensibility. Having studied at Geneva in 1758, where he became acquainted with the writings of Rousseau, he 'instigated a Rousseauesque festival for the local population by a consecrated forest altar in his garden' at Hohenzieritz in 1796.[8] To accompany the garden, he remodelled the house in a provincial Anglo-Palladian manner, providing Sheraton and Hepplewhite furniture in the dining room, and scenic wallpaper depicting country houses in romantic landscapes in the games room.[9]

Other visitors to England, including some not related to the royal family, were Duke Charles Eugene of Württemberg, who built a mosque in the garden at Hohenheim, near Stuttgart, in 1778, doubtless inspired by what he had seen at Kew; Count Friedrich Kielmansegge;[10] Count Karl Friedrich Hardenberg; Prince Ludwig zu Bentheim Steinfurt;[11] the botanist, Jakob Friedrich Erhardt; Count von Brühl, Saxon ambassador and patron of the pioneering watchmaker Thomas Mudge; Count Karl von Zinzendorf, a leading figure at the reforming Enlightenment court of Emperor Joseph II in Vienna;[12] Jobst Anton von Hinüber, the postmaster at Hanover and Counsellor to the Legation of George III as Elector of Hanover; and the scientist, man of letters, and anglophile, Georg Christoph Lichtenberg (1742–99).[13]

Lichtenberg, perhaps the most significant of these, visited England in 1769 and the following year was appointed Assistant Professor of Physics at Göttingen University, which, 'in the absence of a regular court at Hanover, acquired a surrogate courtly role',[14] attracting German, Russian, and English aristocratic students. He came to England as tutor in 1774–5 to two of his pupils at Göttingen, the sons of Lord Boston who was Chamberlain to Augusta, Dowager

---

5 Hirschfeld, *Théorie*, vol. III, p. 284. Translations from Hirschfeld are my own.

6 Hinz, 'Die Parklandschaft Hohenzieritz'.

7 Adamiak, *Schlösser und Gärten in Mecklenburg*, pp. 254–5, and M. Köhler, *Historische Gärten um Neubrandenburg*, pp. 77–8.

8 Information from Professor Marcus Köhler, cited in Campbell Orr,

'Queen Charlotte', p. 257.

9 See Brandt, *Alt-Mecklenburgische Schlösser*, pls. 152–5.

10 See Kielmansegge, *Diary of a Journey to England*.

11 His 'Journal of an English Journey' of 1783, during which the gardens he visited included Richmond and Kew, is in the Fürst zu Bentheim Archive (information from Mr John Harris).

FIG. 111 Johann Zoffany,
*Queen Charlotte with
members of her family*,
(detail), 1771–2. Oil on
canvas. RCIN 401004

Princess of Wales. Lichtenberg was a great admirer of Queen Charlotte and attracted the attention of George III, who spent two hours with him in his Observatory at Kew showing him its instruments.[15] He also employed Lichtenberg to take latitudinal observations around Hanover, Stade, and Osnabrück, while Lichtenberg in turn developed an interest in English life and culture, publishing a volume of letters written from England and also a comprehensive study of Hogarth's engravings.[16] In 1775 he gave his address as Kew Gardens,[17] and his close relation with the King and Queen was doubtless one reason why they sent their three youngest surviving sons, the Dukes of Cumberland, Sussex, and Cambridge, to Göttingen University in 1786.

Jobst Anton von Hinüber kept a diary of his visit to England in 1766–7 in which he recorded Kew.[18] As a result, he laid out an ambitious *jardin anglo-chinois* at Marienwerder, near Herrenhausen, in 1761–81, including a small Chinese pavilion. He was described as 'one of the greatest garden connoisseurs' by Hirschfeld, who published a long account of his achievement

FIG. 111 Johann Zoffany, *Queen Charlotte with members of her family*, (detail), 1771–2. Oil on canvas. RCIN 401004

12   Zinzendorf visited Kew Gardens in March 1768, praising particularly the 'Turkish pavilion', 'the tower of Nankin', and the 'several thousand different sorts of trees' (see Hajós, 'Gardens of the British Isles').

13   See *Georg Christoph Lichtenberg, 1724–99. Wagnis der Aufklärung*, Darmstadt and Göttingen 1992 (exh. cat.).

14   According to Dr Clarissa Campbell Orr.

15   Mare and Quarrell, *Lichtenberg's Visits to England*.

16   *Briefe aus England*, 1776–8, and *Ausführliche Erklärung der Hogarthschen Kupferstiche*, 8 vols., Göttingen 1794–9.

17   Lichtenberg to Ernst Gottfried Baldinger, Kew, 10 January 1775, in Mautner, *Georg Christoph Lichtenberg*, vol. IV, p. 153.

18   Familienarchiv von Hinüber, Burgdorff, Hanover.

at Marienwerder.[19] Another influential English garden, called Georgengarten, was created near Herrenhausen in the late 1760s by Count Johann Ludwig von Wallmoden-Gimborn (1736–1811), an illegitimate son of King George II and Amalie von Wallmoden.[20] Meanwhile, the court gardener of Saarbrücken, Friedrich Koellner, copied plans of Richmond, while his relative, the gardener Johann Ernst August Bernhard Petri, travelled to Kew and to other gardens.[21]

The story we have outlined here of how, from the 1760s, the English landscape garden was adopted in principalities in the Holy Roman Empire can be said to have reached a climax when it came to influence Prussian princely gardening under the leading landscape designer, Peter Joseph Lenné the younger (1789–1866).[22] After a visit to England in 1822, where he had been influenced by the work of William Kent, Lenné returned to Berlin to work for the Crown Prince of Prussia, later King Frederick William IV. The King was a great-nephew of Queen Charlotte: his mother, Louise, was the daughter of Queen Charlotte's brother, Charles. Thus the Mecklenburg-Strelitz family was increasingly drawn into the Prussian orbit. The future Frederick William IV had been trained in architecture by the great architect Karl Friedrich Schinkel (1781–1841), with whom he and Lenné created the perfect house and land-scape of Schloss Charlottenhof at Sanssouci from 1825.

The Central Role of Chambers

Admired on the continent as no other British architect, the King's Anglo-Swedish tutor, William Chambers, was at the heart of the architectural culture of the European Enlightenment. Equally at home in Rome, Paris, London, Gothenburg, and Canton, he urged his pupils to 'Converse much with artists of all Countrys, particularly foreigners, that you may get rid of national prejudices,'[23] and he himself trained in architecture in Paris and Rome. His master-piece was Somerset House (1776–96), a sophisticated essay in the Franco-Italian neo-classical style which was the largest government office in Europe. It was also the home of the Royal Academy which, with the encouragement of Chambers, George III had founded in 1768.

In their return to primary sources, Enlightenment thinkers sought links between different cultures, as Chambers did in suggesting parallels between antique and ancient Chinese architec-ture in his *Designs for Chinese Buildings* (1757), which he dedicated to George, Prince of Wales. His *Dissertation on Oriental Gardening* (1772) was dedicated to the same individual – as George III – while both books were translated into French in the year of their publication. The latter

19   Hirschfeld, *Théorie*, vol. v, 1785, pp. 227–69.

20   See '*Zurück zur Natur'. Idee und Geschichte des Georgengartens in Hannover-Herrenhausen*, Landeshauptstadt Hannover, Göttingen 1997 (exh. cat.).

21   Lohmeyer, *Südwestdeutsche Gärten*, p. 20, and Staatsarchiv

München, MF 18735 (1794–1806).

22   There is a considerable literature on Lenné, but see Butlar, *Peter Joseph Lenné*.

23   Sir John Soane's Museum, SM Private Correspondence i.c.7.1.

even appeared in German as *Über die Orientalische Gartenkunst; eine Abhandlung aus dem Englischen des Herren William Chambers* (Gotha, 1775), the publication of which was doubtless promoted by George III's cousin, Duke Ernest of Saxe-Gotha-Altenburg, of whom more shortly.[24]

Chambers chose to send a copy of his *Dissertation on Oriental Gardening* to Voltaire in 1772, explaining that 'The taste of gardening, as it seems to me, is very indifferent all over Europe: a wish to see it mended, has induced me to th[r]ow out a few hints upon that subject . . . so well deserving the Attention of Genius: 'tis much to be regretted that Monsieur de Voltaire . . . has never employed his thoughts upon this.'[25] Aware of Chambers's popularity on the continent, Voltaire's reply from Ferney included the ironical observation that 'a German prince who sought to be your pupil would ruin himself.'[26]

However, anglomania was the rage in the Europe of the Enlightenment where English liberty was seen as sustained by the British constitutional monarchy. A key figure in Anglo-German connections in garden design was the German-Swiss architect, Johann Heinrich Müntz (1727–98), who worked for Chambers at Kew Gardens, for Chambers's patron, Lord Charlemont, at Marino House, near Dublin, for Horace Walpole at Strawberry Hill, and for Richard Bateman at Old Windsor.[27] At Kew, he designed the 'Gothic Cathedral' in 1759 and probably gave Chambers the drawing which provided the inspiration for the Moorish 'Alhambra'. Müntz later worked in Poland and at Schloss Wilhelmshöhe at Kassel where he seems to have designed the mosque next to the Chinese village.[28] Other mosques close to that of 1761 at Kew were built at Schwetzingen, near Mannheim, and at Steinfurt, near Münster. The former was built in 1778–96 for Charles Theodore, Bavarian Elector, by the French architect, Nicolas de Pigage (1723–96), in the park at Schwetzingen where his other garden buildings, notably the Temples of Minerva and of Apollo of the 1760s, are also close to parallels at Kew. The Temple of Botany which Pigage built at Schwetzingen would have appealed to Lord Bute and Princess Augusta. Trained in Paris, like Chambers, Pigage considered writing a book on English landscaped gardens and may have seen Chambers's mosque at Kew. Certainly, the Turkish taste was very much à la mode in France in the 1780s.

The mosque at Steinfurt was built in the *jardin anglo-chinois* laid out for Prince Ludwig zu Bentheim-Steinfurt in 1780–7.[29] The unexpected frequency of mosques in the Holy Roman Empire, as at Hohenheim, Schwetzingen, and Steinfurt, may possibly be related to memories of the Turkish military frontier with which so many Central European and German princes

24 This family became that of Saxe-Coburg and Gotha, which produced Prince Albert.

25 Besterman, *Correspondence of Voltaire*, vol. LXXXII, p. 101, Chambers to Voltaire, 3 July 1772.

26 *ibid.*, Voltaire to Chambers, 7 August 1772. My translation.

27 See J. Harris, *A Catalogue of British Drawings … in American Collections*, pp. 143–8.

28 Dittscheid, *Kassel-Wilhelmshöhe und die Krise des Schlossbaues*, pl. 184.

29 See Le Rouge, *Jardins anglo-chinois*, Cahier 17/18, pls. 14–16.

serving with the Habsburgs would have become familiar. The fashion for Turkish tents and costume, and the Turkish music of Mozart and Beethoven, was a souvenir of the triumph over Turkey after the Treaty of Passarowitz of 1718, which ended the Turkish War.[30]

It was in garden design rather than architecture that links between England and the Empire were at their closest in the second half of the eighteenth century.[31] Royal patronage in gardening and agriculture in Hanover alone is evident from the establishment of the University and Botanical Garden at Göttingen in 1737–8, the Botanical Garden at Herrenhausen, and the Society for Agriculture at Celle in 1765. The central role played by English gardens such as Kew and by the associated Picturesque theory was clear to Hirschfeld, author of *Theorie der Gartenkunst* (1779–85), which was published simultaneously in German and in French as *Théorie de l'art des jardins*.[32] Hirschfeld, surprisingly little studied by modern garden historians,[33] was a painter and Professor of Philosophy and the Fine Arts at Kiel University. In his remarkably comprehensive aesthetic, theoretical, and historical survey of eighteenth-century gardens throughout Europe and Russia, he established garden design as one of the fine arts. In support of his proposal that garden design is an art which should form impressions on the spirit and the soul, he quoted from authors such as Addison, Chambers, Whately, Banks, Watelet, Winckelmann, and Rousseau, drawing especially on Henry Home's *Elements of Criticism* (1762), which had been dedicated to George III. Hirschfeld's numerous illustrations included one of the Belvedere in Windsor Great Park, built as an eye-catcher by George III's uncle, the Duke of Cumberland (fig. 112). Hirschfeld claimed that the crude strength and 'memories of ancient customs' of such Gothic towers made them appropriate for settings with an 'untamed atmosphere'.[34]

Hirschfeld praised George III for his knowledge of architecture and botany, as well as for 'his soul, full of sweetness and equally open to feelings for nature as for humanity, tenderness and friendship'.[35] He went on to admire him for retreating from public life to the White House at Kew, which he described as 'a house full of simplicity and modest elegance', illustrating both it and Chambers's Temple of Victory at Kew.[36] Praising this temple as 'perfect and superb', he noted that it was built to commemorate the victory near Minden of 1759 by the allied armies under the command of Duke Ferdinand of Brunswick, uncle of George III's future brother-in-law. As we saw in Chapter 2, George III, when Chambers's pupil as Prince of Wales, made a drawing closely based on the Temple of Victory (figs. 35, 36).

30 I owe this suggestion to Bridget Wright.

31 See, for example, Weiss, *Sir William Chambers*.

32 See Schepers, *Hirschfeld's Théorie*.

33 But see Parshall, 'C.C.L. Hirschfeld's Concept of the Garden

in the German Enlightenment'.

34 Hirschfeld, *Théorie*, vol. IV, p. 38.

35 *ibid.*, vol. III p. 86.

36 *ibid.*, vol. II, p. 139, and vol. III, p. 87.

FIG. 112 Pierre Charles Canot after Thomas Sandby, *The Belvedere, Windsor Great Park*, 1754. Engraving. RCIN 814377

The Swedish and Russian Courts

In 1775 a Swedish scholar said of Chambers that he 'considers himself a Swede',[37] for Chambers had been born in Gothenburg and was elected a member of the Swedish Academy of Sciences in 1766. Carl Frederik Adelcrantz (1716–96), Supervisor of Court Buildings in Stockholm, drew on Chambers's *Designs for Chinese Buildings* when creating the enchanting Chinese House at Drottningholm (1763–9) for King Adolphus Frederick of Sweden (1710–71).[38] King Adolphus's wife, Queen Louisa Ulrica (1720–82), a niece of King George II of Great Britain, was a sister of Frederick the Great and part of a complicated network of northern imperial dynastic links. It is within this context that her patronage, as well as that of Catherine the Great and of Prince Franz of Anhalt-Dessau, should be set. She gave Chambers a gold box in 1767, ornamented with images of royal buildings and gardens in Sweden, and about two years later commissioned him to provide designs for a palace and gardens for her at Svartsjö, near Stockholm, which he exhibited at the Royal Academy in London in 1775.

Doubtless with the encouragement of Queen Louisa Ulrica's son, the future King Gustavus III of Sweden (1746–92), Chambers was created a *Chevalier de l'ordre de l'étoile polaire* in April–May 1770, so that, with the special permission of George III, he was styled Sir William Chambers in England. Chambers sent a copy of his *Dissertation on Oriental Gardening* (1772) to a king whose architectural education was a parallel to that which George III received from Chambers and Kirby, for skilled architectural drawings and garden designs survive in his hand.[39] Like George III, Gustavus III also appreciated the importance of academies, creating Swedish academies in 1771 and 1786. He had a passion for architecture throughout his life, was an amateur architect,

The New Building on Shrubs Hill

---

37 J. Harris, *Chambers*, p. 12.

38 See *Chambers & Adelcrantz*.

39 See Olausson, 'Gustav III 1746–92', in Andersson, *et al.*, eds., *Svensk Trädgårdskonst under fyrhundra år*, pp. 97–105, and Alm, *Kina Slott*.

and promoted a French neo-classical style in interior design and furniture which became known as Gustavian. Chambers must have wished that George III would follow his example even more closely. However, such a wish would have served to emphasise the differences in political culture and therefore in spending power between the two kings. Following the unfulfilled ambitions of his mother, Louisa Ulrica, who was not a supporter of the parliamentary style of monarchy which had prevailed in Sweden, Gustavus III adopted a more absolutist style of government. He may thus have been freer to build than George III, but was assassinated in an aristocratic coup.

CATHERINE THE GREAT

Empress Catherine the Great of Russia (1729–96), the former Princess Sophia Frederica of Anhalt-Zerbst, a minor German princely family, was one of the most remarkable eighteenth-century patrons of architecture and landscape design.[40] In 1745, she married, as part of a network of politics and patronage within the northern Holy Roman Empire, the son of Charles Frederick, Duke of Holstein-Gottorp. He was heir to the Russian throne, to which he succeeded as Peter III in 1762, but he was assassinated six months later. While Peter had been a great admirer of Frederick the Great and Prussian culture, Catherine acquired those products of the Industrial Revolution in England which were exported in the last third of the eighteenth century: Wedgwood creamware, ormolu by Boulton, Coade stone, and decorative cast iron.[41] The signing of the second Anglo-Russian trading agreement in 1766 flooded the Russian market with British goods for the next twenty years.

A passionate anglophile, Catherine appointed as her architect Charles Cameron (*c*.1740–1811), a Scot who had dedicated his book, *The Baths of the Ancients Explained and Illustrated* (1772), to Lord Bute in the hope of gaining commissions. She also paid the enormous sum of 1,000 roubles in the early 1780s for two albums of 150 drawings of the buildings, gardens, and park at Hampton Court Palace. These are by John Spyers, who worked as draughtsman to 'Capability' Brown, Royal Gardener at Hampton Court from 1764 to 1783.[42] This purchase can be compared to the Green Frog service which she ordered from Wedgwood in 1773, consisting of 944 pieces decorated at her request with 1,222 examples of medieval and modern British architecture, parks, and gardens. It has been described as 'the largest and most complicated commission ever to be received by an English ceramics firm'.[43]

---

40 To set her interest in context, see Cross, 'British Gardeners and the Vogue of the English Garden in late Eighteenth-century Russia'.

41 See Clifford, 'Anglomania'.

42 The drawings were discovered in the Hermitage store in 2002. See Dedinkin 'Hampton Court Rediscovered', where it is pointed out that

'the total she spent in the 1780s on laying out the vast park surrounding the English Palace [Peterhof] was just over 10,000 roubles, or only 10 times the price of the albums.'

43 Liackhova, 'Wedgwood's Green Frog Service and the Imperial Court', p. 117.

She put a special emphasis on the inclusion of Gothic buildings because the service was to be used in the Kekerekeksinen (frog marsh) Palace, built for her in an English Gothic style in 1774–7 from designs by Yuri Velten (1730–1801) as one of the earliest Gothic Revival buildings in or near St Petersburg.

Familiar with Thomas Whately's *Observations on Modern Gardening* (1770),[44] Catherine translated Chambers's *Designs for Chinese Buildings* into Russian, and created a Chinese Village at Tsarskoe Selo, where she was also responsible for a great landscaped park, the first of its kind in Russia. This was created in two phases between 1770 and 1789, partly by Johann Busch, her gardener from the early 1770s until 1789.[45] Born near Lüneburg, Busch had been a gardener at Kensington Gardens or at one of the local nurseries from about 1744 and eventually became a British subject as John Busch. His daughter Catherine married Charles Cameron in 1784. In Busch's hands, the park at Tsarskoe Selo evolved so that it became a model for many other gardens in Russia. There was also an ambitious pagoda at Tsarskoe Selo, built in 1780 from designs by Cameron, who had for his guidance a model of Chambers's pagoda at Kew that had been commissioned by the Russian Ambassador at the Court of St James's.[46] Catherine wrote to Voltaire from Peterhof in 1772 that

> I now love to distraction gardens in the English style, the curving lines, the gentle slopes, the ponds resembling lakes, the groups of islands on firm land, and I have a profound contempt for straight lines, twinned avenues, I hate fountains which torture water to follow a path contrary to its nature . . . In a word, my anglomania predominates over my plantomania.[47]

As a result, she approached George III in 1793 with a request for plants and seeds to be sent to her from Kew Gardens. After the terrible winter of 1794–5, the King met Joseph Banks at Kew in April 1795, ordering 'as compleat a Collection of Exotic Plants as can possibly be Spard [*sic*]', and was also 'pleased to Direct that Plans & Elevations of the Principal Hothouses at Kew' should accompany them to Russia.[48] The King's foreman at Kew Gardens *c.*1790–1800, the German George Noe, who had been born at Stuttgart, travelled to St Petersburg with the collection.[49]

44 See Cross, 'Catherine the Great'.

45 See M. Köhler, *Frühe Landschaftsgärten in Russland und Deutschland*.

46 Shvidovsky, *Empress and Architect*, pp. 175–6.

47 Besterman, *Correspondence of Voltaire*, vol. LXXXII, p. 130, Catherine II to Voltaire, July 1772. My translation.

48 H. Carter, 'Sir Joseph Banks and the Plant Collection from Kew sent to the Empress Catherine II of Russia 1795', p. 230.

49 In 1800 Noe returned to Stuttgart to work in the gardens of Duke Charles Eugene of Württemberg, who had married George III's eldest daughter, the Princess Royal.

Vue du Belvédére situé vers le Septentrion du Nouveau
Palais &c. Sans-souci

FIG. 113 A.L. Krüger after J.F. Meyer, *Vue du Belvedére situé vers le Septentrion du Nouveau Palais de Sans Souci*, 1772. Engraving, hand-coloured by A. Niegelssohn, 1797. RCIN 704636.f

Courts of the Holy Roman Empire[50]

FREDERICK THE GREAT

One of the most ambitious royal patrons of architecture was George III's first cousin once removed, King Frederick II of Prussia (1712–86),[51] known as Frederick the Great as early as 1745.[52] As we shall see, he sought to appoint William Chambers as his architect in 1752. Britain was allied to Prussia throughout most of the Seven Years War (1756–63), with George II and George III sending annual subsidies to him. Like his father and George III, he also suffered from the appalling hereditary disease of porphyria. His mother was the daughter of George I of England and he long shared her ambition that he should take as his bride Princess Amelia, a daughter of George II. Princess Frederica, the daughter of Frederick the Great's nephew and successor, Frederick William II of Prussia, married George III's favourite son, the Duke of York.

A key figure in the transmission to Frederick the Great of new developments in English architecture was Francesco Algarotti (1712–64),[53] the architectural theorist and courtier, who

50 I am greatly indebted to Professor Marcus Köhler for providing me with information about the relations between the English court and those of the Holy Roman Empire.

51 See Giersberg, *Friedrich als Bauherr*. Though an excellent study, this is narrow in focus and does not relate Frederick II to court patronage as a whole.

52 According to Schieder, *Friedrich der Große*. (For an abbreviated translation of this book, see Sabina Berkeley and H.M. Scott, *Frederick the Great*, London and New York 2000).

53 For correspondence between Frederick the Great and Algarotti, see Wegner, *Nach Albions Stränden*, which concentrates on later architects, notably Langhans, Gentz, and the elder and younger Gilly.

had been a guest of the Earl of Burlington at his Chiswick villa and was made Court Chamberlain by Frederick the Great in 1747. Frederick commissioned his friend, Georg Wenzeslaus von Knobelsdorff (1699–1753), to build the Berlin Opera House in 1740–3 in the Anglo-Palladian manner of buildings such as Colen Campbell's Wanstead House, Essex (c.1714–20), as illustrated in *Vitruvius Britannicus* (vol. I, 1715; vol. III, 1725). Copies of this publication were available in Frederick the Great's library, while Lord Burlington was also asked to send drawings of his work to the King.

The Neues Palais, which the King built in 1763–9 at Sanssouci, Potsdam, was based on the south front of Castle Howard, completed in 1714, again through the medium of engravings in *Vitruvius Britannicus*. The architect of the Neues Palais was Johann Gottfried Büring (1723–c.1788), who had been trained by Jacques-François Blondel at his École des Arts in Paris in 1748, when Chambers was also there. Frederick the Great also rebuilt the town of Potsdam with numerous Anglo-Palladian houses inspired by these engravings, including one described as 'Hiller-Brand's House . . . one of the most splendid ones, a copy of the Royal Palace of Whitehall in England, erected after [Karl von] Gontard's proposal'.[54]

Negotiations were under way in 1752 for the appointment of William Chambers, then in Rome, as 'architect [*sic*] du roy' to Frederick the Great.[55] Nothing came of these and Jean-Laurent Legeay (c.1710–c.1786) was appointed royal architect in 1756. Legeay had been architect to a relative of Queen Charlotte, Duke Christian Louis of Mecklenburg-Schwerin, from 1748 to 1755, in which capacity he designed a formal garden with a canal at Schwerin. In 1766 he sent from London a project for the palace of Ludwigslust,[56] which remained unexecuted. A friend of William Chambers from Paris and Rome, he visited England to seek work in 1767–8 and drew Chambers's Casino at Marino House, Dublin.

Meanwhile, in 1763 Chambers was paid for a set of drawings for chinoiserie bridges[57] for Frederick the Great who, though he did not execute these, built the Dragon House in the park at Sanssouci in 1754–64. Designed by Büring on the basis of Frederick's own designs, this was an echo on a smaller scale of Chambers's pagoda at Kew of 1761–2.[58] It was used for the first time at a dinner in April 1764 attended by Prince Henry of Prussia, two Princes of Brunswick, and George Keith, 10th and last Earl Marischal of Scotland (c.1693–1778), an anti-clerical free-thinker and benefactor of Rousseau. Keith, who lived at Sanssouci, and his brother, Field Marshal James Keith (1696–1758), were two remarkable figures who both

54 Nicolai, *Breschreibung der königlichen Residenzstädte Berlin und Potsdam*, vol. III, p. 1175.

55 Letter from John Forbes to William Chambers, 3 February 1752 (Chambers papers, RIBA). See Huth, 'Chambers and Potsdam'.

56 According to Dobert, *Bauten und Baumeister in Ludwigslust*, pp. 7–8.

57 Giersberg, *Friedrich als Bauherr*, p. 139. One is reproduced in J. Harris,

Chambers, pl. 42. It is close to the pavilions at a Cantonese pagoda illustrated in Chambers's *Designs for Chinese Buildings*, pls. II–III.

58 It was close to the Chinese kiosk at Lunéville of 1740 by Emmanuel Héré de Corny published in 1753 (see *Das Chinesische Haus im Park von Sanssouci*, Berlin 1993). Frederick the Great's sisters commissioned Chinese pavilions at Drottningholm and Bayreuth.

served Frederick the Great. One of them probably provided him with *Vitruvius Britannicus* and also asked Chambers to design the chinoiserie bridges at Sanssouci. Another architect, Karl von Gontard (1731–91), designed the Temples of Friendship and Antiquity for Frederick at Sanssouci in the late 1760s. These were in the Franco-Roman style of William Chambers, whom he probably knew in 1750–2 when he was at J.-F. Blondel's École des Arts, where Büring had also been trained. Similarly elegant was the circular, two-storeyed and colonnaded Belvedere on Klausberg Hill at Sanssouci (fig. 113), built for Frederick the Great in 1770–2 from designs by Georg Christian Unger (1743–1812), a pupil of Gontard.

PRINCESS AUGUSTA OF BRUNSWICK

In 1764 George III's sister, Princess Augusta, married Duke Charles William Ferdinand of Brunswick (1735–1806), who reigned as Charles II from 1780 till 1806.[59] We saw him in Chapter 5 as a Knight of the Garter who contributed to the cost of George III's alterations to St George's Chapel, Windsor. Duke Charles's uncle was Frederick the Great; two great-aunts were an Empress and a Tsar's mother respectively; his sister, Anna Amalia of Weimar, was a patron of Goethe; and his daughter became George's IV's unhappy bride, Queen Caroline. Though only a modest German state, Brunswick thus came to occupy a position at the heart of the courts of Europe. After their marriage in 1764, Augusta and her husband initially remained in

FIG. 114   Caroline, Princess of Wales, *View of Richmond, near Brunswick,* 1810. Pen and ink and wash.
RL K 485

London, travelling to Italy and France, until they settled in Brunswick in 1767.[60] In that year 'Capability' Brown was asked to provide designs for a park for Augusta near Brunswick to be 'laid out in the English Tast [*sic*]'[61] on land she had bought with her dowry. Here she built an elegant summer residence which she called Richmond (fig. 114) because its sloping site, overlooking the River Oker, recalled her family home,[62] though it seems to have served as a retreat from her philandering husband. The grounds of Richmond were laid out for her by Götze as the first English garden of their kind in Germany, based on the designs which had been submitted by 'Capability' Brown.

Built in 1768 from designs by the court architect Karl

59   He was descended from Duke Anton Ulrich of Brunswick-Wolfenbüttel, one of the great collector-princes of the Baroque age who converted to Catholicism and became a friend of Louis XIV. His Baroque gardens at Saltsdahm were, as we have noted, a rival to those at Herrenhausen.

60   In 1764 the Duke built the Kammergebäude (Ducal Council Chamber)

in Brunswick from designs by E.H. Horn. A Palladian building with the ducal arms in the pediment, it was a foretaste of neo-classicism in Brunswick (Watkin and Mellinghoff, *German Architecture*, p. 211 and pl. 165).

61   Letter of 28 October 1767, quoted in M. Köhler, 'German Connection', p. 29.

62   Watkin and Mellinghoff, *German Architecture*, p. 52 and pls. 38–9.

Fleischer (1727–87), the elegant house or *pavillon* at Richmond was praised by Hirschfeld for its 'favourable situation in which one can freely enjoy freely the beauties of nature . . . in a mild spring or a fine autumn'.[63] With its Palladian pedimented windows divided by Corinthian pilasters, it recalls the work of Chambers, whose designs for the new palace for George III at Richmond Princess Augusta and her husband would doubtless have seen while in England in 1765.[64] Its round-headed French windows are certainly close to those of the Orangery at Kew by Chambers of 1757.[65] In the same year in which Princess Augusta built Richmond near Brunswick, 1768, her brother, George III, commissioned William Chambers to create the equally Francophile *pavillon* at Richmond Gardens in which to entertain his cousin and brother-in-law, Christian VII, King of Denmark.

DUKE ERNEST OF SAXE-GOTHA-ALTENBURG

George III's cousin, Duke Ernest II of Saxe-Gotha-Altenburg (1745–1804), was an Enlightenment prince and patron who in 1768 travelled in Holland and England, and in France where he met Diderot and the *Encyclopédistes*. Deciding on his return to create a Picturesque English garden at Gotha, near Schloss Friedenstein, he sought advice from his aunt, George III's mother, Augusta, Princess of Wales, because he had doubtless seen the remarkable gardens which she had created at Kew. She sent him John Haverfield (1705–84), chief gardener of the royal gardens at Richmond and Kew, who had also been involved with 'Capability' Brown on the great park he designed for Lord Bute at Luton Hoo. The garden created during the 1770s at Gotha, which became one of the most celebrated of its day, was described enthusiastically by Hirschfeld, who particularly praised Haverfield as 'the English artist, the initial author of the garden', whose illusionistic skills made the lake seem larger than it is.[66] Haverfield's son, the younger John Haverfield (1744–1820), was an architect and landscape gardener who was frequently employed by Soane, for whom he provided advice on the planting and layout of the grounds of his house, Pitzhanger Manor, Middlesex. The younger Haverfield also maintained his family links with Germany, supplying Soane with the drawing of the gardens at Herrenhausen on which Soane based his illustration of them in his Royal Academy lectures.[67]

One of the most novel features of the garden at Gotha, laid out by the elder John Haverfield for Duke Ernest, was a Greek Doric temple, built of stone.[68] Overlooked by historians of the

63 Hirschfeld, *Théorie*, vol. v, p. 369.

64 However, its diamond-shaped plan may also owe something to the Pavilion de Hanovre in Paris, built in 1761 by the architect, Jean-Michel Chevotet, a work greatly admired by Voltaire. Its façades were removed in 1832 from the Boulevard des Capucines and re-erected in the park at Sceaux, near Paris.

65 A point noted in Cloake, *Richmond and Kew*, p. 54.

66 See M. Köhler, 'Friedrich Karl von Hardenberg's (1696–1763) Journeys to England'.

67 Sir John Soane's Museum, Private Correspondence I.H.10, 1, Haverfield to Soane, 4 August 1812 (quoted in Watkin, *Soane*, p. 375).

68 Hirschfeld, *Théorie*, vol. iv, p. 277.

Greek Revival, this was based on the gateway to the Agora in Athens, as illustrated in the first volume of Stuart and Revett's *Antiquities of Athens*[69] which, as we have seen, was dedicated to King George III. The temple contained a statue of Diana[70] which Duke Ernest commissioned from Jean-Antoine Houdon (1741–1828), noted for his representations of numerous monarchs but also of key Enlightenment and Revolutionary figures such as Diderot, Voltaire, Franklin, and Washington. Houdon also created a handsome portrait of Duke Ernest in the form of a bronzed plaster medallion, combining elements of Greek and Roman coins that represented kings or emperors.[71]

Ernest II founded an art academy at his court and, like George III, spent large sums on his astronomical observatory and his library, while he also used his Privy Purse to promote 'a wide-ranging scientific and educational programme . . . of public benefit to the small duchy of Saxe-Gotha and its citizens'. The eventual abandonment of his project to build a family mausoleum at Gotha[72] has been interpreted as the result of a family 'which found it increasingly difficult to legitimise its claim [to political power] through ostentatious display', so that 'it turned to the creation of educational and scientific institutions aimed at modernising and improving the state.'[73]

THE HESSE-KASSEL FAMILY

In 1740 George III's aunt, Mary (Marie) (1723–72), a daughter of George II, married Landgrave Frederick II of Hesse-Kassel (1720–85) with whom in the late 1760s she introduced for the first time English elements into the great Baroque park of Wilhelmshöhe, outside Kassel, and at Wilhelmsbad, the fashionable spa near Hanau.[74] They sent their court gardener, Schwarzkopf, to England to study the new gardens,[75] while Wilhelmsbad, with its Gothic ruins and pyramid tomb, is also close to Parc Monceau, Paris, the crowded *jardin anglo-chinois* of 1773–8 by Carmontelle. The anglophile Landgrave Frederick II was a model Enlightenment patron, a benefactor of charitable institutions and champion of the arts, sciences, and town planning. At a time when the state was still bankrupt following the Seven Years War, he helped finance these activities by providing a mercenary army of 12,000 men to George III to serve in the American War of Independence. Frederick II's son, William IX (1743–1821) sent his court architect, Heinrich Christoph Jussow (1754–1825), to England in 1787, where his activities included studying gardens such as the King's at Virginia Water.[76] His subsequent design in

69 Vol. I, ch. 1, pl. III.

70 Dated 1776, it is today in the Schloss Museum, Gotha. See Arnason, *Sculptures of Houdon*, pp. 43–4 and fig. 9.

71 Mathias, 'Houdon and the German Courts'.

72 Frank, *et al.*, 'Diderot, Guiard and Houdon'.

73 *ibid.*, part II, pp. 482–3.

74 See Modrow, 'Der Staatspark Wilhelmsbad, Hanau'.

75 I am indebted to Dr Wilfried Rogasch for this information.

76 See J. Harris and Korzus, 'Sich in der Anlegen der englischen Bau Arten wohl zu informiren'.

FIG. 115 H. and J.H. Bleuler, *The Steinhoffer waterfall near the Löwenburg*, 1825. Hand-coloured engraving. RCIN 812807

about 1792 for a waterfall and Devil's bridge, presumably for the park at Wilhelmshöhe, is close to sketches by Thomas Sandby for such features at Virginia Water.[77] The German translation of 1775 of Chambers's *Dissertation on Oriental Gardening* (1772) was in the library of Schloss Wilhelmshöhe.[78]

The Landgrave and Landgravine – both of whom were George III's first cousins – left Wilhelmsbad to take up residence at Kassel. William IX's contributions to the park at Wilhelmshöhe include the astonishing, partly ruinous, castle of Löwenburg, a Picturesque extravaganza designed in 1790 by Jussow and executed in 1793–1802 (fig. 115).[79] It recalls English medieval castles such as Alnwick, Northumberland, largely of the fourteenth century, though rebuilt by George III's friends, the Duke and Duchess of Northumberland.[80] It can also be compared to Robert Adam's designs for buildings such as Culzean Castle (1779–92), which Jussow might have seen on his visit to Britain. The Löwenburg is certainly a building that would have appealed to George III.

77 J. Roberts, *Royal Landscape*, pl. 500.

78 Dittscheid, *Kassel-Wilhelmshöhe und die Krise des Schlossbaues*, p. 220.

79 On Löwenburg, see Dittscheid, *passim*, and Watkin and Mellinghoff, *German Architecture*, pp. 46–9 and 237–44, and pl. 35. A portrait of

Landgrave William IX and his family at Schloss Weissenstein (later Schloss Wilhelmshöhe)near Kassel, painted by Wilhelm Böttner in 1791, is in the Royal Collection (RCIN 401351).

80 See above, ch. 5, pp. 144–5.

PRINCE LEOPOLD FREDERICK FRANCIS OF ANHALT-DESSAU

Antiquity, Anglo-Palladianism, and the Picturesque garden were among the passions of Prince Leopold Frederick Francis of Anhalt-Dessau (1740–1817). Known as Prince Franz, he reigned over Anhalt-Dessau from 1758 to 1817, a period close to the reign of George III. He was a frequent visitor to England, spending several months there in 1763, 1775, and 1785, and over a year in 1766–8, as well as travelling to Glasgow and Edinburgh. He attended the baptism at St James's Palace of Prince Frederick, later Duke of York, in 1763, and was later fond of describing England as his 'second homeland'.[81] Britain was for him the model for the programme of domestic reform, including the introduction of the latest developments in architecture, agriculture, gardening, manufacture, and industry, with which he wished to transform his state of Anhalt-Dessau where the local economy had been destroyed by the Seven Years War. Of course, he spent far more time in Italy and France than in England, yet for a German prince with a serious interest in Italy, the English tradition of the gentleman connoisseur was an obvious short cut to Italy, both antique and modern. It is significant that on all his travels he was accompanied by his friend, the architect Friedrich Wilhelm von Erdmannsdorff (1736–1800),[82] with whom he enjoyed a close association comparable to that between Lord Burlington and William Kent.

A Calvinist, promoting self-improvement and practical good among his subjects, Prince Franz was a defender of the Holy Roman Empire as an umbrella which protected small states such as his own. He was able to devote himself to architectural, antiquarian, agricultural, and pedagogic interests, because he had decided not to follow a military career and because his grandfather had expelled the landed nobility from Anhalt-Dessau, thereby facilitating paternalistic administration of the principality on the lines of one large country estate.

Schloss Wörlitz, near Dessau, which Erdmannsdorff built for him in 1769–73, was stylistically similar to Duddingston House, Edinburgh (1763–8), by William Chambers, whom the Prince knew, but is closer to the later Claremont House, Surrey (1771–4), by 'Capability' Brown. The Chinese Room at Schloss Wörlitz seems related to plates in Chambers's *Designs for Chinese Buildings* (1757). The relation between Prince Franz and his architect has some parallels with that between George III and Chambers. Erdmannsdorff doubtless taught the technique of architectural drawing to the Prince, for several surviving drawings which could be mistaken for George III's are probably in the Prince's hand.[83] When the shell of the building of Schloss Wörlitz was complete, and work began on the interiors, Erdmannsdorff

81   Zeller and Weiss, *Friends of Nature*, pp. 31 and 54.

82   A substantial fragment of Erdmannsdorff's account of his journey with the Prince in 1763–4, written in French in 1764, was recently discovered and published for the first time in Zeller and Weiss, *Friends of Nature*,

pp. 37–71. See also *Friedrich Wilhelm von Erdmannsdorff, 1736–1800: Leben, Werk, Wirkung*, Wörlitz, Oranienbaum, Luisium 1987 (exh. cat.).

83   In the Erdmannsdorff Collection in the possession of Count Waldesee. I am indebted for this information to Mr John Harris.

was living in Rome from where he sent back drawings of correct antique and Renaissance details such as cornices. At least one chimneypiece was acquired from Piranesi, together with work from his associate, Bartolommeo Cavaceppi, while Adam's drawing master, Clérisseau, is also represented at Wörlitz with a set of drawings.

One of Prince Franz's chief contacts in England was the Earl of Shelburne (1737–1805), a reforming Whig, Foreign Secretary in 1782, Prime Minister in 1782–3, and created Marquess of Lansdowne in 1784.[84] Prince Franz visited him at Shelburne House in Berkeley Square, begun for Lord Bute by Robert Adam, and at Bowood, Wiltshire, where Adam also worked for Lord Shelburne.[85] In 1768, Prince Franz asked Shelburne for drawings of Chippendale furniture to imitate at Wörlitz where he established a furniture manufactory, inspired by Chippendale's success in England. As a result, English techniques and furniture design exercised a wide influence in the northern Holy Roman Empire. While in England, Prince Franz also met Josiah Wedgwood, from whom he bought one of the largest collections of Wedgwood outside England.

On his third visit to England in 1775, the Prince visited Lord Shelburne's model farm at Wycombe, Buckinghamshire. Learning from Shelburne to regard agricultural improvement as an area where a new concept of Enlightenment was to be realised, Prince Franz created a model farm at Wörlitz, run along English lines. He and Erdmannsdorff brought back clover seeds from their first journey to England in 1763–4, and introduced English innovations such as clover-based crop rotation which spread to other centres in the Holy Roman Empire. However, in a letter of October 1775 to Lord Shelburne, written in English, he remarked that he had not been able to raise cattle-breeding in Anhalt-Dessau to the level of English standards.

It was on his return from England in 1775 that the Prince met Rousseau, to whom he built a monument in the park at Wörlitz, which he adorned with garden buildings on a scale even more extravagant than Stowe.[86] In 1784, the year in which Shelburne was created Marquess of Lansdowne, he sent his son, Lord Wycombe (1765–1809), on an extensive Grand Tour in northern Europe. Lasting until 1789, this was followed by a long stay in Italy from 1793 to 1796.[87] In 1786 Lord Wycombe visited Prince Franz at Wörlitz, which he compared in a letter to his father to the landscaped park at Stourhead, Wiltshire.[88]

The extensive stylistic and cultural range of the buildings at Wörlitz was intended to educate the subjects of this Enlightenment prince in the history of architecture and world history. In this it was a close parallel to Chambers's buildings at Kew and their relation to his

84 See Norris, *Shelburne and Reform*.

85 A full biography of Lord Shelburne is a desideratum, but for a well-documented account of Prince Franz's relationship with him, see Umbach, *Enlightenment*, pp. 40–5, 96–9, 103, and 123.

86 Of the extensive modern literature on this topic, see in particular Biegel, *Wörlitz*, and Bechthold and Weiss, *Weltbild Wörlitz*.

87 Ingamells, *Dictionary*, pp. 1025–6.

88 Umbach, *Enlightenment*, p. 82.

architectural instruction of the future George III while Prince of Wales. Prince Franz created a *jardin anglo-chinois* at Oranienbaum as late as 1793–7, including a five-storeyed pagoda which still survives.[89] An unexpected feature of the park at Wörlitz is the man-made island of 1788–94 with its miniature Mount Vesuvius, containing red glass windows and belching fire and smoke above the water. This may have been influenced by the description of similar effects in Chinese gardens by William Chambers in his *Dissertation on Oriental Gardening*, a copy of which the Prince owned. With the grottoes below Mount Vesuvius, the combined sensations of sound, light, and darkness could also be seen as a heightened response to creations such as the Duke of Cumberland's great cascade and grotto at Virginia Water, which Prince Franz had seen in 1763.[90] In the late 1780s, when Prince Franz was busy creating his Vesuvius island, George III was restoring the cascade and grotto at Virginia Water. There was also a cast-iron bridge at Wörlitz in 1781, a miniature version of that at Coalbrookdale by Abraham Darby of 1778 and the first of its kind on the continent.

The park at Wörlitz has recently been interpreted by Maiken Umbach as 'a visual manifesto for the German federal Enlightenment',[91] consisting of many gardens expressing a range of different sentiments which could be paralleled in the small political units constituting the Holy Roman Empire. It has been suggested that 'In the German context, the Holy Roman Empire provided the framework in which this pluralistic experimental Enlightenment culture could develop and flourish.'[92] In particular, the Gothic House at Wörlitz has been seen as making explicit references to aspects of the history of the Empire, and the whole garden as related to the federal concept which Prince Franz found in the *Fürstenbund*, the league of princes which George III helped institute in 1783. Prince Franz was one of its most active members and proponents. Indeed, the purpose of the last of Prince Franz's several visits to England in 1785 was principally to persuade George III to reveal to him the secret clauses of the *Fürstenbund*.[93]

The Children of George III and Queen Charlotte

The considerable impact of George III and Queen Charlotte on the architectural and artistic patronage of their children has never been fully acknowledged. We shall see their influence on four of their children in England and on the continent, following the marriages of two daughters to German princes. The career of their eldest son, George IV, as a patron and collector is too well known to need summarising here, though reference will be made to it in the Conclusion.

---

89 Zeller and Weiss, *Friends of Nature*, pp. 96 and 117–20, and pl. 102.
90 *ibid.*, pp. 56 and 69, n. 50.
91 Umbach, *Enlightenment*, p. 191.
92 *ibid.*, p. 192.
93 *ibid.*, pp. 181–2.

FREDERICK, DUKE OF YORK AND ALBANY

After George IV, the most interesting architectural patron among George III's children was his second and favourite son, Frederick, Duke of York and Albany (1763–1827), whose baptism, as we have seen, had been attended by Prince Franz of Anhalt-Dessau. Until at least 1795, when the Prince of Wales, aged 32, married Princess Caroline of Brunswick, his brother Frederick might have expected to inherit the throne. Certainly, Frederick had a more palatial home than any of his brothers. This was the Schloss at Osnabrück, a vast Baroque palace with a façade seventeen bays long, which he inherited as Prince Bishop of Osnabrück. He first visited Osnabrück in August 1783 to receive the homage of the estates of the principality, and from 1784 seems to have spent annually about 8,000 Reichstaler on the Schloss, so that his earliest architectural patronage was in Germany. He was created Duke of York and Albany by George III in 1784, and during a visit to Osnabrück in 1785 he probably discussed the remodelling and decoration of the principal interiors on neo-classical lines. This elegant work was executed from that year by Bartolomeo Verona (1744–1813), a prolific decorative painter who had been employed by Frederick the Great in Berlin and who was then working on the Palais Alten in Hanover.[94] Frederick the Great, who died in 1786, gave Prince Frederick a dinner service made by the Royal Berlin Porcelain Manufactory, handsomely decorated with neo-classical ornament based on antique gemstones.[95]

In December 1787, after returning to England from a six-year stay in Hanover where he had received military training, Prince Frederick bought Fetherstonhaugh House, Whitehall, which he renamed York House. His income as Prince Bishop of Osnabrück enabled him to employ Henry Holland (1745–1806), chosen architect of the Prince of Wales, to remodel and extend York House in an up-to-date neo-classical style. In 1788 Holland thus added a portico and screen wall with engaged columns which recalled his additions for the Prince of Wales at Carlton House. In his sophisticated Parisian manner with touches of Greek, it led to a circular entrance hall ringed with free-standing columns below a glazed dome.[96] Though elegant, it was extremely modest in comparison with the similar but grander entrance vestibule and two-storeyed ballroom which the Duke of York created at Osnabrück. In 1788 the Duke of York employed Holland to make improvements at Allerton Park, Yorkshire, a Palladian mansion which he had bought in 1786 from the 4th Viscount Galway.[97]

The interiors at Osnabrück were probably completed in 1791, in which year Frederick married

---

94 I am indebted to Dr Jarl Kremeier for information on Osnabrück and Hanover. After bomb damage in the Second World War, the Schloss at Osnabrück was rebuilt, but with modern interiors. On Prince Frederick's work there, see Kaster, '"Meliorisierung" und "Möblierung"', in Verspohl, *Das Osnabrücker Schloss.*

95 See *Von Sanssouci nach Europa: Geschenke Friedrich des Grossen an europäische Höfe*, Potsdam 1994, pp. 143–6 (exh. cat.). He was painted by Edward Cunningham being received by Frederick the Great (*ibid.*).

96 Formerly Fetherstonhaugh, later Melbourne, and today Dover House. See *Survey of London*, vol. XIV, *Parish of St Margaret, Westminster*, Part III, pp. 60–5, and Stroud, *Henry Holland*, pp. 92–3.

97 Aslet, 'Early History of Allerton Park'. Nothing is known of Holland's work.

FIG. 116 C. Brauns, *View of Oatlands House with tower and lake*, 1810. Watercolour and body-colour. RL 17962B

FIG. 117 Benjamin and Philip Wyatt, *Design for York House, St James's: south front*, 1825. Watercolour over pencil. RL 18976

Princess Frederica, daughter of King Frederick William II of Prussia. A bridge which Prince Franz of Anhalt-Dessau built at Wörlitz was named after her in 1792 as the 'Princess Bridge', for she was the first person to cross it.[98] The Duke of York employed Henry Holland to add a new Gothic front at Oatlands House, Surrey, in 1794–1800 (fig. 116). Holland was helped in the Gothic detailing here by John Carter, who was shortly to be critical of James Wyatt's Gothic work for George III at Windsor Castle. In June 1804 the Duke appointed as his architectural draughtsman another Gothic specialist, the architect and antiquarian artist William Capon (1757–1827).

After his marriage, the Duke sold Allerton Park and also exchanged York House in Whitehall in 1792 for the grander Melbourne House in Piccadilly, which had been built by William Chambers in 1771–4. He transferred the name of York House to Melbourne House but occupied it for less than a decade before selling it, whereupon it was remodelled in 1803 by Henry Holland as the residential chambers known as Albany. The Duke's standing as heir presumptive, heightened by his role as Commander in Chief of the British Army during most of the Napoleonic Wars, later led him to initiate the building in St James's of the third York House, today Lancaster House (fig. 117), after his wife's death in 1820. He was prompted in this ambitious project by his mistress, the Duchess of Rutland, who laid its foundation stone

98 Zeller and Weiss, *Friends of Nature*, p. 69, n. 46.

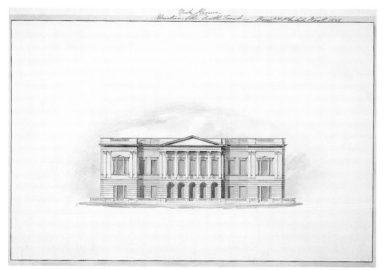

in 1825. The grandest town house in London, it was built from designs by Benjamin Dean Wyatt and Philip Wyatt, sons of George III's architect, James Wyatt.[99]

THE PRINCESS ROYAL

As we have already seen, the King's eldest daughter, Charlotte, the Princess Royal (1766–1828), was also an architectural enthusiast.[100] In 1797 she married Duke Frederick II, Hereditary Prince of Württemberg, whose first wife, Augusta of Brunswick, was George III's niece. It was the Princess Royal who urged George III to build a tower in the Great Park at Windsor in imitation of a medieval ruin she had seen in the Black Forest, and she always encouraged him in his Gothic work at Windsor Castle and Kew Palace. She wrote to him in 1802 that his 'alterations at Windsor Castle must quite restore it to its ancient Gothic beauty, and the new building at Kew be Lulworth improved.' She went on to add that 'I hope your Majesty will allow me to draw you some chairs with a pen on velvet to be placed in this new palace and that you will be so gracious as to decide whether they shall be flowers or landscapes.'[101]

A more original contribution to design than her needlework was her promotion of the Ludwigsburg pottery and porcelain manufactory, established by the house of Württemberg in 1724. This was next to the vast Baroque Residenz of Ludwigsburg, north of Stuttgart, but she eventually acquired her own kiln in the grounds of the palace. She painted many pieces of porcelain for her apartments at Ludwigsburg, including plates, cups, saucers, and vases, but also plaques, which were mounted on furniture by the *ébéniste* Johannes Klinkerfuss (1770–1831). A new technique in German furniture, this may have been inspired by the Wedgwood plaques which were exported to the Continent from the late eighteenth century. Much of this work survives at Ludwigsburg and Friedrichshaven.

In 1797 the architect Nikolaus Friedrich von Thouret (1767–1845) built a Gothic Revival

---

99 Yorke, *Lancaster House*, pp. 15–24, and see Baird, *Mistress of the House*, pp. 245–6.
100 D. Stuart, *Daughters of George III*, pp. 36–8.
101 Aspinall, *Correspondence*, vol. IV, 1968, 22 November 1802, p. 62.

church at Hohenheim, near Stuttgart, with English details and a massive tower, so that it is tempting to suppose that it may have had a connection with Charlotte.[102] In 1799, two years after her marriage to Duke of Württemberg, Thouret was appointed as court architect, though he was also skilled as a furniture designer and decorative painter.[103] The Duke and Duchess employed him in that capacity to remodel in the most elegant Empire style the interiors of the palaces at Stuttgart, Ludwigsburg, and Hohenheim, from 1803 to 1815. After a training in Paris and Rome, Thouret had worked with Goethe in 1798–1800 on the Schloss and court theatre at Weimar for Duke (later Grand Duke) Charles Augustus of Saxe-Weimar. His surviving state rooms of 1805–12, in the *corps de logis* which had been added to Schloss Ludwigsburg in 1724, are an impressive tribute to the Empire style of Napoleon's architects, Percier and Fontaine. This was appropriate in view of the fact that Napoleon elevated the Duchy of Württemberg to the status of a kingdom in 1806, with Frederick II as its first king.

After Frederick's death in 1816, his widow remained in Germany as Queen Dowager until her death in 1828. Her stepson, who reigned as King William I of Württemberg from 1816 to 1864 formed the 'intention to Anglicise some of the Royal Domains'.[104] He furthered this ambition by commissioning John Buonarotti Papworth (1775–1847) to prepare three sets of designs in 1817–20 for an ambitious summer palace in the Corinthian order at Cannstadt, Stuttgart.[105] In 1816 Papworth had built conservatories, cottages, and a Gothic summerhouse at Claremont, Surrey, for George III's grand-daughter, Princess Charlotte and her husband, Prince Leopold of Saxe-Coburg-Saalfeld, the future King Leopold I of the Belgians. Papworth worked at Claremont in association with John William Hiort (1772–1861), who had been promoted in the Office of Works by Sir William Chambers.

Some of Papworth's designs for Cannstadt were exhibited at the Royal Academy in 1823 and 1827, but they were unexecuted, and the palace, known as Schloss Rosenstein, was built in 1824–9 in the Greek Revival style from designs by the Italian architect, Giovanni Salucci (1769–1845), court architect from 1817 to 1839.[106] Papworth's designs for laying out the park at Cannstadt in the English manner were partly carried out and in 1820 he was given a diploma signed by the King appointing him 'Architect to the King of Württemberg'.

We might note in passing that similar work was carried out in Hanover by the court architect from 1816, Georg Laves (1788–1864), who rebuilt the Residenz, the Leineschloss, in

102 The church was re-erected in 1803 at Montrepos at Ludwigsburg, where it survives, partly ruined.

103 There is no satisfactory modern monograph on Thouret, but see Faerber, *Nikolaus Friedrich von Thouret*.

104 Papworth, *John B. Papworth*, pp. 40–3.

105 McHardy, *Office of J.B. Papworth, Catalogue of the Drawings Collection of the Royal Institute of British Architects*, pp. 83–4 and pls. 72–8.

106 Watkin and Mellinghoff, *German Architecture*, pp. 185 and 258 and pls. 149 and 232.

1817–35, following a study tour in France and England from 1814 to 1817.[107] In the form in which he first left the Leineschloss, with its entrance front sporting a Corinthian porte-cochère, it was probably inspired by Henry Holland's Carlton House for the Prince of Wales. This major work at the Leineschloss was carried out under George III's youngest surviving son, Prince Adolphus, Duke of Cambridge (1774–1850), who was Viceroy of Hanover from 1816 to 1837. Perhaps the most Hanoverian of the King's sons, he had already lived away from England for fifteen years, first at Göttingen University and then fighting in the Hanoverian army from the outbreak of war in 1793 until after the peace of 1802.

Georg Laves revisited England in 1826, when he met John Nash, and in 1830, 1834, and finally in 1851. In 1842–7 he built a handsome domed Greek Doric mausoleum in the gardens at Herrenhausen for the tomb of Queen Frederica of Hanover, who died in 1841. As we noted in the Introduction, she was a daughter of Grand Duke Charles II of Mecklenburg-Strelitz and therefore a niece of Queen Charlotte, whose son, Ernest Augustus, Duke of Cumberland, she had married in 1815.[108] The mausoleum today also contains the tomb of King George I of England, moved from the now destroyed court chapel at the Leineschloss in Hanover.

PRINCESS ELIZABETH

Princess Elizabeth (1770–1840)[109] made several additions to the grounds at Frogmore, including a circular thatched hermitage which was built from her designs in 1793 and for which she asked Lady Harcourt to provide a suitable inscription. She also painted scarlet panels of simulated lacquer in the Red Japan Room at Frogmore. Only three of the six daughters of George III and Queen Charlotte managed to escape, eventually, from the close family circle. Princess Elizabeth achieved this in 1818 when, in her forty-eighth year, she married Landgrave Frederick VI Joseph of Hesse-Homburg (1769–1829). Her dowry later enabled her to employ Georg Moller (1784–1852) to build the castellated Gothic House at Tannenwald, near Bad Homburg, in 1823–6. Inspired by the Castellated Palace at Kew, designed for her father by Wyatt, it had the same ultimate model as Kew – Lulworth Castle, Dorset – though the central hall was not executed. Wyatville also sent designs for a Gothic conservatory for her Gothic House.[110] As Princess Elizabeth she had begun assembling at Windsor an outstanding collection of prints which she continued in Homburg and concluded in Frankfurt.[111] The largest collection of eighteenth-century British mezzotints outside the

---

107 Hammer-Schenk, *et al.*, eds., *Laves und Hannover*.

108 For a well-documented study, see G.M. Willis, *Ernest Augustus*, ch. XI.

109 On Princess Elizabeth, see *'Ich schreibe, lese und male ohne Unterlass …'. Elizabeth, englische Prinzessin und Landgräfin von Hessen-Homburg (1770–1840) als Künstlerin und Sammlerin*, Museum in Gotischen Haus, Bad Homburg n.d. (*c.*2000; exh. cat.).

110 Six drawings for two projects (Technische Universität, Berlin, Plansammlung, Inv. Nr.10325–10327; 10328–10330).

111 It is housed today in the Sommerpalais, Greiz, Thuringia. I am indebted to Dr Wilfried Rogasch for information about this collection.

British Museum, it consists mainly of portraits but also includes architectural views. She also built up a large library which echoed the scientific and literary interests of her mother.[112]

Further building work after her marriage to the Landgrave of Hesse-Homburg included the remodelling of the seventeenth-century Schloss at Bad Homburg with the so-called English Wing in a restrained neo-classical mode by Moller in 1825–41.[113] In 1810 Moller was appointed court architect to Louis I, Grand Duke of Hesse-Darmstadt, who married his cousin, Louisa, who was herself the sister of two aunts by marriage of Princess Elizabeth.[114] Moller published *Denkmäler der deutschen Baukunst* (3 vols., Darmstadt 1815–21), a work which made him popular in England where it was translated as *An Essay on the Origin and Progress of Gothic Architecture* (1824), and as *Moller's Memorials of German-Gothic Architecture* (1836). He was one of the first elected members of the (Royal) Institute of British Architects in 1835. All this activity was an important development from the time when George III was deploying Gothic at Windsor Castle in the years around 1800.

AUGUSTUS, DUKE OF SUSSEX

Though he was scarcely an architectural patron, George III's sixth son, Prince Augustus Frederick (1773–1843),[115] should be noted here for his cultural interests. The King sent him to study with his brothers Ernest and Adolphus at the University of Göttingen in 1786. In December 1789 Prince Augustus arrived in Florence, partly because it was thought that his health would improve in a warmer climate. He spent much of the next ten years in Italy where, around 1792, he commissioned from Jacob More a panoramic view of Rome, 20 feet long, for Buckingham House.[116] In 1793 he obtained a licence to excavate with Robert Fagan at Ostia, where he discovered a statue of Venus which he presented to the Prince of Wales. It was subsequently given to the British Museum by King William IV. With Thomas Jenkins as his agent, he acquired further antique sculpture, and also gave numerous commissions to British artists then in Rome, including Christopher Hewetson, John Deare, Robert Fagan, Guy Head, and Angelica Kauffman. In 1795 he bought a marble chimneypiece, carved with masks and vines, which was designed by the architect, George Hadfield, and executed by Deare and Vincenzo Pacetti. It was installed in the dining room at Frogmore House where it remains to this day. Prince Augustus purchased a further two chimneypieces, also by Deare, intended for the Prince of Wales at Carlton House.

112 *A Catalogue of the Valuable and Choice Library of HRH The Princess Elizabeth*, London 1863 (copy in the Royal Library, Windsor Castle).

113 Fröhlich and Sperlich, *Georg Moller*, pp. 260–75 and 358.

114 These were Frederica Caroline and Charlotte Wilhelmine, first and second wives of Grand Duke Charles of Mecklenburg-Strelitz.

115 There is no serious study of the intellectual and political positions of the Duke of Sussex, but for basic biographical information, see Gillen, *Royal Duke*.

116 Untraced. See Ingamells, *Dictionary*, p. 36.

Returning to England, he was created Duke of Sussex in 1801, but he was unwelcome at court as a man of advanced liberal views with a romantic admiration for Napoleon. He devoted himself to literature, science, and the arts, was appointed President of the Society of Arts in 1816, and served as President of the Royal Society from 1830 to 1839. A Freemason who was a close friend of Sir John Soane,[117] he formed an impressive library of 50,000 volumes at Kensington Palace.[118]

An American Parallel: Thomas Jefferson

Thomas Jefferson (1743–1826), a near contemporary of George III and President of the United States of America 1801–9, spent six weeks in London in 1786, including a week in April touring the country to inspect Picturesque parks and gardens in the company of John Adams whom he was to succeed as President.[119] Jefferson remarked that 'The gardening in that country is the article in which it surpasses all the earth, I mean their pleasure gardening [*sic*]. This indeed went far beyond my ideas.'[120] Jefferson took with him Thomas Whately's *Observations on the Art of Gardening* (1770) and recorded that 'I always walked the gardens with his book in hand'; he and Adams visited sixteen gardens including Stowe, Blenheim, Hagley, the Leasowes, and Kew, where the only feature Jefferson noted was an 'Archimedes' screw for raising water', to which he devoted two diagrams and numerous detailed notes.[121] With his own interest in machinery, George III would have been in complete sympathy with this response to Kew. This ambitious water engine, designed by the famous civil engineer John Smeaton (1724–92), was illustrated in the book which Chambers had dedicated to the King's mother, *Plans, Elevations, Sections, and Perspective Views of the Gardens and Buildings at Kew* (1763); in it (fig. 118) Chambers explained that 'this Engine works with two horses, and raises 300 hogsheads of Water in an hour.' Jefferson thought that such a device might be used for the springs at Monticello, the house he designed for himself near Charlottesville. Noting with admiration in 1786 that 'The mechanical arts in London are carried to a wonderful perfection,'[122] Jefferson toured the continent in March and April 1788,[123] describing buildings and drawing diagrams of the kind of mechanical devices which appealed to George III.

Jefferson was presented to the King and Queen at St James's Palace on 3 March 1786, but the King turned his back on him, perhaps understandably in view of the insults hurled at him years earlier in the Declaration of Independence, which included describing him as 'a

117 On their association, see Watkin, 'Freemasonry and Sir John Soane'.

118 See *Bibliotheca Sussexiana. A … catalogue … of the manuscripts and printed books … of the Duke of Sussex*, 2 vols., London, 1827–39.

119 Boyd *et al.*, *Papers of Thomas Jefferson*, vol. IX, 'Notes of a Tour of English Gardens', pp. 369–75. For Adams's account of this tour, see C. F. Adams, *Works of John Adams*, vol. III, pp. 394–5.

120 Boyd, *Papers of Thomas Jefferson*, vol. IX, Jefferson to John Page, Paris, 4 May 1786, p. 445.

121 *ibid.*, p. 373.

122 *ibid.*, p. 445.

123 *ibid.*, vol. XIII, 'Notes of a Tour Through Holland and the Rhine Valley', pp. 8–36.

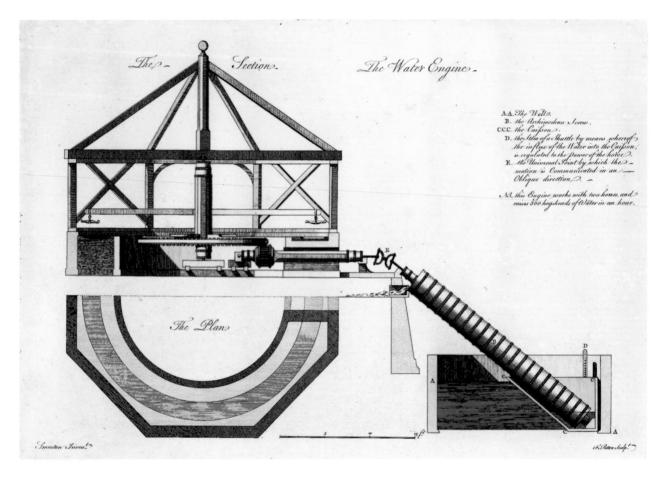

prince whose character is marked by every act which may define a tyrant' and 'unfit to be the ruler of a free people'. Jefferson was annoyed because, as he noted, John Adams had been received far more graciously in June in the previous year on the important occasion of his reception as the first American Minister to Great Britain.[124] Nonetheless, even in the first year of the war of American Independence, Jefferson declared that 'there is not in the British Empire a man who more cordially loves a Union with Gr. Britain than I do,'[125] though rejecting totally the current proposals of the British parliament for maintaining that union.

124   *ibid.*, vol. IX, p. 364. For Adams's account of his courteous treatment
      on this occasion, see C. F. Adams, *Works of John Adams*, vol. VIII, pp. 255–8.
125   *ibid.*, vol. I, Thomas Jefferson to John Randolph, Philadelphia,
      29 November 1775, p. 269.

FIG. 118 F. Patton after J. Smeaton, *The Water Engine, Kew Gardens*, 1763 (from W. Chambers, *Kew*). Engraving. RCIN 1150769

The marked similarities between George III and Thomas Jefferson included their interests in architecture, gardening, music, science, and machinery; their devotion to their family; and their dislike of ostentation and preference for the simple life of the country gentleman.[126] Like George III, Jefferson was an amateur architect although, in contrast to the monarch, he had to teach himself architectural draughtsmanship. He is supposed to have declared that, 'architecture is my delight, and putting up and pulling down one of my favourite amusements', while what we may call his 'hands-on' approach, similar to that of George III, is typified by the detailed instructions he sent from Paris in August 1785 about the materials and construction of the State Capitol of Virginia in Richmond, largely designed by himself.[127] Finally, his years in Paris as American Ambassador from 1784 to 1789[128] also gave him an intense admiration for modern French architecture, akin to that of George III's architect, William Chambers.

In comparing figures so contrasted as Jefferson and George III, whom we can hardly imagine owning slaves and siring children by them, we should note that during his long reign, the King came to be seen as a broad central figure, attempting, with various degrees of success, to defuse dissension between his subjects, so that he was able to grant pensions to both Rousseau, an arch-enemy of courts, like Jefferson, and to Rousseau's benevolent friend, David Hume (1711–76), agnostic philosopher of the Enlightenment, historian, and diplomat. Fanny Burney recorded that although George III condemned Voltaire to her, 'He next named Rousseau, who he seemed to think of with more favour, though by no means with approbation.'[129] This might have brought some small comfort to her father, Dr Charles Burney, the music historian, who was an admirer and translator of Rousseau whom he visited in Paris where he was well received by him. He noticed on this occasion that Rousseau had retained an engraving of Ramsay's portrait of the King when, on leaving England in 1766 and advised by the King's friend, Lord Harcourt, he sold most of his prints and books.

126 See W. H. Adams, *Eye of Jefferson*.
127 Boyd, *Papers of Thomas Jefferson*, vol. VIII, pp. 366–8.
128 Rice, *Jefferson's Paris*.
129 Barrett, *D'Arblay Diary*, vol. II, p. 342.

CONCLUSION

George III has emerged as a complex figure who was associated with some of the traditions of the *ancien régime* through which he lived, as well as with some of the contrasting ideals of the European Enlightenment. Historians have debated how far Britain was an *ancien-régime* society, some historians promoting the concept,[1] others querying it on the grounds that, as a parliamentary monarchy, it possessed equality before the law, few instances of legal privilege, and a free press, and was not fundamentally a confessional state in the continental sense since it permitted some degree of religious toleration. The relation of George III to the Enlightenment had something of the ambiguity of his relation to the *ancien régime*. He may have been little involved with the philosophy and politics of the Enlightenment, but echoed some of its characteristics such as the cult of simplicity, of civic virtue, naturalness, and the conceding of validity to non-classical traditions in architecture. Thus Chinese architecture was promoted by the King's architect and architectural tutor, William Chambers, while the King himself commissioned buildings in both classical and Gothic styles. His devotion to science, improvement, arts, and manufactures was also in tune with Enlightenment concerns.

However, by the 1770s, the Enlightenment coexisted with, or was being replaced by, the age of sensibility and sentiment in which the naturalism of Rousseau was a critical commentary on both the Enlightenment and on court values. Recent research into Queen Charlotte has shown that several of her associates and relatives in Germany were friends or followers of Rousseau.[2] In England, these included Lord and Lady Harcourt whose natural flower garden at Nuneham Courtenay, inspired by Rousseau's *Julie, ou la Nouvelle Héloïse*, was much admired by George III. The Duchess of Leinster, the sister of Lady Sarah Lennox[3] with whom the King was in love in 1759–60, was also a disciple of Rousseau. In 1766 she set up a school for her children at Black Rock on the coast near Dublin, inspired by the programme in Rousseau's *Émile* (1762).[4] She even invited Rousseau to come to it as tutor, but he declined and left England for France in May 1767.

It is therefore a remarkable irony that George III should have given a pension to Rousseau at this moment. Rousseau's initial sponsor was his friend David Hume, to whom the King also gave a pension. Under the impression that Rousseau was about to arrive in England, Hume wrote in 1762 that 'We are happy at present in a king who has a taste for literature, and I hope M. Rousseau will find the advantage of it, and that he will not disdain to receive benefits from a great monarch, who is sensible of his merit.'[5] In fact, Rousseau had previously been offered pensions by Louis XV and Frederick the Great but he had declined them both on the grounds of his republican principles.

---

1   For example, the revisionist approach of J. Clark, *English Society, 1660–1832*.

2   See Campbell Orr, 'Geneva in England'. I am indebted to Dr Campbell Orr for allowing me to see this valuable essay before publication.

3   Lady Sarah, who was a bridesmaid at the King's wedding, is familiar from the portrait of her as *Lady Sarah Bunbury Sacrificing to the Graces* (1764–5) by Sir Joshua Reynolds.

4   Tillyard, *Aristocrats*, pp. 240–5.

5   David Hume to Madame de Boufflers, 1 July 1762 (cited in Leigh, 'Rousseau's English Pension', p. 116). Surprisingly, the story of Rousseau's pension does not appear in biographies of George III, so that Leigh's fascinating account is especially valuable.

It was General Henry Seymour Conway (1719–95), the Rockingham Whig MP, who approached the King on Rousseau's behalf when he arrived in England in 1766. The King agreed to grant him a pension of £100 a year, whereas Dr Johnson's was £300, but it was even paid after Rousseau's death in 1778 to his mistress, Thérèse Levasseur. It was decided, significantly, that it should not be a Treasury pension but should come from the Privy Purse. The great Rousseau scholar, R.A. Leigh, referred in the context of Rousseau's pension to the 'enthusiasm for the enlightenment and culture of "Farmer George" which is apt to seem somewhat strange today, but which was widely shared in the 1760s and even later.'[6] Indeed, Rousseau's belief that man is by nature good, but has been corrupted and depraved by society so that he needs to return to nature, is not too far distant from aspects of the King's lifestyle: the simplicity of his private life, his interest in agriculture and farming, and his easy familiarity with his humbler subjects. The King, however, would never have countenanced Rousseau's rejection of original sin. Nonetheless, the landscaped parks created by his gardener 'Capability' Brown, could be interpreted as echoing the pursuit of 'naturalness' promoted by the *philosophes*. We have seen the King and Queen Charlotte entertaining their German cousins, who took back these ideals, and in some cases gardeners, to the courts of the Holy Roman Empire.

In 1774, Omai, the South Sea Islander, was brought to England where he was regarded as one of Rousseau's 'noble savages' and remained for two years before returning to Tahiti with Captain Cook. He was introduced to the expert on the Pacific, Sir Joseph Banks, who presented him to the King at Kew in July 1774, three days after his arrival. 'His Majesty very familiarly took him by the hand and made several very kind enquiries concerning him,'[7] giving him an allowance and recommending that he be inoculated. In her forthcoming study of Queen Charlotte, Clarissa Campbell Orr goes so far as to suggest that, with the links of the King and Queen with figures of the late Enlightenment such as Banks and Dr Charles Burney, Windsor could be seen as a significant centre of the Enlightenment in England.[8] Its 'combination of piety, science, and sensibility, typical of the smaller German courts', made Windsor 'one of the nodal points in the northern sector of the Republic of Letters',[9] which is taken to include the Danish and Prussian courts, as well as those of Hanover, Saxony, Brunswick, Dessau, Weimar, and Mecklenburg-Strelitz, and the city of Geneva. The Enlightenment of George III, however, was always a Christian Enlightenment, in contrast to the free-thinking and proto-materialist Enlightenment of a monarch like Frederick the Great. One of the most notable aspects of George's reign, not always stressed in accounts of him, is the extent to which he demonstrated in his religious activities the

6   Leigh, *loc. cit.*, p. 115–16.
7   *Gentleman's Magazine*, vol. XLIV, 1774, p. 330.
8   See Gascoigne, *Joseph Banks and the English Enlightenment*.
9   Campbell Orr, 'Charlotte of Mecklenburg-Strelitz'.

exemplary piety of kingship which was certainly a preoccupation of *ancien-régime* monarchies.

The religious position of George III was close in many ways to that of his admirer, Dr Johnson, to whom he had given a pension from 1762 and whose record of his conversation with the King in the library at Buckingham House in 1767 is well known. Johnson has himself been interpreted in the context of the Enlightenment on the grounds that in most European countries except France, the *philosophes* were Christian. Though the Enlightenment was associated in France with philosophy and literature, in England it was closer to the sciences and the promotion of a popular press.[10]

The King would have agreed with Henry Home, Lord Kames, the Enlightenment philosopher who chose to dedicate to him his book, *Elements of Criticism*, that 'Riches [properly] employed, instead of encouraging vice, will excite both public and private virtues.' According to Kames, royal patronage should not be exercised exclusively to celebrate the glory of kingship, but to encourage the arts 'for their beneficial influence in society': this was because 'By uniting the different ranks in the same elegant pleasures, they promote benevolence.' When, by contrast, the opulence provided by commerce is 'vented on luxury, and on every sensual gratification . . . it extinguishes the *amor patriae* and every spark of public spirit.' Pointing to ancient Greece as a model, he recommended that England should now follow its example. This George III did in his extensive patronage of the American Republican artist, Benjamin West, whom he employed to represent the Enlightenment cult of ancient Roman Republican virtues. The King's evident religious piety also manifested itself as the expression of simplicity.

His formation of topographical and geographical collections in his extensive library had a universalist scope which was akin to that of the *Encyclopédie*. The *Gentleman's Magazine*, one of the sources used in writing this book, tells us much about the world of George III, with its lively articles on topics such as science, literature, architecture, humanitarianism, representative politics, colonial expansion, and commercial enterprise.[11] It is in such a context that we should place Sir Joseph Banks, the botanist and student of natural history who joined Captain Cook's ship, HMS *Endeavour*, for 'the advancement of useful knowledge'. Banks was received by George III on his return in 1771 after which he played a key advisory role from 1773 at Kew, where his aim, as he explained in 1787 to David Dundas, was to turn the Royal Gardens 'into a great botanical exchange for the empire'.[12]

The King's interest in the scientific revolution and its products led to his enthusiasm for varied topics such as agriculture, machinery, and astronomy, as well as for new techniques and

---

10   See Cannon, *Samuel Johnson and the Politics of Hanoverian England*, ch. 6, 'Johnson and the Enlightenment'.

11   Founded in 1731, the magazine did much to promote the career of Dr Johnson. See Carson, *The First Magazine*.

12   Joseph Banks to David Dundas, 15 June 1787 (Botany Library, Natural History Museum), quoted in Desmond, *Kew*, p. 126. Dundas was the Windsor apothecary who attended the King in 1788 and during his final illness.

materials, as in Wedgwood wares, Coade stone, and ormolu. Wedgwood and Bentley were advised on the design of their Etruscan ware by the antiquarian and collector Thomas Hollis, the passionate Whig who, as we have seen, advised Cipriani on the decorative programme of the King's Gold State Coach. An *éminence grise*, devoted to the promotion of civil and religious liberty, Hollis was associated with the three architects who were close to the King at the start of the reign: Chambers, Robert Adam, and 'Athenian' Stuart.

Consideration has also been given in this book to the relation between England and the Holy Roman Empire in the hierarchy of European diplomacy. This was suggested by George III's claim to an imperial status, inevitably rivalling that of the Habsburgs, and by his role in the founding of the *Fürstenbund*. The imperial theme occurs in the symbolic decoration of the Gold State Coach and of Somerset House, while the King followed practice within the Holy Roman Empire in creating the 'Windsor uniform' in 1779. A dark blue coat with gold facings and red collar and cuffs to be worn by the royal family, their servants, retainers, and, if they wished, ministers of state, it is still in occasional use. Here he was following the example of Frederick the Great, while the Bavarian court had adopted a household uniform to be worn by all courtiers by the early eighteenth century. Such uniforms had the effect of diminishing the isolation of the monarch and of tying him in more closely with those who served him.

The immense emphasis which George III placed on the Order of Garter relates to its role as an independent Order, the rival of the prestigious *Toison d'Or*, the Order of the Golden Fleece of the Holy Roman Empire, founded in 1430. With his imperial standing, and as head of the premier court of the Protestant world, George III conferred the honour of the Knighthood of the Garter on several princes of the Holy Roman Empire between 1760 and 1801.[13] George IV followed more spectacularly, as often, a path initially trodden by his father, by making the Kings of France, Prussia, and Spain, and even the Emperor of Austria, Knights of the Garter in 1814–15.

The recoveries of George III from illness served, perhaps unexpectedly, to bolster support for him, the occasions being carefully orchestrated with the production of commemorative porcelain, medals, and loyal addresses.[14] The patriotic sentiments naturally aroused by the war with France also established the King as father of his people. At the time when he was remodelling Windsor Castle in the Gothic style, John Carter was promoting Gothic architecture as a bulwark against Napoleon. This helped the King to fulfil the testament left to him by his father, Frederick, Prince of Wales, 'Convince this nation that you are not only an Englishman born and bred, but that you are also this by inclination.' George III echoed this statement in his first speech before

13   The full list is as follows: his uncles, Frederick, Landgrave of Hesse-Kassel, and Frederick III, Duke of Saxe-Gotha; his brothers-in-law, Adolphus Frederick IV, Duke of Mecklenburg-Strelitz, and Charles William Ferdinand, Hereditary Prince, afterwards Duke of Brunswick-Wolfenbüttel; his cousins, William, Landgrave of Hesse-Kassel, and Ernest II, Duke of Saxe-Gotha-Altenburg; Charles William Frederick, 8th Margrave of Brandenburg-Ansbach; and Ferdinand, Prince of Brunswick-Beiern.

14   See, for example, Bellaigue, 'Huzza the King is Well!'

Parliament in November 1760: 'born and educated in this country I glory in the name of Briton.'
The height of his popularity was probably reached at his Jubilee which was celebrated throughout
the country on 25 October 1809.[15] An address distributed at all the festivities provided by public
subscription, at a time when the war against Napoleonic France was at its height, stressed the
King's role as 'The father of his people'. In that capacity he had preserved his country from 'the
dreadful evils' prevailing on the continent where 'we have seen kings hurled from their thrones,
and constituted authorities (venerated and admired for ages) trodden under foot'. In pointed
reference to the enemies of King and country, attention was also drawn to 'the efforts that were
then made by wicked and designing men, at home and abroad, to introduce them [these evils]
into England'.[16]

Just as George III inherited much from his gifted father, so he passed on many architectural
ambitions to his sons and daughters, notably, Frederick, Duke of York and Albany, sometimes
overlooked in this context, and to his eldest son, despite the political and financial problems
which divided him from his father. The ambition to build a grandiose new royal palace, which
George III shared with so many other monarchs, went back at least to the designs for Whitehall
Palace by Inigo Jones and John Webb. Though no British monarch has been able to realise this
ambition, George IV came closest to creating a metropolitan palace with his transformation of
George III's Buckingham House into Buckingham Palace.

As a collector of Old Master drawings, George IV did not begin to equal his father, but as a
collector and commissioner of pictures, furniture, and other works of art, he undoubtedly
outshone him. However, even here, though admittedly in a small way, George III led the way,
for example, in visiting the porcelain shop and manufactory of Flight and Barr in Worcester in
1788, making orders for porcelain. The future George IV followed his example on a visit to
Worcester in 1807, ordering dinner, dessert, and breakfast services and granting the firm his
Royal Warrant.[17] Father and son both gave extensive commissions to the Coade stone manufactory at Lambeth. Also, the way in which George III commissioned paintings by Benjamin West
for specific rooms at Buckingham House and Windsor Castle, creating interiors with a total
visual coherence, anticipated some of his son's activities.

Though George IV took more interest in royal ceremonial and display than his father, it was
for George III that Sir John Soane first envisaged the creation of a Scala Regia and Royal Gallery
at the House of Lords for use by the sovereign at the State Opening of Parliament. We have
already seen in Chapter 4 Soane's eternal gratitude to George III for granting him a travelling

15   The celebration of the jubilee after 49 years followed an ancient
     precedent of Jewish law. See also Preston, *Jubilee of George the Third*,
     where it is claimed that the celebrations began, unexpectedly, with 'a
     splendid fête at Bombay, given by the Governor' on the King's

birthday, 4 June, 'attended by ambassadors from all parts of the Indian
Empire, and neighbouring countries' (p. ix).

16   *ibid.*, p. xxiii.

17   *Royal Treasures*, pp. 189–90.

scholarship to Italy, so that it would have been a pleasure as well as an honour for him to show his drawings for the Scala Regia to the King at Windsor in 1794. He claimed that the King professed himself delighted with the patriotic sculpture and paintings with which he had proposed to adorn these interiors. These reappeared in the Scala Regia and Royal Gallery which Soane eventually built for George IV at the House of Lords in 1822–3.

However, we can agree that 'It seems fitting, for a monarchy whose political strength rested on tax-efficiency and public credit, that the great public building of George III's reign was not a home for the royal family but John Soane's . . . Bank of England.'[18] Soane arranged the illuminations and transparencies which decorated the Bank at the Thanksgiving for the King's Recovery in 1789. Though a palace of public credit rather than a royal palace, the Bank filled the role of a palace as a destination for dignitaries, led by Queen Charlotte and several of her children who, in the presence of Soane, paid a lengthy visit on 12 June 1805. She was followed by Alexander, Emperor of Russia, who was taken to the Bank on his visit to London with the Allied Sovereigns in June 1814. Accompanied by his sister, the Grand Duchess of Oldenburg, he, too, was shown round by Soane.[19]

What was unique in George III's patronage was the exceptional way in which he worked *with* and *for* his architects and designers such as Chambers and Boulton. This contrasts with the essentially bossy approach to his architects adopted by George IV. It cannot in the end be denied that the high hopes at the start of the reign of George III were never fully realised in his architectural commissions. The explanation for this can only partly be the problems caused by his recurrent illness, the American War, and the wars against Revolutionary and Napoleonic France. Perhaps the extremely conscientious character, which led to his near-obsessive attention to detail, impeded the development of a larger vision. At the same time, it should never be forgotten that, unlike their continental counterparts, George III, Queen Charlotte, and their children, were always under public scrutiny from the press as well as accountable to Parliament for their expenditure. Though the King was well aware that extravagant spending on royal buildings would have alienated many of his subjects, it was fortunate for us that his eldest son was content to forfeit all popularity by his lavish spending on architecture and works of art. When George IV commissioned Wyatville to complete the Gothic transformation of Windsor Castle which had been initiated by George III with Wyatville's uncle, James Wyatt, as architect, he created a statement of national identity which must represent the climax of George III's influence, and remains today the central image of the monarchy.

18   Campbell Orr, 'Queen Charlotte', p. 28.
19   Darley, *John Soane*, pp. 174 and 225.

BIBLIOGRAPHY

A King's Purchase. King George III and the Collection of Consul Smith, The Queen's Gallery, Buckingham Palace, 1993 (exh. cat.)

Abrams, Ann Uhry, *The Valiant Hero. Benjamin West and Grand-Style History Painting*, Washington, D.C. 1985

Achilles, Walter 'George III. als Königlicher Landwirt. Eine Bestätigung zur Personalunion', *Niedersächsisches Jahrbuch für Landesgeschichte*, vol. LXXIII, 2001, pp. 351–408

Adam, Bernd, 'Die Grotten im Grossen Garten von Hannover-Herrenhausen und im Park von Richmond (Surrey)', in *Bericht über die 40. Tagung für Ausgrabungswissenschaft und Bauforschung*, Stuttgart 2000

Adam, Robert, *Ruins of the Palace of the Emperor Diocletian at Spalatro*, London 1764

– and James Adam, *The Works in Architecture of Robert and James Adam*, 2 vols., London 1773–9

Adamiak, Josef, *Schlösser und Gärten in Mecklenburg*, Leipzig 1980

Adams, Charles Francis, ed., *The Works of John Adams*, 10 vols., Boston 1851–6

Adams, William Howard, ed., *The Eye of Jefferson*, National Gallery of Art, Washington 1976 (exh. cat.)

Adamson, John, ed., *The Princely Courts of Europe, 1500–1750*, London 1999

Airs, Malcolm, ed., *The Regency Great House*, Oxford 1999

Allen, Brian, 'Royal Portraits. Convention and Domesticity', in *Buckingham Palace: A Complete Guide. Part 1*, Apollo, August 1993, pp. 131–40

– and Larissa Dukelskaya, eds., *British Art Treasures from Russian Imperial Collections in the Hermitage*, New Haven and London 1997

Alm, Göran, ed., *Kina Slott: de Kungliga Slotten*, Stockholm 2002

Altick, Richard D., *The Shows of London*, Cambridge, Mass., and London 1978

Andersson, Thorbjörn, *et al.*, eds., *Svensk Trädgårdskonst under fyrhundra år*, Stockholm 2000

Angelo, Henry, *Reminiscences*, 2 vols., London 1828–30

Arciszewska, Barbara, *The Hanoverian Court and the Triumph of Palladio. The Palladian Revival in Hanover and England*, Warsaw 2002

Arnason, H. Harvard, *The Sculptures of Houdon*, London 1975

Ashmole, Elias, *The Institution, Laws and Ceremonies of the Most Noble Order of the Garter*, London 1672

Aslet, Clive, 'The Early History of Allerton Park', *Country Life*, 26 January 1989, pp. 92–5

Aspinall, John, ed., *The Later Correspondence of George III, 1783–1810*, 5 vols., Cambridge 1962–70

Ayling, Stanley, *George the Third*, London 1972

Baird, Rosemary, *Mistress of the House. Great Ladies and Grand Houses 1670–1830*, London 2003

Barbaro, Daniele, *I dieci libri dell'architettura di M. Vitruvio*, Venice 1556

Barber, Peter, 'Maps and Monarchs in Europe 1500–1800', in Oresko, *Sovereignty*

– 'Royal Geography: The Development and Destiny of King George's Geographical Collections', typescript, 2000

– 'George III's Topographical Collection. A Georgian View of Britain and the World', in Kim Sloan, ed., *Enlightenment. Discovering the World in the 18th Century*, London 2003

Barbier, Carl, *William Gilpin. His Drawings, Teaching, and Theory of the Picturesque*, Oxford 1963

Baretti, Joseph, *Guide through the Royal Academy*, London 1781

Barnard, Toby and Jane Clark, eds., *Lord Burlington. Architecture, Art and Life*, London and Rio Grande 1995

Barrett, Charlotte, ed., *Diary and Letters of Madame D'Arblay 1778–1840*, 6 vols., London 1904

Barrier, Janine, 'The Franco-Italian Album', in Michael Snodin, ed., *Catalogues of Architectural Drawings in the Victoria and Albert Museum. Sir William Chambers*, London 1996, pp. 20–6

Bauman, Thomas, 'Courts and Municipalities in North Germany', in Neal Zaslaw, ed., *The Classical Era. From the 1740s to the End of the Eighteenth Century*, London 1989

Baylis, Sarah, '"Absolute Magic". A Portrait of George III on Glass by James Pearson', in *Journal of Stained Glass*, vol. XXII, 1998, pp. 16–30

Beattie, John M., *The English Court in the Reign of George I*, Cambridge 1967

Bechthold, Frank-Andreas, and Thomas Weiss eds., *Weltbild Wörlitz: Entwurf einer Kulturlandschaft*, Wörlitz 1996 (exh. cat.)

Bellaigue, Geoffrey de, 'Huzza the King is Well!', *Burlington Magazine*, June 1984, pp. 325–32

Belsham, William, *Memoirs of the Reign of George III*, London 1824

Berger, Robert, *A Royal Passion. Louis XIV as Patron of Architecture*, Cambridge 1994

Bermingham, Ann, *Learning to Draw. Studies in the Cultural History of a Polite and Useful Art*, New Haven and London 2000

Besterman, Theodor, ed., *Correspondence of Voltaire*, 107 vols., Geneva 1953–65

Biegel, Gerd, ed., *Wörlitz. ein Garten der Aufklärung*, Brunswick 1992

Bignamini, Ilaria, 'George Vertue. Art Historian, and Art Institutions in London, 1689–1769', *Walpole Society*, vol. LIV, 1988, pp. 1–148

Black, Jeremy, ed., *Knights Errant and True Englishmen. British Foreign Policy, 1660–1800*, Edinburgh 1989

Blackwood, John, *London's Immortals. The Complete Outdoor Commemorative Statues*, London 1989

Blanning, T.C.W., '"That Horrid Electorate" or "Ma patrie germanique"? George III, Hanover, and the Fürstenbund of 1785', *The Historical Journal*, vol. XX, no. 2, 1977, pp. 311–44

– *The Culture of Power and the Power of Culture. Old Regime Europe, 1660–1789*, Oxford 2002

Bolton, Arthur T., *The Architecture of Robert and James Adam*, 2 vols., London 1922

– ed., *The Portrait of Sir John Soane, R.A.*, London 1927

Bond, Shelagh M., 'Henry Emlyn of Windsor. A Craftsman of Skill and Invention', *Report of the Society of the Friends of St George's*, vol. IV, no. 3, 1962, pp. 99–103

Bond, William Henry, *Thomas Hollis of Lincoln's Inn. A Whig and his Books*, Cambridge 1990

Boyd, John, *et al.*, eds., *The Papers of Thomas Jefferson*, 27 vols., Princeton 1950–97

Brandt, Jürgen, *Alt-Mecklenburgische Schlösser und Herrensitz*, Berlin 1925

Brewer, John, *Pleasures of the Imagination. English Culture in the Eighteenth Century*, London 1997

Bristol, Kerry, *James 'Athenian' Stuart (1713–1788) and the Genesis of the Greek Revival in British Architecture*, Ph.D. thesis, University of London 1997

Brooke, John, *King George III*, London 1972

– 'The Library of George III', *Yale University Gazette*, vol. 52, 1977, pp. 33–45

Brooks, Christopher, *The Gothic Revival*, London 1999

Bucholz, Robert, and John Sainty, *Officials of the Royal Household, 1660–1837*, University of London, Institute of Historical Research, 2 vols., 1997–98

Burke, Edmund, *Reflections on the Revolution in France*, London 1790

– *Correspondence*, 10 vols., Cambridge and Chicago 1958–78

Burney, Charles, *The Present State of Music in Germany, the Netherlands, and United Provinces*,

2 vols., London 1773

– *General History of Music*, 4 vols., London 1776–89

Butlar, F. von, ed., *Peter Joseph Lenné*, Berlin 1989

Cameron, Charles, *The Baths of the Ancients Explained and Illustrated*, London 1772

Campbell, Colen, *Vitruvius Britannicus*, 3 vols., London 1715–25

Campbell Orr, Clarissa, 'Queen Charlotte as Patron: Some Intellectual and Social Contexts', *Journal of the Society for Court Studies*, vol. VI, 2001, pp. 183–212

– *Queenship in Britain, 1660–1837. Royal Patronage, Court Culture and Dynastic Politics*, Manchester and New York 2002

– 'Queen Charlotte, "Scientific Queen"', in Campbell Orr, ed., *Queenship in Britain*

– 'Lost Royal Libraries and Hanoverian Court Culture', in James Raven, ed., *Lost Libraries*, London 2003

– 'Geneva in England: Rousseau's Disciples at the Court of George III and Queen Charlotte', in V. Crossy and S. Bahar, eds., *Travaux sur le dix-huitième siècle*, Geneva 2003

– *Charlotte of Mecklenburg-Strelitz, Queen of Great Britain and Electress of Hanover. Northern Dynasties and the Northern Republic of Letters*, forthcoming

Cannon, John, *Samuel Johnson and the Politics of Hanoverian England*, Oxford 1994

Carson, C. Lennart, *The First Magazine. A History of the Gentleman's Magazine*, Providence, R.I. 1938

Carter, Harold, 'Sir Joseph Banks and the Plant Collection from Kew sent to the Empress Catherine II of Russia 1795', *Bulletin of the British Museum (Natural History)*, Historical Series, vol. 4, no. 5 (1974), London 1983

– *Sir Joseph Banks, 1743–1820*, London 1987

Carter, John, *The Ancient Architecture of England*, 2 vols., London 1795–1814

Chambers & Adelcrantz, Nationalmuseum, Stockholm 1997 (exh. cat.)

Chambers, William, *Designs of Chinese Buildings*, London 1757

– *Treatise on Civil Architecture*, London 1759; 3rd edn as *Treatise on the Decorative Part of Civil Architecture*, London 1791

– *Plans, Elevations, Sections, and Perspective Views of the Gardens and Buildings at Kew in Surrey*, London 1763

– *Dissertation on Oriental Gardening*, London 1772

Charles de Wailly. Peintre architecte dans l'europe des lumières, Caisse Nationale des Monuments Historiques et des Sites, Paris 1979 (exh. cat.)

Chennevières, H. de, *Les Menus-plaisirs du roi et leur artistes*, Paris 1882

Chesterfield, 5th Earl of, *Letters written by the Late Right Honourable Philip Dormer Stanhope, Earl of Chesterfield, to his son, Philip Stanhope, Esq.*, 4 vols., London 1800

Clark, Jonathan, *English Society, 1660–1832. Religion, Ideology and Politics During the Ancien Regime*, Cambridge 2000

Clark, Kenneth, *The Gothic Revival: An Essay in the History of Taste*, London 1928

Clifford, Timothy, 'John Bacon and the Manufacturers', *Apollo*, October 1985, pp. 288–304

– 'Anglomania: Catherine's Patronage of British Decorative Arts', *British Art Journal*, vol. II, no. ii, Winter 2000/2001, pp. 119–20

Cloake, John, *Palaces and Parks of Richmond and Kew*, 2 vols., 1995–6, vol. II, *Richmond Lodge and the Kew Palaces*, Chichester 1996

Colley, Linda, 'The Apotheosis of George III. Loyalty, Royalty and the British Nation 1769–1820', *Past and Present*, no. 102, February 1984, pp. 94–129

– *Britons. Forging the Nation 1707–1837*, London 1992

Colton, Judith, 'Kent's Hermitage for Queen Caroline at Richmond', *Architectura*, 1974, pp. 181–91

Colvin, Howard, ed., *The History of the King's Works*, 6 vols., London 1963–73

– *Royal Buildings*, London 1968

– *A Biographical Dictionary of British Architects, 1600–1840*, 3rd edn., New Haven and London 1995

Conrady, S., 'Die Wirksamkeit Königs Georgs III. für die hannoverschen Kurlande', *Niedersächsisches Jahrbuch für Landesgeschichte*, vol. XXXIX, 1967, pp. 150–91

Coombs, David, 'The Garden at Carlton House of Frederick Prince of Wales and Augusta Princess and Dowager of Wales', *Garden History*, vol. XXV, pt 2, Winter 1997, pp. 153–77

Cornforth, John, 'Cotehele, Cornwall', *Country Life*, 1 and 8 February 1990, pp. 52–5 and 68–71

Crathorne, James, *Cliveden. The Place and the People*, London 1995

Croft-Murray, Edward, *Decorative Painting in England 1537–1837*, 2 vols., Feltham 1970

Crook, J. Mordaunt, *John Carter and the Mind of the Gothic Revival*, vol. 17 of Occasional Papers from the Society of Antiquaries of London, 1995

Cross, Anthony, 'Catherine the Great and Whately's *Observations on Modern Gardening*', *Study Group on Eighteenth-Century Russia,*

Newsletter, vol. 18, 1990, pp. 21–9

– 'British Gardeners and the Vogue of the English Garden in late Eighteenth-century Russia', in Allen and Dukelskaya, eds., *British Art Treasures from Russian Imperial Collections*

Daniels, Stephen, *Humphry Repton. Landscape Gardening and the Geography of Georgian England*, New Haven and London 1999

Darley, Gillian, *John Soane. An Accidental Romantic*, London and New Haven 1999

Dedinkin, Mikhail, 'Hampton Court Rediscovered', *Hermitage Magazine*, issue 1, Summer 2003, pp. 48–52

DeLorme, Eleanor, *Garden Pavilions and the 18th Century French Court*, Woodbridge 1996

Desgodetz, Antoine, *Les Édifices antiques de Rome*, Paris 1682, translated by George Marshall as *The Ancient Buildings of Rome*, 2 vols., London 1771–95

Desmond, Ray, *Kew: The History of the Royal Botanic Gardens*, London 1995

Dillenberger, John, *Benjamin West. The Context of his Life's Work with Particular Attention to Paintings with Religious Subject Matter*, San Antonio 1977

Dittscheid, Hans-Christoph, *Kassel-Wilhelmshöhe und die Krise des Schlossbaues am Ende des Ancien Régime. Charles de Wailly, Simon Louis Du Ry und Christopher Jussow als Architekten von Schloss und Löwenburg in Wilhelmshöhe*, Worms 1987

Dobert, Johannes Paul, *Bauten und Baumeister in Ludwigslust*, Magdeburg 1920

Donaldson, William, *Agriculture Considered as a Moral and Political Duty; in a Series of Letters, inscribed to His Majesty*, London 1775

Downes, Kerry, *Vanbrugh*, London 1977

Eddy, Donald, *A Bibliography of Richard Hurd*, New Castle, Delaware 1999

Ellis, K.L., 'The Administrative Connection between Britain and Hanover', *Journal of the Society of Archivists*, vol. III, no. 10, October 1969, pp. 546–66

Emlyn, Henry, *A Proposition for a New Order of Architecture. With Rules for Drawing the Several Parts*, London 1781; 2nd edn 1787; 3rd edn 1797

Erffa, Helmut von and Allen Staley, *The Paintings of Benjamin West*, New Haven and London 1986

Faerber, P., *Nikolaus Friedrich von Thouret. Ein Baumeister des Klassizismus*, Stuttgart 1949

Farington, Joseph, *Diary*, Kenneth Garlick *et al.*, eds., 17 vols., New Haven and London 1978–98

Fischer von Erlach, Johann Bernhard, *Entwurff einer historischen Architektur*, Vienna 1721;

translated as *A Plan of Civil and Historical Architecture*, London 1730 and 1737

Fleming, John, *Robert Adam and His Circle in Edinburgh and Rome*, London 1962

Fletcher, Ernest, ed., *Conversations of James Northcote, R.A., with James Ward on Art and Artists*, London 1901

Fortescue, John, ed., *The Correspondence of King George the Third*, 6 vols., London 1927–8

Frank, Christoph, *et al.*, 'Diderot, Guiard and Houdon. Projects for a Funerary Monument at Gotha', *Burlington Magazine*, part I, April 2002, pp. 213–21, and part II, August 2002, pp. 475–85

Fraser, William, *The Chiefs of Grant*, 3 vols., Edinburgh 1883

Fréart de Chambray, Roland, *Parallel of the Antient Architecture with the Modern*, translated by John Evelyn, London 1664

Frew, John, 'Gothic is English. John Carter and the Revival of the Gothic as England's National Style', *Art Bulletin*, vol. LXIV, June 1982, pp. 315–19

Frölich, Marie, and Hans-Günther Sperlich, *Georg Moller. Baumeister der Romantik*, Darmstadt 1959

Gagliardo, John, *Reich and Nation. The Holy Roman Empire as Idea and Reality, 1763–1806*, Bloomington 1980

Galt, John, *The Life and Studies of Benjamin West, Esq., ... Prior to his Arrival in England*, London 1816; *The Life and Works of Benjamin West, Esq., ... , Subsequent to his Arrival in England, Part II*, London 1820

Gascoigne, John, *Joseph Banks and the English Enlightenment. Useful Knowledge and Polite Culture*, Cambridge 1994

– 'Sir Joseph Banks and his Abiding Legacy', in *London Papers in Australian Studies*, no. 2, King's College, London 2001

George III and Queen Charlotte. Patronage, Collecting and Court Taste, London 2004, ed. J. Roberts (exh. cat.)

George III, Collector and Patron, The Queen's Gallery, 1974, ed. G. de Bellaigue (exh. cat.)

Giersberg, Hans-Joachim, *Friedrich als Bauherr: Studien zur Architektur des 18.Jahrhunderts in Berlin und Potsdam*, Berlin 1986

– and Claudia Meckel, eds., *Friedrich II. und die Kunst*, 2 vols. in 1, Sanssouci 1986 (exh. cat.)

Gillen, Mollie, *Royal Duke. Augustus, Duke of Sussex (1773–1843)*, London 1976

Giometti, Cristiano, 'Giovanni Battista Guelfi. New Discoveries', *The Sculpture Journal*, vol. III, 1999, pp. 26–43

Girouard, Mark, *The Return to Camelot. Chivalry and the English Gentleman*, London 1981

Glanville, Philippa, 'A George III Silver Service at Waddesdon Manor', *Apollo*, April 2003, p. 29

Gondoin, Jacques, *Description des écoles de chirurgie*, Paris 1780

Goodison, Nicholas, *Ormolu: The Work of Matthew Boulton* (1974), revised, London 2002

Green, Valentine, *The History and Antiquities of the City and Suburbs of Worcester*, 2 vols., London 1796

Greenhouse, Wendy, 'Benjamin West and Edward III: A Neoclassical Painter and Medieval History', *Art History*, vol. VIII, 1985, pp. 178–91

Greig, James, ed., *The Diaries of a Duchess. Extracts from the Diaries of the First Duchess of Northumberland (1716–1776)*, London 1926

Günther, Harri, ed., *Gärten der Goethe-Zeit*, Leipzig 1993

Gwynn, John, *Essay upon Design*, London 1749

– *London and Westminster Improved*, London 1766

Habermas, Jürgen, *The Structural Transformation of the Public Sphere. An Inquiry into a Category of Bourgeois Society* (1962), Cambridge 1989

Hajós, Géza, 'The Gardens of the British Isles in the Diary of the Austrian Count Karl von Zinzendorf in the Year 1768', *Garden History*, vol. 9, i, 1989, pp. 44–7

Hall, Michael, 'Arbury Hall, Warwickshire', *Country Life*, 7–14 January 1999, pp. 30–5 and 40–3

– ed., *Gothic Architecture and its Meanings. 1550–1839*, Reading 2002

Hammer-Schenk, Harold, *et al.*, eds., *Laves und Hannover. Niedersächsische Architektur im neunzehnten Jahrhundert*, Hanover 1989

Harris, Eileen, and Nicholas Savage, *British Architectural Books and Writers 1556–1785*, Cambridge 1990

Harris, John, 'Sir William Chambers and his Parisian Album', *Architectural History*, vol. 6, 1963, pp. 54–90

– *Sir William Chambers, Knight of the Polar Star*, London 1970

– *A Catalogue of British Drawings for Architecture, Decoration, Sculpture and Landscape Gardening 1550–1900 in American Collections*, New Jersey 1971

– and Bernhard Korzus, '"Sich in der Anlegen der englischen Bau Arten wohl zu informiren": Das Englische bei Jussow', in *Heinrich Christoph Jussow 1754–1825: Ein hessischer Architekt des Klassizismus*, Staatliche Museen, Kassel, 1999, pp. 53–66 (exh. cat.)

– and Michael Snodin, eds., *William Chambers, Architect to George III*, New Haven and London 1996

Hart, Vaughan, *Nicholas Hawksmoor. Building*

Ancient Wonders, New Haven and London 2002

Hatton, Ragnhild, *George I. Elector and King*, London 1978

Hedley, Olwen, *Queen Charlotte*, London 1975

Herrmann, Wolfgang, 'Antoine Desgodets and the Académie Royale d'Architecture', *Art Bulletin*, vol. XL, March 1958, pp. 23–53

Hewlings, Richard, 'Chiswick House and Gardens. Appearance and Meaning', in Barnard and Clark, eds., *Lord Burlington*

Hibbert, Christopher, *George III. A Personal History*, London 1998

Hinz, Christine, 'Die Parklandschaft Hohenzieritz', in Günther, ed., *Gärten der Goethe-Zeit*

Hirschfeld, Christian, *Théorie de l'art des jardins*, 5 vols., Leipzig 1779–85

Holmes, Oliver Wendell, *The Poet at the Breakfast Table* (1872), Oxford 1906

Home, Henry (Lord Kames), *Elements of Criticism*, Edinburgh 1762

– *The Gentleman Farmer, being an Attempt to improve Agriculture by subjecting it to the Test of Rational Principles*, Edinburgh 1776

Home, James, ed., *The Letters and Journals of Lady Mary Coke*, 4 vols., Edinburgh 1889–96

Hoock, Holger, *The King's Artists. The Royal Academy of Arts and the Politics of British Culture, 1760–1840*, Oxford 2003

Horn, D.B., ed., *British Diplomatic Representatives 1689–1789*, Royal Historical Society, Camden Third Series, vol. XLVI, 1932

Hoskin, Michael, 'Herschel's 40 ft reflector', *Journal for the History of Astronomy*, vol. XXXIV, 2003, pp. 1–32

Hudson, Helen, *Cumberland Lodge. A House Through History*, Chichester 1989

Hurd, Richard, *Moral and Political Dialogues*, London 1759; 3rd edn., as *Moral and Political Dialogues. With Letters on Chivalry and Romance*, 3 vols., London 1765

– *Letters on Chivalry and Romance*, London 1762

Hutchinson, Sidney, *The History of the Royal Academy, 1768–1968* (1968), London 1986

Huth, Hans, 'Chambers and Potsdam', in D. Fraser *et al.*, eds., *Essays in the History of Architecture Presented to Rudolf Wittkower*, London 1967

Ingamells, John, ed., *A Dictionary of British and Irish Travellers in Italy, 1701–1800*, New Haven and London 1997

Jackson-Stops, Gervase, '"A Noble Simplicity". Pyne's views of Buckingham House', in *Buckingham Palace: A Complete Guide*, *Apollo*, August 1993, pp. 44–56

Jacques, David, '"Capability" Brown at Hampton Court', *Hermitage Magazine*, issue 1, Summer 2003, pp. 52–5

James, M.R., *St George's Chapel, Windsor. The Woodwork of the Choir*, Windsor 1933

Jenkins, Susan, 'The External Sculptural decoration of Somerset House and the Documentary Sources', *British Art Journal*, vol. II, no. ii, Winter 2000/2001, pp. 22–8

Johnson, Samuel, *Thoughts on the Coronation of His Present Majesty King George the Third*, London 1761, in *Works*, Donald Greene, ed., vol. x, *Political Writings*, New Haven and London 1977, pp. 292–300

Kaster, Karl, '"Meliorisierung" und "Möblierung". Das Schloss als hannoversches Allod zwischen 1698 und 1802', in Verspohl, *Das Osnabrücker Schloss*, pp. 248–66

Kelly, Alison, *Mrs Coade's Stone*, Upton-upon-Severn 1990

Kent, Nathaniel, *Hints to Gentlemen of Landed Property* (1775), 3rd edn., London 1793

Kielmansegge, Count Frederick, *Diary of a Journey to England in the Years 1761–1762*, London 1902

Kilvert, Joseph, *Memoirs of the Life and Writings of the Right Rev. Richard Hurd, DD*, London 1860

Kirby, Joshua, *Dr Brook Taylor's Method of Perspective Made Easy*, London 1754

– *The Perspective of Architecture*, London 1761

– *The Description and Use of a New Instrument Called, an Architectonic Sector*, London 1761

Knight, Charles, *Windsor Guide*, Windsor 1796

– *Passages of a Working Life*, London 1864

Köhler, Marcus, 'Friedrich Karl von Hardenberg's (1696–1763) Journeys to England and his Contribution to the Introduction of the English Landscape Garden to Germany', *Garden History*, vol. 25, ii, 1997, pp. 212–18

– 'The German Connection: Richmond in Braunschweig', *Garden History*, vol. 29, i, 2001, pp. 29–35

– *Historische Gärten um Neubrandenburg*, Berlin 2002

– *Frühe Landschaftsgärten in Russland und Deutschland. Johann Busch als Mentor eines neuen Stils*, Berlin 2003

Köhler, Volkmar, 'Jagdschloss Göhrde', *Niederdeutsche Beiträge zur Kunstgeschichte*, vol. VIII, 1969, pp. 169–200

Kremeier, Jarl, 'Iburg, Osnabrück, Hannover – Sophie Charlottes Eltern und ihre Residenzen', in *Sophie Charlotte und ihr Schloss*, Schloss Charlottenburg, Berlin 1999, pp. 67–75 (exh. cat.)

Laird, Mark, '"Our equally favorite hobby horse". The Flower Gardens of Lady Elizabeth Lee at Hartwell and the 2nd Earl Harcourt at Nuneham Courtenay', *Garden History*, vol. 18, ii, 1990, pp. 103–54

Langley, Batty, *Ancient Masonry*, London 1733–6

– *The Builder's Jewel*, London 1741

– *Ancient Architecture, Restored, and Improved*, London 1742

Le Clerc, Sébastien, *Pratique de la géométrie*, Paris 1669

– *Traité d'architecture*, 2 vols., Paris 1714

Leigh, R.A., 'Rousseau's English Pension', in J.H. Fox, *et al.*, eds., *Studies in Eighteenth-century French Literature. Presented to Robert Niklaus*, Exeter 1975

Le Rouge, Georges Louis, *Détails des nouveaux jardins à la mode*, 21 cahiers (some entitled *Jardins anglo-chinois*), Paris 1774–89

Leroy, Julien-David, *Les Ruines des plus beaux monuments de la Grèce*, Paris 1758

Leslie, Charles, and Tom Taylor, *Life and Times of Sir Joshua Reynolds*, 2 vols., London 1865

Liackhova, Lydia, 'Wedgwood's Green Frog Service and the Imperial Court', in Allen and Dukelskaya, eds., *British Art Treasures from Russian Imperial Collections*

Lloyd, Christopher, *The Quest for Albion. Monarchy and the Patronage of British Painting*, London 1998

Lohmeyer, Karl, *Südwestdeutsche Gärten des Barock und der Romantik*, Saarbrücken 1937

Lomas, Richard, *A Power in the Land. The Percys*, East Linton 1999

Lonsdale, Roger, *Dr Charles Burney. A Literary Biography*, Oxford 1965

Loudon, John, ed., *The Landscape Gardening and Landscape Architecture of the Late Humphry Repton, Esq.*, London 1840

Lubbock, Constance, ed., *The Herschel Chronicle. The Life-Story of William Herschel and his Sister Caroline Herschel*, Cambridge 1933

Lysons, Daniel, *The Environs of London* (1792–6), 5 vols., London 1796–1800

– and Samuel Lysons, *Magna Britannia. Berkshire*, London 1806

Macalpine, Ida, and Richard Hunter, *George III and the Mad Business*, London 1969

Macdonagh, Giles, *Frederick the Great. A Life in Deed and Letters*, London 1999

McHardy, George, *Office of J. B. Papworth, Catalogue of the Drawings Collection of the Royal Institute of British Architects*, Farnborough 1977

Manco, Jean, *et al.*, 'Lulworth Castle in the Seventeenth Century', *Architectural History*, vol. 33, 1990, pp. 29–53

– and Francis Kelly, 'Lulworth Castle from 1700', *Architectural History*, vol. 34, 1991, pp. 145–70

Mare, Margaret, and W.H. Quarrell, transl. and ed., *Lichtenberg's Visits to England, as described in his Letters and Diaries*, Oxford 1938

Marschner, Joanna, 'Queen Caroline of Anspach and the European princely museum tradition', in Campbell Orr, ed., *Queenship in Britain*

Marsden, Jonathan, and John Hardy, '"O fair Britannia Hail": The "Most Superb" State Coach', *Apollo*, February 2001, pp. 3–12

Mason, William, *The English Garden. A Poem in Four Books*, London 1771–81

Mathias, Ulrike D., 'Houdon and the German Courts: Serving the Francophile Princes', in Anne Poulet, ed., *Jean-Antoine Houdon. Sculptor of the Enlightenment*, Washington 2003, pp. 299–303 (exh. cat.)

Maurer, Michael, *Aufklärung und Anglophilie in Deutschland*, Göttingen 1987

Mautner, Franz, ed., *Georg Christoph Lichtenberg. Schriften und Briefe*, 6 vols., Frankfurt-am-Main 1983

Meyer, Jerry D., 'Benjamin West's Window Designs for St George's, Windsor', *American Art Journal*, vol. XI, 1979, pp. 53–65

– 'Benjamin West's Chapel of Revealed Religion. A Study in Eighteenth-Century Protestant Religious Art', *Art Bulletin*, vol. LVII, June 1975, pp. 247–65

Millar, Oliver, *Zoffany and his Tribuna*, London 1967

– *Later Georgian Pictures in the Royal Collection*, 2 vols., London 1976

Miller, Edward, *That Noble Cabinet. A History of the British Museum*, London 1973

Millon, Henry, ed., *The Triumph of the Baroque*, London 1999 (exh. cat.)

Mittig, Hans-Ernst, *Kloster Medingen. Ein protestantischer Stiftsbau, 1781–1788*, Museumsverein für das Fürstentum, Lüneburg 1971

Modrow, Bernd, 'Der Staatspark Wilhelmsbad, Hanau', in Günther, *Gärten der Goethe-Zeit*

Moller, Georg, *An Essay on the Origin and Progress of Gothic Architecture*, London 1824

– *Moller's Memorials of German-Gothic Architecture*, London 1836

Morris, Marilyn, *The British Monarchy and the French Revolution*, New Haven and London 1998

Morris, Mowbray, ed., *Boswell's Life of Johnson* (1893), London 1929

Morton, Alan, and Jane Wess, *Public and Private Science. The King George III Collection*, Oxford 1993

Mowl, Timothy, and Brian Earnshaw, *An Insular Rococo. Architecture, Politics and Society in Ireland and England, 1710–1770*, London 1999

Myers, Sylvia Harcstark, *The Bluestocking Circle. Women, Friendship, and the Life of the Mind in Eighteenth-Century England*, Oxford 1990

Newman, John, 'Somerset House and Other Public Buildings', in Harris and Snodin, *Chambers*

Newton, Thomas, *The Works of the Right Reverend Thomas Newton, D.D, … with Some Account of his Life*, 3 vols., London 1782

Nichols, John, *Literary Anecdotes of the Eighteenth Century*, 9 vols., London 1812–15

Nicolai, Friedrich, *Breschreibung der königlichen Residenzstädte Berlin und Potsdam*, Berlin 1786

Nicolas, Nicholas Harris, *History of the Orders of Knighthood of the British Empire*, 4 vols., London 1842

Norris, John, *Shelburne and Reform*, London 1963

Nugent, Thomas, *Travels through Germany … with a Particular Account of the Courts of Mecklenburg*, 2 vols., London 1768

Olausson, Magnus, 'Gustav III 1746–92', in Andersson *et al.*, *Svensk Trädgårdskonst under fyrhundra år*

Oppé, Adolf, *The Drawings of William Hogarth*, London 1948

– *English Drawings, Stuart and Georgian Periods, in the Collection of His Majesty the King at Windsor Castle*, London 1950

Oresko, Robert, *et al.*, eds, *Royal and Republican Sovereignty in Early Modern Europe. Essays in Memory of Ragnhild Hatton*, Cambridge 1997

Packe, Michael, *Edward III*, London 1983

Palladio, Andrea, *I Quattro Libri dell'Architettura*, Vicenza 1570

Papendiek, Charlotte, *Court and Private Life in the Time of Queen Charlotte*, 2 vols., London 1887

Papworth, Wyatt, *John B. Papworth, Architect to the King of Wurtemberg. A Brief Record of his Life and Works*, privately printed 1879

Parshall, Linda, 'C.C.L. Hirschfeld's Concept of the Garden in the German Enlightenment', *Journal of Garden History*, vol. XIII, 3, 1993, pp. 125–71

Patterson, Stephen, *Royal Insignia. British and Foreign Orders of Chivalry from the Royal Collection*, London 1986

Paulson, Ronald, *Hogarth's Graphic Work*, 3rd revised edn., London 1989

Pearce, Ernest Harold, *Hartlebury Castle*, London 1926

Percy, Thomas, *Reliques of Antient English Poetry*, 3 vols., London 1765

– *Northern Antiquities, with a Translation of the Edda and Other Pieces from the Ancient Icelandic Tongue*, 2 vols., London 1770

– ed., *The Regulations and Establishment of the Household Book of Algernon Percy, the Fifth Earl of Northumberland*, London 1770

Percy, Victoria, and Gervase Jackson-Stops, '"Exquisite Taste and Tawdry Ornament". The Travel Journals of the 1st Duchess of Northumberland – II', *Country Life*, 7 February 1974, pp. 250–2

Perrault, Claude, *Les dix Livres d'architecture de Vitruve*, Paris 1673

Peyre, Marie-Joseph, *Oeuvres d'Architecture*, Paris 1765

Plumb, J.H., *The First Four Georges* (1956), London 1966

Postle, Martin, 'A Taste for History. Reynolds, West, George III, and George IV', *Apollo*, September 1993, pp. 186–91

Pottle, Frederick, ed., *Boswell's London Journal 1762–1763*, London 1950

Pressly, Nancy L., *Revealed Religion: Benjamin West's Commissions for Windsor Castle and Fonthill Abbey*, San Antonio 1983

Preston, Thomas, *The Jubilee of George the Third. 25th October, 1809. A Record of the Festivities*, London 1887

Prochaska, Frank, *Royal Bounty. The Making of a Welfare Monarchy*, New Haven and London 1995

Prüser, Jürgen, *Die Göhrde. Ein Beitrag zur Geschichte des Jagd- und Forstwesens in Niedersaschsen*, Hildesheim 1969

Pye, John, *Patronage of British Art. An Historical Sketch*, London 1845

Pyne, W.H., *History of the Royal Residences*, 3 vols., London 1819

Quill, Humphrey, *John Harrison. The Man who Found Longitude*, London 1966

Reilly, Robin, *Wedgwood*, 2 vols., New York 1989

Repton, Humphry, *Sketches and Hints on Landscape Gardening*, London 1795

– *Fragments on the Theory and Practice of Landscape Gardening*, London 1816

Reynolds, Joshua, *Discourses*, Robert Wark, ed. (1959), New Haven and London 1975

Rice, Howard, *Jefferson's Paris*, Princeton 1976

Roberts, Hugh, 'Metamorphoses in Wood. Royal Library Furniture in the Eighteenth and Nineteenth Centuries', *Apollo*, June 1990, pp. 382–90 and 441–2

– 'A Neoclassical Episode at Windsor', *Furniture*

History, vol. XXXIII, 1997, pp. 176–87

– *For the King's Pleasure. The Furnishing and Decoration of George IV's Apartments at Windsor Castle*, London 2001

Roberts, Jane, 'Henry Emlyn's Restoration of St George's Chapel', *Report of the Society of the Friends of St George's*, vol. V, no. 8, Windsor 1977, pp. 331–8

– *Royal Artists from Mary Queen of Scots to the Present Day*, London 1987

– *Royal Landscape. The Gardens and Parks of Windsor*, New Haven and London 1997

– 'Sir William Chambers and George III' in Harris and Snodin, eds., *Chambers*

Robinson, John Martin, *Georgian Model Farms*, Oxford 1983

– *Arundel Castle*, Chichester 1994

Rorschach, Kimerly, 'Frederick, Prince of Wales (1707–51), as Collector and Patron', *Walpole Society*, vol. LV, 1993, pp. 1–76

Rosenthal, Michael, *The Art of Thomas Gainsborough*, New Haven and London 1999

Rousseau, Jean-Jacques, *Julie, ou la nouvelle Héloïse*, Paris 1761

– *Émile, ou, De l'éducation*, Amsterdam 1762

Rowan, Alistair, *'Bob the Roman'. Heroic Antiquity & The Architecture of Robert Adam*, Sir John Soane's Museum 2003 (exh. cat.)

Royal Treasures. A Golden Jubilee Celebration, London 2002, ed. J. Roberts (exh. cat.)

Russell, Francis, 'King George III's Picture Hang at Buckingham House', *Burlington Magazine*, vol. CXXIX, August 1987, pp. 524–31

– *John, 3rd Earl of Bute. Patron and Collector*, London 2004

St John Hope, W.H., *Windsor Castle. An Architectural History*, 2 vols., London 1913

Sandon, Henry, *Flight and Barr, Worcester Porcelain, 1783–1840*, Woodbridge 1978

Savage, Nicholas, 'The "Viceroy" of the Royal Academy. Sir William Chambers and the Royal Protection of the Arts', in Harris and Snodin, *Chambers*

Schepers, Wolfgang, *Hirschfeld's Théorie der Gartenkunst, 1779–85*, Worms 1980

Schieder, Theodor, *Friedrich der Große. Ein Königtum der Widersprüche*, Frankfurt-am-Main, Berlin, and Vienna 1983

Schnath, Georg, *Das Leineschloss. Kloster, Fürstensitz, Landtagsgebäude*, Hanover 1962

Scott, Jonathan, *The Pleasures of Antiquity. British Collectors of Greece and Rome*, New Haven and London 2003

Sedgwick, Romney, ed., *Letters from George III to*

Lord Bute 1756–1766, London 1939

Seymour, W.A., ed., *A History of the Ordnance Survey*, Folkestone 1980

Shvidovsky, Dimitri, *The Empress and the Architect. British Architecture and Gardens at the Court of Catherine the Great*, New Haven and London 1996

Simms, Brendan, '"An Odd Question Enough". Charles James Fox, the Crown and British Policy during the Hanoverian Crisis of 1806', *The Historical Journal*, vol. XXXVIII, no. 3, 1995, p. 594

– *The Impact of Napoleon. Prussian High Politics, Foreign Policy and the Crisis of the Executive, 1797–1806*, Cambridge 1997

Sloan, Kim, *'A Noble Art'. Amateur Artists and Drawing Masters c.1600–1800*, British Museum 2000 (exh. cat.)

Smith, Ann, and Michael Hall, 'Sherborne Castle, Dorset', *Country Life*, 10 and 17 August 2000, pp. 38–41, 44–6

Smith, Charles Saumarez, *Eighteenth-Century Decoration. Design and the Domestic Interior in England*, London 1993

Smith, Nicola, *The Royal Image and the English People*, Aldershot 2001

Strange, Robert, *An Inquiry into the Establishment of the Royal Academy of Arts. To Which is prefixed, a letter to the Earl of Bute* (1775), William Coningham, ed., London 1850

Strong, Roy, *And When Did You Last See Your Father?*, London 1978

Stroud, Dorothy, *Henry Holland. His Life and Architecture*, London 1966

– *Capability Brown*, London 1975

Strutt, Joseph, *The Regal and Ecclesiastical Antiquities of England*, London 1773

Stuart, Dorothy, *The Daughters of George III*, London 1939

Stuart, James, and Nicholas Revett, *The Antiquities of Athens*, 4 vols., London 1762–1816

Survey of London, London County Council, 45 vols., 1900– (in progress)

Tait, Alastair, *Robert Adam, Drawings and Imagination*, Cambridge 1993

Taylor, Brandon, *Art for the Nation. Exhibitions and the London Public 1747–2001*, Manchester 1999

Tighe, Robert, and James Davis, *Annals of Windsor*, London 1858

Tillyard, Stella, *Aristocrats. Caroline, Emily, Louisa and Sarah Lennox 1740–1832*, London 1994

Turner, G.L.'E., 'The Auction Sales of the Earl of Bute's Instruments, 1793', *Annals of Science*, vol. XXIII, 1967, pp. 213–42

Uglow, Jenny, *Lunar Men. The Friends who Made the Future 1730–1810*, London 2002

Umbach, Maiken, *Federalism and Enlightenment in Germany, 1760–1810*, London and Rio Grande 2000

Vale, Juliet, *Edward III and Chivalry. Chivalric Society and its Context 1270–1350*, Woodbridge 1988

Verspohl, Franz-Joachim, ed., *Das Osnabrücker Schloss: Stadtresidenz, Villa, Verwaltungssitz*, Bramsche 1991

Vertue, George, 'Notebooks', *Walpole Society*, vol. XVIII, 1930

Vitruvius, *De architectura, see under* Barbaro *and* Perrault

Vivian, Frances, 'Joseph Smith, Antonio Visentini, el il movimento neoclassico', *Bollettino del Centro Internazionale di Studi di Architettura Andrea Palladio*, vol. V, 1963, pp. 340–58

– *The Consul Smith Collection*, Munich 1989 (exh. cat.)

Wackernagel, Rudolph, 'Carlton House Mews. The State Coach of the Prince of Wales and of the Later Kings of Hanover', *Furniture History*, vol. XXXI, 1995, pp. 47–115

Wales, H.R.H. The Prince of, *A Vision of Britain. A Personal View of Architecture*, London 1989

Walpole, Horace, *Anecdotes of Painting in England* (1762), James Dallaway, ed., 5 vols., London 1828

– *Correspondence*, 48 vols., 1937–83, vol. XVI, New Haven 1951

Watkin, David, *Athenian Stuart. Pioneer of the Greek Revival*, London 1982

– *The English Vision. The Picturesque in Architecture, Garden and Landscape Design*, London 1982

– *The Royal Interiors of Regency England*, London 1984

– 'Freemasonry and Sir John Soane', *Journal of the Society of Architectural Historians*, vol. LIV, December 1995, pp. 402–17

– *Sir John Soane. Enlightenment Thought and the Royal Academy Lectures*, Cambridge 1996

– 'Greek and Gothic Country Houses. The Impact of Napoleon', in Malcolm Airs, ed., *The Regency Great House*

– and Tilman Mellinghoff, *German Architecture and the Classical Ideal, 1740–1840*, London 1987

Watkins, John, *Memoirs of … Her Most Excellent Majesty Sophie Charlotte*, London 1819

Wegner, Reinhard, *Nach Albions Stränden. Die Bedeutung Englands für die Architektur des Klassizismus und der Romantik in Preussen*, Munich 1994

Weiss, Thomas, ed., *Sir William Chambers und der Englisch-chinesische Garten in Europa*, Wörlitz 1996 (symposium proceedings, 1995)

Whately, Thomas, *Observations on Modern Gardening*, London 1770

White, Philip, *A Gentleman of Fine Taste. The Watercolours of Coplestone Warre Bampfylde (1720–1791)*, Taunton 1995

Whitley, William T., *Artists and Their Friends in England 1700–1799*, 2 vols., London and Boston 1928

Williams, Clare, ed., *Sophie in London 1786 being the Diary of Sophie v. la Roche*, London 1933

Willis, G.M., *Ernest Augustus, Duke of Cumberland and King of Hanover*, London 1954

Willis, Peter, *Charles Bridgeman and the English Landscape Garden* (1977), reprinted Newcastle upon Tyne 2002

Wilson, Christopher, 'The Royal Lodgings of Edward III at Windsor Castle. Form, Function, Representation', *British Archaeological Association: Conference Transactions*, vol. XXV, 2002, pp. 15–94

Wilson, Peter, *The Holy Roman Empire, 1495–1806*, Basingstoke 2000

Wood, Robert, *The Ruins of Palmyra, otherwise Tedmor, in the Desart*, London, 1753

– *The Ruins of Balbec, otherwise Heliopolis, in Coelosyria*, London 1757

Woodbridge, Kenneth, *Landscape and Antiquity. Aspects of English Culture at Stourhead 1718 to 1838*, Oxford 1970

– 'Bélanger en Angleterre. Son Carnet de Voyage', *Architectural History*, vol. 25, 1982, pp. 8–19

Woolf, H., *The Transit of Venus. A Study in Eighteenth-Century Science*, Princeton 1959

Worsley, Giles, 'Out of Adam's Shadow', *Country Life*, 14 May 1992, pp. 101–2

– *Classical Architecture in Britain. The Heroic Age*, New Haven and London 1995

Yorke, James, *Lancaster House. London's Greatest Town House*, London 2001

Young, Arthur, *The Farmer's Tour through the East of England*, 4 vols., London 1771

– *Annals of Agriculture*, vol. VII, 1787

Zeller, Ursula, and Thomas Weiss, eds., *For the Friends of Nature and Art. The Garden Kingdom of Prince Franz von Anhalt-Dessau in [sic] Age of Enlightenment*, Dessau, Wörlitz 1997 (exh. cat.)

Zouch, Henry, *Catalogue of the Royal and Noble Authors of England, with Lists of Their Works. Printed at Strawberry Hill*, 1758

INDEX

Numbers in *italic* type indicate pages on which illustrations occur.

PHOTOGRAPHIC ACKNOWLEDGEMENTS

All works reproduced are in the Royal Collection unless otherwise indicated. Royal Collection Enterprises is grateful for permission to reproduce the following: figs. 3, 39, 67 By permission of the British Library; fig. 7 Photographer Michael Hoskin; figs. 42, 43, 58, 105, 107 By courtesy of the Trustees of Sir John Soane's Museum; fig. 44 The City of Westminster Archives Centre, photographer Geremy Butler; fig. 55 English Heritage Photographic Library, Photographer Jonathan Bailey; fig. 56 Photographer John Freeman; fig. 62 RIBA Library Photographs Collection; fig. 65 Photographer Harland Walshaw; fig. 66 Science Museum/Science and Society Picture Library; figs. 68–9 Crown copyright: Historic Royal Palaces; fig. 81 Collection of Hirschl & Adler Galleries, New York; fig. 82 By kind permission of the Bishop of Worcester; figs. 89–91, 93–6 Reproduced by permission of the Dean and Canons of Windsor; fig. 98 Copyright Royal Academy of Arts, London; fig. 109 Photograph by courtesy of Sandra Willson, King George VI and Queen Elizabeth Foundation of St Catharine's, Cumberland Lodge.

Every effort has been made to contact the copyright holders of material reproduced in this publication. Any omissions are inadvertent and will be rectified in future editions if notification of the correct credit is sent to the publisher in writing.